ADVANCE PRAISE

"This is more than the celebration of a great American original. This is the inside dope on a whole way of life, the stuff of legend, and reading *The Art Pepper Companion* allows us to see and hear how that tortured life produced one of the most haunting voices in jazz."
—**Ben Sidran**, author of *Talking Jazz: An Oral History* and *Black Talk*

"Art Pepper embodied so many of the qualities of jazz in his time. . . . It would be great to think that players such as Art Pepper will come along again, but I wouldn't bet on it. Meanwhile, we have this handsome, intriguing collection as a memorial."
—**Derek Bailey**, author of *Improvisation: Its Nature and Practice in Music*

"Despite the turmoil of his private life, Art Pepper always created inspired jazz; his peerless improvising consistently induced leading writers to sing his praises. Todd Selbert has done the jazz world a great service in bringing together the best of these articles. They highlight the achievements of a jazzman whose playing has gathered a remarkably durable international following."
—**John Chilton**, author of *Sidney Bechet: The Wizard of Jazz*

"This varied, finely spiced collection contains bravura performances by well-known and outspoken jazz writers. In the aggregate, they present everything you ever wanted to know about a crucial era in jazz history as seen through the microcosm of the life and music of one troubled but extraordinarily gifted alto saxophonist. . . . Don't miss these riches."
—**Leslie Gourse**, author of *Unforgettable: The Life and Mystique of Nat King Cole* and *Louis' Children: American Jazz Singers*

THE
ART PEPPER
COMPANION

WRITINGS ON A JAZZ ORIGINAL

edited by TODD SELBERT

Cooper Square Press

First Cooper Square Press edition 2000. This Cooper Square Press hardcover edition of *The Art Pepper Companion* is an original publication.

Published by Cooper Square Press
An Imprint of the Rowman & Littlefield Publishing Group
150 Fifth Aventue, Suite 911
New York, New York 10011

Distributed by National Book Network

Library of Congress Cataloging-in-Publication Data

The Art Pepper companion : writings on a jazz original / edited by Todd Selbert
    p. cm.
  Includes bibliographical refrences and discography.
    ISBN 0-8154-1067-0 (pbk. : alk. paper)
    1. Pepper, Art, 1925-   . 2. Saxophonists–United States–Biography.
I. Selbert Todd.
  ML419.P48 A78 2000

788.7'3165'092–dc21
00-064395

∞ ™ The paper used in this publication meets the minimum requirements of American National Standard for Information Sciences–Permanence of Paper for Printed Library Materials, ANSI/NISO Z39.48-1992.
Manufactured in the United States of America.

To my mind, no jazzman has ever surpassed him in the balanced artistry of the several ingredients that make for great music. His is a nearly ideal tone, hot, but harsh only when intentionally so, and singingly alive with clear-pitched beauty. His is the nearly perfect attack, easily flowing with the rhythm section, in command at all tempos, and masculinely assertive with the jazz-cry.

—*John William Hardy*

CONTENTS

INTRODUCTION

Although the millennium is accompanied by the seventy-fifth anniversary of the birth of Art Pepper, there will be no torrent of memorial albums or "Altos for Art" concerts commemorating Pepper's life and music. But the absence of celebration will not be due to the lack of inspired music by Pepper—it will be owing to the wayward life he led, a life impacted by his neglect of his gift and archaic U.S. narcotics laws. So let this volume of writing celebrate Pepper, one of the great alto saxophonists jazz has known, perhaps the greatest.

Of the hundreds of pieces written on Art Pepper over a brilliant but crosswired career spanning forty years, the selected pieces tended to be published toward the latter part of his career; most pieces which appeared when he was in his prime either focused on his private life or contained the vapid writing of the day. This collection of prose is drawn from magazine and newspaper articles and interviews, book chapters, liner notes and record and book reviews. Although the focus of *The Art Pepper Companion* is on Pepper's music, the Chronology section does include information concerning his drug use and the corresponding results because it impacted his career in music so, and is virtually required in order to explain his frequent and lengthy absences from the jazz scene. For a full and personal account of Pepper's life, one has only to look to *Straight Life: The Story of Art Pepper*, his autobiography.

The wonder of Pepper's career is that he was able to fashion a name for himself despite being incarcerated for many of his prime years. But the beauty of his music is so striking that it etches the brain, and so remains with us despite prison bars and, finally, his death in 1982. It is said that the best jazz musicians draw on life experience. In the case of Art Pepper, his music was drawn from a life with more than its share of harrowing experience, yet this experience enabled him to develop the soul that is at the heart of his music.

Art Pepper started out in music as Horatio Alger but became Lemuel Pitkin and, finally, someone in between. He gave us inspired music but promised it in greater quantity during his peak years. But what he gave us is rare and unique.

In his last recorded performance, just two weeks prior to his death, he was still wailing. For his farewell piece of the concert and, as it turned out, his discography, as if to conclude matters full-circle, the horn he raised was not alto or even tenor, but clarinet—the first instrument he had played. And what tune did he select? "When You're Smiling," of all things! Inside, he must have been smiling; against all odds he had lived a full albeit checkered life, and he had created some memorable music. You *bet* he was smiling!

TODD SELBERT
New York, New York
August 2000

1

GETTIN' TOGETHER

Martin Williams

The square's question about jazz may not be such a bad question if you think about it. I mean the one that goes, "Where's my melody?" or "Why don't they play the melody?" We could borrow the famous mountain climber George Mallory's answer, "Because it's there." But a more helpful one might be, the melody is whatever they are playing, or to put it more directly, they don't play it because they can make up better ones. And if I wanted to introduce the square to that fact, one of the first people whose work I would use to show it would be Art Pepper.

This album is a sort of sequel to the earlier *Art Pepper Meets The Rhythm Section* (Contemporary C3532, stereo S7018), a set I would call one of the best in the Contemporary catalog. That one was made in 1957 and the rhythm section of the title was the very special one of the Miles Davis quintet of the time: Red Garland, piano; Paul Chambers, bass; Philly Joe Jones, drums. This one is made with the (again special) Miles Davis rhythm section of February 1960. Paul Chambers is still there, Wynton Kelly is on piano, Jimmie Cobb is on drums. That former session was made under pressure, for not only was the section available only briefly, Pepper himself had not played for two weeks before the night it was done. For this one, the Davis group was again in town only briefly, and again, there was only one recording session. In fact, the last track, *Gettin' Together*, made because Art wanted to record a blues on tenor, is just Pepper, Kelly, and the rest playing ad lib while the tape was kept rolling.

All of which obviously does not mean that either session was made with the kind of haste that makes waste.

I began by saying that I would use Art Pepper's playing to convince our square friend that jazzmen can make up better melodies than the ones they start with. (Others I would use for similar reasons might be Jack Teagarden, Lester Young, Duke Jordan, Miles Davis, and Benny Morton.) And I could well begin with an Art Pepper record like *Softly, As in a Morning Sunrise*, for Pepper states that theme with none of its usual melodramatics and proceeds to make up melodic lines spontaneously that are superior to those he began with. And I might also use it as an example of the emotional range he can develop within a solo from a very limited point of departure, and without eccentricity or crowding.

Pepper is a lyric or melodic player (those words are vague but when you have heard him, you know what they mean). Very good test pieces for such qualities are slow ballads—and many a jazzman of Pepper's generation wanders aimlessly and apologetically through such tests. There are two ballads here. *Why Are We Afraid?* is a piece Art Pepper plays in the movie *The Subterrraneans*. *Diane* is named for Art Pepper's wife; he has recorded it before but he prefers this version. So do I. It especially seems to me an *emotionally* sustained piece of improvised impressionism, and Kelly also captures and elaborates its mood both in his accompaniment and solo. Unlike many comparable players of his generation in jazz Art is not so preoccupied with making a melody that is "pretty" that he falls into lushness or weakness in his melodic line. What saves him is a kind of rhythmic fibre and strength that some lyric and "cool" players decidedly lack. (*Softly, As in a Morning Sunrise* is again a very good example.) For that reason, it should surprise no one to

2

hear him, particularly on the tracks where he plays tenor here, absorbing some rhythmic ideas from the better players in the current Eastern "hard" school. And to show how well they fit and are assimilated, that ad lib blues, *Gettin' Together*, is prime evidence. Surely one of the things that makes jazz so unsentimental and fluent an art is the jazzman's rhythmic flexibility, and that is something Art Pepper has always been on to.

It should come as no surprise that Art finds playing with a rhythm section picked by Miles Davis such a pleasure and stimulation. It is true that those two hornmen "use the time" (as musicians put it) differently; Pepper is closer to the beat in his phrasing for one thing. But Miles Davis is a unique combination of surface lyricism, concentrated emotion, and a decided, but not always obvious rhythmic flexibility. (He has been called a man walking on eggshells; a man with his kind of inner emotional terseness would surely crush eggshells to powder.) The sections he picks for himself might therefore be ideal for Art Pepper, for, although I don't think they convey emotion in the same way, they have many qualities in common. Miles' rhythm sections have been accused of playing "too loud" by some people. I am not sure what that means exactly, but I am sure that they are *never* heavy and always swing at any dynamic level they happen to be using, and that is a very rare quality. Their swing always has the secret kind of forward movement that is so important to jazz. (A handy explanation of "swing" might be "any two successive notes played by Paul Chambers.")

There are several other things on this record that gave me pleasure that I would recommend you listen for. One of the first is the unity of Pepper's solo on *Whims of Chambers* and the way it builds. (You cannot make a good solo just by stringing phrases together to fit the chord changes—but nobody admits how many players don't try to do much more than that.) The unity is subtle, but it is not obscure, and once grasped it becomes a delightful part of experiencing the solo. For instance, if you keep the phrase he opens with in mind, then notice how much of the solo is melodically related to that phrase. And also how much of it is related to Chambers' theme. Such unity is never monotonous because Art Pepper gets inside of these melodic ideas, finds their meaning, and develops them musically—he is never just playing their notes or playing notes mechanically related to their notes. The curve of the solo is also a delight. In a very logical way, more complex lines of shorter notes begin in Art's third chorus (that is the one where Kelly re-enters behind him). They reach a peak of dexterity in the fourth, tapering to a more lyric simplicity at its end. There is a very effective echo of those more complex melodies at the end of the fifth chorus, as the solo is gradually returning to the simpler lines it began with. (There is nothing really difficult or forbidding about following these things; if you can follow a "tune" you can follow these melodic structures, although they are far more subtle and artful than a "tune" is. And following them gives the kind of pleasure that digging deeper always does.)

Thelonious Monk's *Rhythm-A-Ning* may sound like only a visit to that "other" jazz standard (other than the blues, that is) which its title indicates. It isn't just that. And the best part is the "middle" or "bridge." Most popular songs are written with two melodies and if we give each a letter to identify it, the form of them comes out to be AABA. That B part of *Rhythm-A-Ning* is an integral part of the piece because its melody is a development of one of the ideas in the A part. The other thing is the way it is harmonized. You can easily hear that it is unusual when they play it the first time. Hearing what they do with it in the solos I leave to you to enjoy. I was also intrigued with the idea that Monk would get a smile out of Pepper's writing on *Bijou*.

A musician friend who had recently returned from California and was answering my questions about Art Pepper said, "I think maybe Art knows now that he plays not to win polls or be famous or any of that, but just because he has it in him to play and he just needs to."

If a man has come to that insight, I think you can hear it in the way he plays. I think I hear it here.

2

INTENSITY

Richard Hadlock with Lester Koenig

Intensity is a particularly apt word to describe Art Pepper. The dictionary defines it as "great energy or vehemence of emotion, thought, or activity." These are the qualities which have marked Art's playing for twenty years, from his first sessions on Los Angeles' Central Avenue in the early 1940s, through his association with Stan Kenton before and after World War II, and with his own groups in the 1950s. In reviewing Art's Contemporary album, *Smack Up!* M3602/stereo S7602, *Down Beat's* editor, Don DeMicheal, used the word: "Of all who were lumped together in the so-called West Coast school, Pepper was the one with the most to say, the one who seemed to consume himself and the listener with a searing fire that, for all its intensity, seemed never quite to express the emotion Pepper was feeling. Judging from his recorded work, this man whiplashed himself every time he soloed; the result was one of the most moving experiences to be had in jazz."

DeMicheal makes an interesting point. Despite the intensity, one always felt that there was more Pepper struggled to say—like the jazz artist in *Young Man with a Horn* who, unable to make his trumpet express *all* he felt, threw it across the room. The sensitive listener must hear this in performances by great jazzmen: Miles, Coltrane, Rollins—all seem frustrated by the limitations of their instruments and of music itself in expressing the totality of their emotions. This may explain why Ornette Coleman's attempt to reach beyond the rules of "natural" music has had such appeal for critics and musicians. If it is true that "a man's reach should exceed his grasp," it is especially true for artists everywhere, and Art Pepper is no exception.

"Art's life," writes Richard Hadlock, jazz editor of the San Francisco *Examiner,* "has been one of wild ups and downs. His employment history contains a file of top names plus countless forgotten rock and roll units, Latin bands and hastily assembled jazz combinations. Not to mention jobs that had nothing to do with music at all.

"I seldom made much money when I worked in Los Angeles," Pepper told me, "Usually about a hundred dollars a week. But there were many weeks I couldn't find a job at union scale. Somebody once even offered me a casual for five dollars."

"Art was understandably, something of a loner, and I think it shows in his playing. Pepper persisted in going his own way. There is and always has been an identifiable sense of urgency and emotional candor in Art's playing. He is a true individualist, in the same musical way that Pee Wee Russell, Ben Webster and Thelonious Monk are individualists. Pepper just plays Pepper, completely ignoring fad and fashion in the process.

"For him, sincere music of any kind seems to have instant, absolute value. He has spoken warmly of his stint in one rock and roll band ('. . . they really *felt* it') and of an early love for good Dixieland. It is as easy to imagine him playing decades ago with, say, Jimmy Blanton, Dave Tough or Earl Hines as with the best of today's or tomorrow's jazzmen. In short because he plays himself, Pepper cannot be dated. This fact is made abundantly clear by the present album of standards, as it is by his previous recordings.

"Listen, for example, to *I Can't Believe that You're in Love with Me*. From Art's rather traditional opening and closing statements to his unfettered improvisations in the core of the performance, it is unclassifiable Pepper-style jazz—modern and historically sound at the same time.

"Note, too, the time-honored devices by which the altoist communicates his feelings: the variable vibrato; bent notes; intuitive control over growth and decay of each tone; the injection of blues like phrases; arrangement and rearrangement of melodic fragments; the development of contrasting rhythmic figures. All these things and more make up Pepper's unique and compelling manner of talking on the alto saxophone. They are basically the same devices employed for decades by great jazz individualists such as Sidney Bechet, Frank Teschemacher, Bunny Berigan, Bill Harris and Miles Davis, and the approach remains as valid as ever.

"As this and his last Contemporary release, *Smack Up!*, demonstrate, Art was well on his way toward a new kind of playing freedom in 1960. He had, partly through the examples of John Coltrane and Ornette Coleman, begun to set aside his few remaining inhibitions and reach out for still more direct contact with his emotions. And, like most jazz musicians who have accomplished much, he was not afraid of taking musical chances, or even of stumbling from time to time.

"A musician friend told me recently that sometimes Pepper's playing 'sounds like a man crying—it just tears you up.' I agree."

3

ART PEPPER
—MARTY PAICH INC.

Alun Morgan

In the spring of 1956 Marty Paich came to London as accompanist to Dorothy Dandridge. Raymond Horricks and I were fortunate enough to spend some time with Marty and this was my first
"live" contact with the currently popular West Coast jazz movement. Identifying terms are convenient but invariably misleading and a great deal of misconception has arisen through this glib
method of pigeon-holing. "West Coast jazz" eventually rebounded
on its creators and developed into a term of derision in certain
circles although, strictly speaking, the description covered the
music of such California-based jazzmen as Kid Ory, Dexter Gordon, Earl Hines, Teddy Buckner and Maxwell Davis as well as
Lennie Niehaus, Shorty Rogers and Shelly Manne. A recession
in jazz interest in the area during the late fifties has led to a
reduction in the amount of work for men such as Bill Perkins,
Niehaus, Russ Freeman, etc., but the stigma has remained. This
bias is depressingly unfair, for it means that many collectors and
critics have pre-judged new records bearing the "made in Los
Angeles" tag. When this method of assessing value and importance is applied to the work of musicians such as Marty Paich,

"Art Pepper—Marty Paich Inc." by Alun Morgan originally appeared in the November 1960 issue
of *Jazz Monthly* magazine, and is reprinted by permission of the author.

Art Pepper, Bill Perkins, Alvin Stoller, Charlie Mariano and Jack Sheldon it is time to call a halt so that a few critical blinkers might be removed.

Marty Paich, as I soon discovered, is a man with an acute awareness of tradition and a love of all that is good in jazz. He spoke to me with relish of his then recent engagement with Harry Edison and Buddy Rich and revealed an extensive knowledge of the first Basie band culled direct from Edison. "When the band left Kansas City for New York in 1936," he remarked, "the book, the *entire* set of parts, travelled in Harry's trumpet case." His eyes glowed with pleasure at the thought of an orchestra which achieved so much largely on the strength of its head arrangements. Our conversation turned to a big band of more recent vintage, the fine orchestra put together by Shorty Rogers for the "Cool and Crazy" album (HMV DLP1030, Victor LPM1350). Marty played piano on the two dates for the LP and had based the broad outline of his style on the orchestral keyboard work of the Count. "We used five trumpets," he said. "Four played the opening ensemble chorus first time round with Conrad Gozzo on lead. (You know, Gozzo's one of the greatest lead men of all time.) Then when we'd given the impression that that was our full power we repeated the passage but this time we brought in Maynard Ferguson doubling the lead an octave above. It was quite a sound." Art Pepper had been one of the featured soloists on the "Cool and Crazy" LP and gradually we found ourselves talking of Pepper who, at the time of our conversation, was serving a sentence for narcotic addiction. Pepper had long been a particular favourite of mine (the only Kenton records I ever bought have been the ones with solos by Art) and I was anxious to learn of his whereabouts. Marty spoke at length and with obvious warmth about the alto player, regretting his absence from the Los Angeles circle at a time when there was so much work for jazz musicians and bemoaning the circumstances which had ensnared this superb soloist. It became obvious that Paich's love for Pepper's music was enormous.

Some months after Marty returned home I was surprised and delighted to learn of Art Pepper's release and I guessed that Paich's reactions would be the same. Within weeks of his reappearance Art had recorded an LP with Marty (Tampa TP28, London LZ-U14040) and it seemed that the Old Firm was back in business. Since that date Paich has worked and recorded with Pepper on a number of occasions but the surprising truth of the matter is that Art has found difficulty in breaking into the circle of musicians commanding the studio jobs and jazz club engagements. *Down Beat* dated April 14, 1960, carried a revealing feature on Pepper (the author was uncredited) which contained the information that at the beginning of 1959 Art was selling piano-accordions, complete with lessons on the instrument, to make a living. Less than three years before it seemed that Pepper was destined for a triumphant re-entry into the jazz world which had, in 1949, 1951, 1952, 1953 and 1954, placed him amongst the leading three or four alto saxists in referendums organised by *Metronome* magazine. A relatively brief spell of recording activity during 1957 and the latter half of 1956 left him high and dry. Warding off the narcotic peddlers who thought he might be easy meat having once experienced this deadly and easy way of nullifying frustrations, hardly helped matters, and the accordion-selling job seemed the only way he could earn a living for Diane (his wife) and himself. "It's true I was pretty disinterested in music at that time," he told *Down Beat*, "But I began to put down the *music* rather than the circumstances. The guy who really made me want to play again was John Coltrane. The fact that he'd come up with an original style struck me strongly. In the past there was Pres, then Charlie Parker. Now there's Coltrane. He starts playing and just flows through the rhythm. And I like his sound. Many people object to his sound, they say it's too rough and hard. Not me. He plays an awful lot of notes but as beautifully as anyone ever played. The way he plays with a chord and with scales is really remarkable."

When his interest in music was rekindled by Coltrane, Pepper cast about for a job in which he could get back to the music he loved. Strangely enough the only offer seemed to come from a rock and roll unit playing at a club in San Fernando Valley. "This was an *authentic* rock and roll band," he insists. "Most of the guys were from Shreveport, Louisiana, and they didn't fool around with the music. I began to dig music again from working with them. Because they really *felt* it. The music swung." Pepper was not the first to discover the importance of the rhythm and blues group to the jazz musician. Most of the leading soloists of today have come up through the ranks of r. and b. bands, bands in which the beat is important and the projection of the solo voice above a strongly riffing background leads to a tone and volume control which can never be achieved through working only with small jazz groups. By the middle of 1959 Art was anxious to get back into jazz proper and he jumped at the chance to join Bud Shank's new quartet at the Drift Inn at Malibu for week-end engagements. Soon afterwards he was signed up as a full-time member of the Lighthouse club band along with Conte Candoli, Vince Guaraldi, Bob Cooper and drummer Nick Martinis. Yet a man of his stature should be in a position to command a higher salary and to reckon on a fairly steady supply of day jobs in radio and television studios. "The truth is," Art confessed to the *Down Beat* reporter, "Marty Paich is the only leader in town who has called me for record dates, and who still does whenever he records. Even if he has an arrangement, say, on a vocal album with all strings, he'll even write in an alto part for me to blow on." About Pepper, Marty replies, "There's no-one else I would rather write for because the minute he hears the background, he makes an immediate adjustment to the arrangement. Art never stops listening to what's happening in the background; in reverse, it's like a pianist working with a singer."

The finest collaborative work featuring Pepper and Paich is the album entitled "Art Pepper plus Eleven: Modern Jazz Classics" (Vogue LAC12229, American Contemporary M3568) recorded at three sessions in March and May, 1959. Art and

Marty chose twelve outstanding jazz compositions dating from the 1944-vintage *'Round about midnight* to Sonny Rollins's 1954 *Airegin* by way of *Move, Groovin' high, Opus de funk, Four brothers, Shaw 'nuff, Bernie's tune, Walkin' shoes, Anthropology, Walkin'* and *Donna Lee.* Paich used a modified version of 'Dektette'-type instrumentation to support Pepper, the 'Dek-tette' being itself a development of the famous Miles Davis band. Marty was fortunate to have the services of Bob Enevoldsen, for this versatile musician was at home either on valve-trombone or tenor sax, thus giving the arranger the choice of five brass and three saxes or four brass and four reeds. Pepper played clarinet on one number (*Anthropology*), alto on seven, tenor on three, and both alto and tenor on one. An excellent transcription of the original Woody Herman sound was achieved on *Four Brothers* when Pepper played lead tenor in a sax section completed by Enevoldsen and Richie Kamuca, also on tenors, and Med Flory on baritone. Rarely in jazz can there have been more sympathy between arranger and soloist or a greater affinity of purpose. I must disagree wholeheartedly with the review of the record which appeared in this magazine for it contained the misleading statement, "in view of the lack of stimulating *rapport* between soloist and accompaniment here one feels that *Art Pepper meets the rhythm section* (Vogue-Contemporary LAC12066) remains this artist's best record." This is one of those cases (by no means rare in jazz criticism) when the reverse is actually the truth. Vogue LAC12066 features Pepper with Miles Davis's rhythm section (Red Garland, Paul Chambers and Philly Joe Jones); Art had never played with the rhythm section before and there are a number of occasions on the LP when the quartet seems to be heading in two directions at once. Philly Joe, for example, is such a strong individualist that there are few groups in which he can play his part to maximum effect; his trick of doubling the tempo for no apparent reason (it seems to take control of him like a nervous twitch) appears to surprise and annoy Pepper. Chambers's habit of playing a kind of running solo also runs counter to the ideas of the alto saxist who had previously enjoyed the superior class playing of Ben Tucker or Leroy Vinnegar in his rhythm sections. Most jazz enthusiasts (and surely all musicians) hearing *Art Pepper plus eleven* will sense at once the stimulating *rapport* between arranger and soloist, a truth which is borne out by the statements appearing in the *Down Beat* article. "I feel the situation between Art and myself is similar to that between Miles Davis and Gil Evans" stated Paich. "We understand each other. I've played with him long enough to understand his feelings. Because Art's usually recorded with a quartet or similar group, I tried to write for the *Eleven* album in a manner that would make him feel that he was playing with a small band." Marty expands the argument on the sleeve to the LP: "I wanted to give him a different kind of inspiration than he's been used to with just a quartet behind him. I wanted Art to feel the *impact* of the band, and I thought this setting would spur him to play differently than usual–though still freely within his natural style. And it did. Art and I have always thought very much alike. I couldn't have asked for a more compatible soloist." Pepper's agreement is implicit in his statement: "Seems like everything I've ever done with Marty came out good–from the first quartet we did on the Tampa label. He writes very interestingly–just listen to the latest album–and it always swings. That *Eleven* album is written with a lot of taste, and the voicing is excellent. Between him and me, it's a feeling . . . Like, some people make it together and some don't. We do."

Paich's writing for the *Eleven* album is something of a highspot in a consistently excellent arranging career. A knowledge of, and love for, the subject matter has meant that each number is not only treated with respect but with circumspection. On *Groovin' high,* for example, Marty has transcribed Parker's solo from the original Musicraft record and handed it to the saxes to play as a section; *Jeru* makes its appearance, in part, as an ensemble figure towards the end of *Walkin shoes* while the opening half chorus of *Donna Lee* captures the spirit and hope inherent in the music of Parker's quintet. The attention to detail not only in the writing but also in the playing means that Pepper has been given a series of springboards from which to launch himself into inspired solo passages, and the scoring of *Groovin' high, Airegin* and *Anthropology* in particular boosts Art up into the clouds. Always a lyrical, passionate player, Pepper is heard at his best on *Groovin' high* where his sense of occasion stands him in good stead. Stylistically he descends from an admixture of Parker, Lee Konitz and Benny Carter and the singing quality of his improvised lines would do credit to Carter or Lester Young. Alto remains his most effective instrument, the one on which he seems best able to communicate his thoughts, but his tenor playing in this album indicates that he could also become a major voice on the larger saxophone. His clarinet feature, *Anthropology*, is a revelation, for it is the first clarinet playing in the modern idiom I have heard which is warm-toned and free-swinging. "Art Pepper is probably one of the most dedicated musicians I know," maintains Paich. "He just lives for his horn." It is certainly true that he immerses himself in his music whenever he is called upon to solo. There is never a feeling of superficiality nor insincerity but always an impression of deep-seated emotion and a desire to get at the truth.

In recent months I have read full-page advertisements in American magazines calling attention to "soul" music which, if I have read the announcements correctly, is the prerogative of the Riverside and Prestige record companies. I am not sure of the exact meaning of "soul music" in this context but it seems to comprise a crude, insincere imitation of Negro gospel diluted with a generous helping of the vastly overrated Ray Charles. The result is more contrived than the most extreme examples of Illinois Jacquet's crowd-rousing screams. My conception of music which has heartfelt emotion or soul is the kind of jazz produced by trumpeter Joe Thomas or Art Pepper, for both these men play with a simple directness and poetic lyricism. Pepper can, and does, play the blues with more conviction than many of his so-called "soul" brothers and I would recommend in particular his

Blues out from Score SLP4030, an extended performance on alto backed only by Ben Tucker's bass. Unfortunately the hippies of this world are not likely to accept Pepper at his true value for, not to put too fine a point on it, Art, in their eyes, is not only resident on the wrong coast but is of the wrong colour. This is one of the fundamental injustices which no amount of preaching will put to rights, nevertheless my aim in writing this brief appraisal of an outstanding record is an attempt to set things in their correct perspective.

Art Pepper plus eleven is a superb album in every way. Not only does it showcase one of the really important soloists of our times but it focuses attention on one of jazz's brightest arrangers. It also indicates that Jack Sheldon, who shares the solo space with Pepper, is potentially the best of the newer jazz trumpeters resident in California and that Mel Lewis is a drummer with an enviable sense of timing and a Don Lamond-like approach to big band work. Further, it revives at least four masterpieces of a decade or so ago, tunes which are likely to retain their validity long after many of today's "originals" are forgotten. For some years I have looked on Art Pepper as the greatest solo player in jazz since Charlie Parker and this present LP, which I cannot recommend too highly, merely reinforces that opinion.

4

ART PEPPER'S THANKSGIVING
Cold Turkey a la Anslinger

Dave Solomon

Every jazz fan knows, by now, that Art Pepper was busted recently for possession of heroin, and given the traditionally sadistic and dangerous cold turkey treatment in a bare cell. Such unattended treatment, in cases of severe withdrawal symptoms, can result in death, and *always* produces the most excruciatingly severe physical agony. (Withdrawal illness is never pleasant, but can be made safe and far less agonizing by the use of proper medications.) But for Art Pepper, America's medieval drug laws and federal drug administration have once again decreed that a desperately ill man spend years rotting in a prison cell rather than a few rehabilitational months in a hospital bed. A few facts about drugs: heroin addiction is, in particular and primarily, a medically definable physical and emotional illness. It is a serious illness, but one that can be treated and cured by proper and humane medical attention. Certain drugs, especially the opiates (morphine, heroin and codeine) and the barbiturates (the common sleeping pill) cause a *physical addiction*. A physical addiction is not merely a strong habit: *it is an actual physical dependence that becomes part of the body chemistry.* Non-addicting drugs,

"Art Pepper's Thanksgiving" by Dave Solomon originally appeared in the March 1961 issue of *Metronome* magazine.

such as marijuana, may cause a mild habit, no stronger to break than our socially approved national drug habits: distilled and fermented beverages (alcohol), coffee (caffeine), tea (caffeine), and cigarettes (nicotine). Marijuana does not *addict*, does not create a physical dependence. It is, in point of scientific fact, less toxic and far milder than whiskey. (Alcohol is a *really* dangerous drug, which though accepted by our society, and the source of billions of dollars of government tax revenue, cripples millions of Americans annually.) Cocaine, though not addicting, is quite poisonous and dangerous to use.

In England and in certain Scandinavian nations, there is no serious drug problem because opiate and barbiturate addictions are successfully treated as illnesses, not crimes. America's cruel and vicious federal drug laws support and perpetuate drug addiction by forcing addicts to resort to pushers rather than doctors. *These laws should be repealed and replaced with more enlightened and constructive legislation. An important first step, however, would be for President Kennedy to fire Narcotics Commissioner Anslinger, whose administration has been both ignorant and inhumane.*

Art Pepper's career—as well as the lives and careers of thousands of other sick men and women *from all walks of life*—can still be saved. President Kennedy and our legislators can be moved to pass new laws that would open up hospitals and clinics, rather than cell doors, to the Art Peppers of America. METRONOME advises its readers to send letters to the President requesting that he call for the passage of new federal legislation, and that he replace Commissioner Anslinger with a more capable, knowledgeable and sympathetic administrator.

5

ART PEPPER

Clive Loveless

On October 25th, 1960, Art Pepper, who to my mind is the greatest modern alto player in jazz today, was arrested on charges of narcotic addiction. It was his third arrest for similar charges.

The relative arguments concerning his imprisonment and the whole question of narcotic addiction and its place in the American Penal Code are of no specific importance to this article. What is of importance though is, not how and for what reason he did become addicted, but rather that, despite his addiction and its ensuing mental and physical breakdown, Pepper, like Charlie Parker before him, was still able to remain in contact with his art, and even extend and develop it.

A comparison between Pepper and Parker's musical stature, however, is useless. Parker was a giant of jazz, an innovator and a man who changed the whole course of jazz history. However great Pepper is, he is still only a developer and consolidator of Parker's musical language. Yet though he cannot compete with Parker's flow and spontaneity of melodic ideas, his fire and his sheer force of musical character—(What present day saxophonist

"Art Pepper" by Clive Loveless originally appeared in the May 1963 issue of *Jazz Journal*. Reprinted by permission of *Jazz Journal*.

can?)—Pepper is Parker's logical successor and the only truly individual modern altoist today.

Not only has Pepper had to fight the temptations and effects of his addiction and pay for them in terms of social degradation and imprisonment, but he has not as yet been accorded the acclaim and respect which is owing, and certainly long overdue, by the jazz-listening public. It is only Sonny Stitt or Jackie McLean, both of whom have been highly praised, who can come anywhere near challenging him, and neither of these two great musicians are gifted with Art Pepper's breadth of emotional content and skill of dynamics in solo.

Pepper came to jazz at the age of eighteen, and eventually joined the Kenton Band, where he soon made a name for himself on the West Coast. At this time his playing, which had a thin, floating sound, was reminiscent of Paul Desmond or Lee Konitz, and he earned himself high ratings in the popularity polls of the early 1950s, during the West Coast jazz craze.

Then came Pepper's arrest and imprisonment for narcotic addition. 1956, though, brought Pepper's return to jazz, and a short but prolific output of recordings, including those with his own quartet (LONDON LZ-U 14038) and also with his friend and musical associate, Marty Paich (LONDON LZ-U 14040).

During this time Pepper's sound had undergone considerable change, now being noticeably fuller and thicker in texture, with much of Benny Carter's poise. For instead of his former wispy and rather antiseptic tone, his playing had now taken on a more "tenor-like" sound with out-bursts of restrained passion, which would then melt back into the overall quiet lyricism of his improvisation. An example of this can be found on *I Can't Give You Anything But Love* (VOGUE LAE 12106), where he is ably supported by only bass and drums.

Recordings made with Hoagy Carmichael (VOGUE VA 160112) and tenorist Bill Perkins (VOGUE LAE 122088) are also worthwhile, though not outstanding examples of his gradual development throughout this phase. However, it is with the release of *Art Pepper Meets the Rhythm Section* (VOGUE LAE 12066) that his latent potential and signs of his true stature are made obvious.

There has been much discussion and argument over this record, and the effects that the rhythm section, comprising Red Garland, Paul Chambers and Philly Joe Jones, had on Pepper's playing. It is clear the rhythm of these men is not wholly compatible with Pepper's sense of time and not every track, especially the fast ones, is an unqualified success. Yet, as always, Pepper does succeed in communicating his taut though lyric emotionalism, most notably in his versions of *Jazz Me Blues* and *Star Eyes*, the latter being a classic of its kind.

This brief spell of recording came to an abrupt halt at the end of 1957, and it seems that it was difficult for Pepper to find work in the studios. He became dispirited and disinterested in his music, and to complicate these frustrations it seems he was pestered by "junk peddlers," who felt he would be easy prey to their temptings. However, after a stint at selling piano-accordions, Pepper began to take new interest and pride in his music— as he said, "The guy who really made me want to play again was John Coltrane." The end of 1959 found him back in the recording studios, this time with Barney Kessel (VOGUE LAC 12206) and once again with Marty Paich (VOGUE LAC 12225).

On the latter disc, *Art Pepper Plays Modern Jazz Standards*, Pepper forsook his alto on five tracks, playing warm, Zoot Sims-styled tenor on *Move, Four Brothers* and *Walkin'*, and turning in a swinging, expressive, modern jazz clarinet solo on *Anthropology*, which should safely quieten down any who thinks Tony Scott is "something else." Once again, this record is not a complete success, for it leaves Pepper too restricted by the shortness of tracks and he is unable to cut loose and find his usual freedom in these heavily arranged surroundings.

Musically speaking, 1960 became Art Pepper's most satisfying year. In two LP records, *Gettin' Together* (VOGUE LAC 12262) and *Smack-Up* (VOGUE LAC 12316), can at least be seen the full achievement and still developing aims of Pepper's style. *Gettin' Together*, recorded in February, contains the most successful of Pepper's quartet sides, producing a ravishing version of *Why Are We Afraid?* and the beautiful floating lyricism of *Diane*, which he wrote for his wife. On three other tracks of this album he is joined by Conte Candoli who, though once showing promise, is particularly inept here, trying to equal the quiet warmth of his leader, but only succeeding in producing totally gutless solos. Yet it is on these tracks that Pepper is most inspired, producing solos of the highest quality, using stark melodic fragments interspersed with rests, in their construction.

On these tracks, *Whims of Chambers*, *Bijou the Poodle* and *Rhythm-a-ning*, Pepper sounds like a less acid, more restrained Thelonious Monk, but on alto. The best example of this manner of playing is contained on the Monk original, *Rhythm-a-ning*, where Pepper creates, in total, a united, yet subtly poised solo of great worth.

On *Smack-Up* the results are even more exceptional, due in no small way to the superlative bass and drums playing of Jimmy Bond and Frank Butler (indeed the same complementary relationship between drummer and leader can be found here as with Danny Richmond and Mingus, Billy Higgins and Ornette Coleman on their albums). Also Pepper finds a better front-line partnership with the welcome return of Jack Sheldon.

The tunes were all written by saxophonists, and once again it is interesting to note the way in which Pepper uses characteristics which suit his own musical ideas, from the styles of other musicians, while still creating a solo which is completely his own. Here reference may be made to Parker, Konitz, Monk, and in this album one can find a definite Ornette Coleman influence, particularly at the searching, probing beginning of *Smack-Up*, and in his *Tears Inside* solo. In all, despite Pete Jolly's rather mannered piano playing, this is Pepper's most satisfying album to date and the hopes and resolutions of his playing can all be found in the attractive 5/4 theme, *Las Cuevas de Mario*.

Unfortunately the day that this album was recorded was the day of Pepper's arrest, and we do not know how much longer it will be before he will once again be recording and producing discs of such high quality.

It is sad and ironic that such a great artist as this, still only at the age of thirty-eight, should remain almost unknown but for a trickle of records, which for the time being seems to have dried up, while someone like Paul Desmond is voted top alto of the year for his vapid meanderings, Cannonball Adderley is acclaimed by the "soul-searchers" for his hysterical squawks, and Eric Dolphy is lauded by the "hippies" for every "bubble and squeak" he regurgitates on his bass clarinet. But of course the inverted "snobbism" of many jazz fans today finds sheer beauty of sound, technical mastery, lyricism and restraint poor excuses for a jazz-man who does not submit to a formula, resides on the wrong coast and is unfortunately—dare I say it—white!

6

ART PEPPER
Towards A New White Jazz

T. E. Martin

The fact of Art Pepper's arrest several years ago on a charge of drug addiction is by now widely known and many critics have lamented this unfortunate termination of his creative output, quite apart from the sad state of legal consciousness it implies. His work is generally respected and several writers, notably Alun Morgan, consider him to be the greatest altoist in the modern idiom. It is very pleasing therefore to note a report of his impending release on March 22nd.

Consideration raises several problems however, not least of these being "why if he justifies such praise is he not worthy of more frequent mention in studies of jazz styles and achievements?" The answer, I think, we shall find is in the colour of his skin or more precisely the colour of his culture. But first this seems an important opportunity to form a clear idea of the origins of the style of a singular musician, to see how he can assemble them to signify his own meanings and perhaps finally to recognise the seeds of an attempt to go beyond his beginnings. Above all, this essay is an attempt to focus some attention on a

"Art Pepper: Toward a New White Jazz" by Terry Martin. This is a slightly edited reprint of the article originally appearing in the February 1964 and August 1964 issues of *Jazz Monthly*, and is reprinted by permission of the author.

jazzman of supreme integrity who unfortunately is in many ways unappreciated and who has contributed much to this writer's love for jazz.

THE ELEMENTS

White saxophone playing in recent years has been dominated by the twin influences of Parker, harmonically, and Young, tonally and melodically. Its sources reach back into the melting pot of the forties with the crumbling swing bands and emergent bop. The present essay is mainly concerned with the recordings (to be discussed specifically in the second part) made since the time when Pepper first proved that he was a true soloist, an integral musical personality capable of independent and coherent statements rather than being merely one solo voice among many. This is taken to begin, on record, with the quartet dates of '52, but some résumé, and frequent reconsideration, of his background will be useful. Born of a musical family in Gardena, Calif., on September 1, 1925, he served his apprenticeship during the forties in an environment of big bands and dixieland groups; he no doubt heard many of the great Negro stylists including Benny Carter with whom he worked in 1943, an important formative period. But he moved to the brink of maturity as a member of the Kenton band and appears to have been greatly stimulated towards the end of his second stay with this orchestra by Lee Konitz's example, as any young saxophonist might by this doggedly individual player who, in addition, bore the same cultural marks. He had of course recorded many fine solos before this in a manner suspended between those of Parker, Carter, and Willie Smith, whose work on the Lunceford performances was particularly admired by the young musician. At the time it might have seemed that the influence of Konitz was to be detrimental to the hitherto robust playing of Pepper who produced a simple modification of the former's style retaining much of the mentor's abstraction. Konitz himself was to develop the line of abstraction to the point of involution and so achieve by devious means his own expressive ends where he would finally cage himself in a hyper-sensitive but limited art. (Konitz also is in urgent need of careful revaluation and greater appreciation, for he is one of the true ascetics of jazz and as such, has carried one of the elements of the white style to its logical conclusion.) However it was an affinity for other aspects of the two Negro musicians who had inspired the white moderns that allows Pepper to transcend his fellows. We shall have cause to return to this problem of race (culture) shortly but first I shall attempt to indicate the mainstream origins of Pepper's techniques.

Parker's fragmentation of traditional forms, with the reassembly of new contorted structures, is an obvious source but Pepper has modified this process in his mature work under the direct influence of Lester Young's rhythmic innovations. It must be realised immediately that the contortions apparent in Pepper's solos arise from only one of Bird's methods, that is the counterpoising of differently moving lines within a melodic sentence, and rarely are they fused and concentrated to distortions at the note level as they are in Parker or Ornette Coleman. He has been more conservative in this sense than the last named innovators, indeed more so than many of the better Negro consolidators e.g. Rollins, McLean, et al., but his ability to build the mosaic patterns of the modern idiom is considerably greater than that of his white contemporaries, who generally found it easier to approximate the desired aesthetic ends by pursuing endless even lines to the limits of the harmonies. Brief reflection will indicate that the variety and immediacy of emotional impact open to the former method are by far the greater (a fact apparently now being realised by the masters of the latter, viz. Getz and Konitz, allowing the possibility of their escape from the bonds of their exquisite miniatures). This ability I feel springs from a surety strange in a white musician, rhythmic confidence, and the corollary, rhythmic freedom. Again the technique used is simpler than Parker's staggering sequence of metric suggestions but that it begins to rival the perfection of Pres's refined sensibility is recommendation in itself.

It is remarkable that the school most devoted to the work of Lester Young should be so rhythmically unvaried; though I don't mean uninteresting. Sims has a fine swing and Lee Konitz's rhythm goes hand in hand with his aesthetic of purism. Parker was the true heir of his innovations and exploited their implications more fully than any other jazzman. While there is an obvious effect of Parker on Pepper, witness the rare Parkerism, the latter by direct reference to the source made a similar but distinct, if less extensive, exploitation of rhythmic shifts. Parker replaces the indolent perfection with all the concentrated desperation of the modern aesthetic; less the iconoclast, Pepper is recognisably modern, and a disturbed urgency permeates his work. Whereas the former's lines contort and pulsate with constantly changing patterns, Pepper relies more on a knife edge precision of note placement in relation to the beat. As with Pres himself it is not that the rhythms used are complex but that the placement is always fresh and refreshing; this clearly demands a highly refined rhythmic sense. The four square placement is constantly avoided by means beyond those of a mere craftsman, they are expressive means. If one should doubt Pepper's ability in this sphere I suggest that the reader, if possible, attempt to achieve a similar effect, or more simply, listen again to the way he invariably ends "right side up" after astounding multinoted passages such as occur in *Besame Mucho, Rhythm-a-ning* etc. Despite the more involved investigations of rhythm which appear in the work of the shamefully ignored Lennie Tristano and Warne Marsh whose use of the mode is often inconsistent, brilliant and imperfect, one is led easily to the conclusion that Pepper's rhythmic sense is unrivalled by any other white jazz musician.

However, melodic fragments dealt out with a sharp sense of time require reassembly if a coherent expressive end is to be served. Again Pepper seems to have delved back into the middle era independent of Parker; despite the fragmentation there is a constant sense of formal resolution, a tendency to symmetry which is absent from Bird's boldly asymmetric patterns. It should be stressed that total asymmetry is not essential to the modern style but its imprint must remain. Pepper in his own way attempts to regain a classical order from the chaos revealed by the bop greats just as Rollins has done to his. It seems that his stint with the Benny Carter band may have been critical in moulding this sense of form since Carter is the master of construction (Pepper may also have aspired to the master's clarity of tone). Certainly, he relies strongly on similarities of melodic shapes, these stemming from the choice and direction of intervals not from resemblances of melody as such. Rollins is the obvious example of a musician who uses the latter method. The altoist on the other hand builds not on the original melodic figure laid down at the beginning of the solo but on its shape, thus the melodies developed later need have no close relation to the germ cell in melodic terms. Here is a reason for the absence of note distortions which are often used, e.g., by Parker and Rollins, to create the required ambiguity. The shapes themselves must be kept clean and unambiguous if they are to form the main constructive element; the ambiguity undeniably present springs from Pepper's individual use of rests. Carter's melodic figures which are placed symmetrically result in symmetry, Pepper (who has absorbed Young) places his asymmetrically and thus only tends toward overall symmetry. This is one source of his lyrical tension.

Pepper has never sought beautiful melodies for their own sake and cannot be regarded as a great melodist. Rather his melody is completely absorbed in the expressive fabric of the music. It would be wrong to assume from this that he would have simply adopted some previously established melodic approach—e.g., from Parker as Stitt and others have. Rarely does he strive for a melodic paraphrase of the theme, being generally more interested in the emotive possibilities of interlocking fragments arising from germ cells of the theme and the effect of altered dynamics. Melody suffers change under a constant redistribution of the pattern of rests; in this respect we may note the mastery of Monk, another who is more concerned in reading meaning into the melody rather than extending further the melodic limits during his improvisations. Pepper's approach to ballads is almost invariably that of lending weight to themes; he does not attempt the creation of ingratiating melodic variations (contrast Paul Desmond for example), although I do not mean to imply that he is any way lacking in melodic ability.

One other striking feature of the altoist's technical vocabulary also deserves mention as it occurs more and more frequently in his recorded work. Again the source is Lester Young (and further back Bubber Miley et al. at a rough guess); in this case Pepper, probably more than any other, had adapted the use of a varied tonal density to the needs of the lighter instrument and the modern aesthetic. He uses this in the way that Parker often employs a pitch slur, to dramatise a phrase. It is at once less forthright, less confident and more subtle. Again it has been a Negro, viz Coleman, who has taken up the slur, a most dangerous and vertiginous technique.

Before approaching his records we should perhaps consider a crucial aspect of Pepper's position that we have avoided so far, viz his aesthetic position as an American White. Some writers have attempted to create the impression that there is no distinction between white and Negro jazz. This is purely wishful thinking. While there is segregation, physical and cultural, it is impossible. Parker and Pepper hold differing positions in relation to the background of American culture. We must still insist that beyond the particular differences between individual musicians there remain general differences between white and Negro. We cannot hasten assimilation, if that is what we seek, by ignoring obvious divergences (nor, in passing, should we imagine differences that have ceased to exist). Bird is part of a rapidly fluxing culture whereas Pepper's is relatively static; by now the aesthetic prospect is almost the same for black and white but the reactions necessarily differ. I have recently expressed some views on the peculiar position of the white musician in jazz (*Jazz Monthly*,

Dec. 1962, Jan. 1963). The archetypal figure is of course Bix. I hope that I may be able to justify Pepper's role as the modern counterpart, albeit lacking the romance and legend if not the tragedy, and indicate that the apparent aesthetic of the two men is the same (given some doubt as to the implications of recent modifications in Pepper's style; I feel by the way that these are not incompatible with the general thesis but merely the logical outcome). I do not wish to give the impression that Bix and Pepper are the only worthwhile white musicians; the examples of Rappolo, Lang, Freeman, Russell, Teagarden, Eager, Getz, Tristano, Konitz, Marsh, Woods, et al., would make such a conclusion ridiculous, but both stand out by their consistent ability to express themselves freely in the medium. How the estimates may change given the new breadth in the work of Getz and Woods, the possible re-emergence of the Tristano school or even the rejuvenation of Pee Wee Russell, is impossible to say. Nevertheless at the moment of his incarceration it seems to this writer that Art Pepper was without peer amongst his race.

I would like now to mention a few frequent characteristics of white jazz in relation to Pepper, his choice of techniques and hence this aesthetic character. Needless to say I feel some trepidation in plunging deeply into the complex of psychological and sociological motives that underlie any musician's creative work especially at this distance from the subject, but it is a quest that promises immense interest. To begin, it is a commonplace to note the work of Europeans is decidedly more nervous but less vigorous than that of the Negro. The cases where this is not so are often those which involve "sound and fury" rather than depth, e.g., Wild Bill Davison in his less coherent moments, and the occasionally spurious use of "growl" that mars some of Phil Woods's solos. A common "fault" with even some of the best white jazzmen is that of uncertainty. Now it may be argued I think that this uncertainty is a basic property, not necessarily one of technique or purely personal psyche. In the end it must be admitted that aesthetically at least even Getz and Konitz have fallen before uncertainty. They have both in the past created consistent but essentially "tangential" modes; they have preferred a hermetic world which must be approached rather than approaches. This makes it superficially comfortable for the listener as well, but the last century has shown that such an attitude is not that which produces transcendent art. Their quality stems from the undoubted truth within limitation, their imperfection from the fact of limitation. Beiderbecke, Pepper and few others survive the aesthetic struggle by admission and expression of uncertainty, though it may be suggested that there has been a personal defeat in the case of these two men. To go beyond their charm Getz and Konitz (vide essays by Michael James in his *Ten Modern Jazzmen*) both require a prior or learned disposition in favour of their means of expression, whereas Pepper, at times, demands our attention as do the great Negro musicians. He will go to the listener and grasp him, he does not hold back, the declaration is emotionally unambiguous thanks to a clarity of conception and absolute rhythmic precision, of Bix. It is obvious however that his work is far less aggressive than Parker's or Coleman's, but this is the "difference of reaction," Bix never showed the adventurous, if occasionally fumbled, strokes of the maturing Armstrong. There has been no white iconoclast in jazz. Bix's advantage over all other white musicians in terms of jazz memory is the revelation by him that there could be a truly expressive white jazz.

It would be interesting to know the broader musical taste of the developing Art Pepper. Did he share with Bix, Pee Wee and others an interest in Debussy and the moderns for example? He at least reveals his cultural relation to these men. But in jazz the whites have developed only conservative styles avoiding the iconoclastic which are apparently required for a strong tradition. The greater musicians have appeared to have attained their positions independently of earlier white masters, Bix in particular, by necessarily (because of their cultural background) similar views of the main stream of jazz evolution. Beiderbecke left no heirs. White jazz has existed in clusters, the Chicagoans, the dix-

ielanders, the West Coasters . . . . No one hears (aesthetically) Lee
Konitz, Tristano, Getz . . . . The reason is to a large extent the aesthetic of isolationism that lies at the base of contemporary Western art. However the sparks of iconoclasm have remained in the
air of European art; if the best of white jazz relates to the tense
lyricism of, say, a Braque, where is the Picasso? Must we look
solely amongst Negroes, who created bop, thus bridging, for jazz,
in one great stride the gap between Manet and Picasso, Wagner
and Stravinsky, Baudelaire and Joyce? It seems so. The white
man still strives to find a voice in jazz evolution. He has found
how to create in spite of our ambiguous existence in contemporary society, Getz, Konitz; how to admit and express these ambi-
guities, Bix and Pepper, but he has not yet managed to challenge
and shatter them, despite the rise of "action" and "rigorous"
forms in the traditional arts. Now the Negroes (with voices of
Coleman and Coltrane) again steal a lead and begin once more
to renew the jazz language virtually unaided by those whom we
might expect could excel within the new aesthetic. The white
musicians appear as separate branches of the main flux, all
admittedly moving in the same direction, but as yet only con-
nected and sustained by the central stream.

We have now reached a point which is peripheral to this essay,
but its importance to the future development of the white style
and jazz as a whole persuades me to return to this later, particularly as Pepper's last recordings suggest some relevant possibilities.

When the altoist departed from the Kenton organisation after
his second stint his style was in ferment. . . . This schizophrenia
was to prevail for several years and was prolonged by Pepper's
sheer technical ease; it seems that he was to use this unconsciously to play the chameleon, fitting himself to the concepts of
West Coast academicism and merging, albeit without ever resort-
ing to the prevalent and rarefied banality, then in another solo
from the very same session bursting out with an approach completely mature and without precedent. We may contrast this with

the dogged individualism developing in Lee Konitz and Stan Getz. If I may simplify, I picture three main poles of distraction at this time which ironically are also the foundations of his individuality. These are: the direct neo-swing approach of his early Kenton period owing much to Willie Smith, the disturbing influence of Konitz's clearly impressive but introspective solos, and the developing Kenton tradition and the allied West Coast formalism of the early-'fifties. They do in fact symbolise the three attributes that fuse in his best work, yet each in itself is guilty of aesthetic bias: the Smith influence represents the enduring fiery Negroid tradition which supports the entire jazz superstructure— i.e., jazz as emotion, an extrovert content.

Konitz's asceticism doubtless finds cultural sympathy in Pepper and introduces the idea of jazz as a self-question—i.e., an introvert content.

The West Coast school came to stand for precision and formalism, at its worst a complete atrophy of what Pepper must have gained from Benny Carter. It stands for a preoccupation with jazz as form or in its less desirable manifestation jazz as presentation. Although now in danger of neglect the West Coasters represented a dangerously polarised and polarising school of jazz thought and the young altoist seems to shift between the various masks and himself, pre-occupation and integration in the most disconcerting manner.

It is my opinion that each of the masks separately was futile for the young white musician. The first was unobtainable without the denial of cultural integrity, the second without loss of personal integrity in favour of what after all was only a part solution anyway (vide earlier remarks on the limitations of the Konitz style particularly as it was at the time, also Michael James's sympathetic essay on "The Cool Deviations" in *Jazz Monthly* for April), while the depersonalisation engendered by the third dogma should be obvious to all. The odd thing is that all these masks could coexist with a Pepper who was completely himself, a true extension and fusion of his influences.

THE FIRST QUARTETS

Stylistic diversities are seen immediately in the first sides he made under his own name. The first quartet recorded for Discovery in February 1952 and included Hampton Hawes (pno), Joe Mondragon (bass) and Larry Bunker (dms). These performances along with those of the second session were released on Vogue LDE067. The matrix numbers indicate that quite a few takes were required before the final polished performances were obtained; *Brown Gold* as issued being a seventh take. Certainly the construction of the alto solos here is immaculate but beneath the surface one can detect a variable expressive quality. The tone employed is light and clear but the retreat from the Konitz sound is already apparent. The Konitz influence had been strongly apparent in the latter half of his stay with Kenton; in the 1947 *How High the Moon* the tone was strong and the deployment of rests prophetic, but by 1950 in *Jolly Rogers, Art Pepper* and the Rogers's Giants version of *Over the Rainbow* (1951), the Konitzian world is clearly evoked (on the other hand one could mention this impressive Pepper-ish version of the exotic *Francesca* and the original harp-like phrases of *Street of Dreams* both of 1951). By '52 however the eventual direction seems to have been determined and it seems on recorded evidence that he could no longer don the Konitz mask without his own features distorting it and compromising the expressive quality of the solo. These quartet sides indicate that the flexible immaturity was near its end.

Before leaving the subject of the Konitz bias one should state that only Konitz himself could surpass Pepper's better essays in the genre, because up to the quartet sides Pepper had shown an amazing aptitude to be truly creative in existent styles and there can be no doubt that he felt the "cool" aesthetic. But in depth the two altoists were at odds; Pepper's need to create by form, to expand his palette, could only destroy the austere isolation of Lee's pure conception. Since this was what the latter was indeed expressing the entire basis of a hybrid is compromised and as such invalid. This danger would haunt Pepper's work for some years and is clearly apparent in the quartet's *Brown Gold* where after an expressive Pres-like phrase with notable use of timbral variations on a repeated note in the first eight bars the fluency of the rest of the solo is anticlimactic. This is unfortunate, for the line provides the rhythmic platform for the movements through the upper register that follow, but there the chastity of timbre and phrase works against the precise structures that provide the expressive force in his music. True, it is the interaction of defined forms, timbral and rhythmic emphases with a quiet fluency that defines his "passionate lyricism," but the tendency to make fluency itself an avenue of exploration allows the hint of underlying uncertainty.

However, the four tracks show abundant awareness of the tricks of fusing choruses into a unit. Notice for example the remarkable welding of his second and third choruses on the medium pace blues *Holiday Flight*. The first and second choruses move by symmetrical stepping figures in the upper and middle range but as he moves towards the last he moves to the lower range lifting slightly in bar 24 to lead to the emphasis of the first note of bar 25 from which as the lowest note the ascent suggested in bars 23-24 can take place throughout the rest of the chorus. Thus bar 25 is the natural outcome of the suggestive descents in the second half of chorus two and the foundation for the ascents of chorus three, itself an expansion of bars 23-24, while being bound by parallel motion to bar 24 and being the reversed tonic accent of the unit 22-28. This crucial position is underlined by the timbral peculiarities of the lowest notes on the instrument. So carefully contrived is the construction and accent of this passage that the movement to the upper register is felt as release, indeed as anticlimax, for he allows it to trail away in a rather fibreless manner.

I do not wish to give the impression that *Holiday Flight* is greatly superior to the other tracks but chose it merely for this clear example that Pepper is intuitively a musical architect—his materials, forms, rhythms, textures and their interactions—I hope that it is not necessary to explain that one can achieve emotional statement equally well with these as with the colour and free arabesque of a more romantic artist. The gift of melodic form hardly ever deserts him even when he is not greatly involved in the proceedings and probably explains the incredible surface consistency of his recorded solos. It is easily apparent on *Surf Ride,* a fine fast blues on which he employs the familiar pattern of breaking and sparring with the melodic line though more significant in his exceptional ease with that most difficult genre— the four bar exchange. Even the greatest musicians come to grief here; even Parker. Generally the most successful essays result from an excited dialogue or duel between the performers—e.g., the Navarro-McGhee sides, Parker-Navarro on *Ornithology* (Le Jazz Cool), Hawkins-Shavers on *Hawk Eyes* etc.; if there is no interaction we are left with ill-assorted fragments. Pepper does not interact to any great extent with the other "speaker." He does, however, interact with the basic pulse and uses it to carry over the "gap." In other words while formally dropping out for every alternate four bars he can often create the illusion of a continuous solo; the suggestions of space inherent in his solo style obviously aid him in this. I shall return to this topic when we come to his great performances, but for the moment let us see what other characteristics may be detected in these early recordings.

I have suggested that the altoist is not a great melodist and one might expect that he would generally eschew ballad-playing. This seems to be so, but his ballads remain impressive. Of the three white moderns I have used for comparison, viz Pepper, Konitz and Stan Getz, only the last had at that time a style which could use the ballad as a base for ballad extension. Konitz's melodic invention was too esoteric and intractable to stick to the ballad's own terms. Art Pepper could not (just as Lester Young) fragment and reassemble the ballad line because of the slow tempo and the highly developed character of the material; though the unique Thelonious Monk solved this problem. He resolved this by an approach which did not extend but rather reinforced and deepened the given melody line. For example, in the fourth title from the 1952 date, *These Foolish Things*, the theme is treated with the utmost respect, there is no attempt to "pretty it up" (as a Getz or Desmond might do), but there are some apparently minor changes, at least at first sight they seem minor. The melody has been pruned a little, the superfluous tails of the main line having been cut away. Reconsideration will show that he uses this strengthened phrase to evolve the sinuous nature of the first sixteen bars. An example of his strengthening of the line is seen in the way he counters the upward melody movement in bars 1-2 by a symmetrical descent in bar 3 and the treatment of certain notes as recapitulation points a few bars later. The bridge and final theme are treated very tenderly and prophesy the later versions of his own tune *Diane*. The whole solo is reticent in the manner of a Getz, indeed the embellishment in bars 7-8 is very like a Getz line. Though possibly lacking the melodic fertility of the tenorist, he gains in tension by the pervading interplay of lyricism and organisation.

The ballad of the following year, *Everything Happens to Me*, is played much more brilliantly and remains a model of the West Coast style; many of the effects of later Bud Shank performances are apparent here, the sandwiching of double-time between the phrases of the theme and the tremolo phrasing (a very dubious device) though Shank denies Pepper's influence. However, though lacking the integrity of *These Foolish Things*, the timbral and rhythmic effects achieved on re-entry after Russ Freeman's piano passage are intriguing. On the whole this second session is of lower tension; *Chile Pepper*, a rather glib Latinized *Tea for Two*, *Suzy the Poodle*, a fast and fluent *Indiana*, but *Tickle Toe* is clearly an outstanding exception to this and is perhaps the best quartet side. Here we may sense an atmosphere peculiar to Pepper's work and it is present in all of the best uptempo solos of his maturity.

From the opening break his playing is elated, a tense pulse dances through his theme statement and the sense of "wanting to blow" is wonderfully expressed, driving frustrated amateurs like myself in search of our discarded instruments. The sheer mastery of the breaks at the close is enough to make us cast them aside once more. But a second look at the solo (the lilt of the theme fuses it with the improvised chorus) reveals a painful edge to the élan, the poignancy reinforced by the pleasure. The inspired melodic figures developed in the breaks, which have the beauty and surprise of no less than Pres himself, bear an emotive ambiguity, a latent anguish that the altoist can generate so unexpectedly in his best work at middle and uptempo. This is a crucial point and should be borne in mind by anybody approaching Pepper's music; it is the expansion of this unique expressive quality that endows elements of greatness to his later achievements.

WITH SHORTY ROGERS

Art Pepper's recordings with his ex-Kenton colleague conveniently span the period under discussion and they are seminal to the entire West Coast movement. In retrospect the Capitol sides of October 1951 (reissued with the similarly styled Mulligan tentet session of two years later on Capitol T2025) supply the key to the Californian aesthetic; the instrumentation recalls that of the Davis '49 band as does the superficial aspect of the arrangements but that's all that remains of the penetrating artistry, the surface. It might be said that an unsaleable triumph of the East when hollowed out by ex-Kentonites and later by Mulligan, a Davis sideman, became a commercial rage in the West. But this is an overly misanthropic view, for Rogers's scores are very fine in their way and become excellent settings for Pepper who has no trouble in standing out in this company despite some scraps of fine Hampton Hawes.

Nowadays one has to make some adjustments to the low key of these distillations but from the first side, *Four Mothers*, we see the trend; Rogers and even more Giuffre are bound by the circumstances and strive to fill their time; Hawes, brittle and Parker-ish, strives for the autonomy that Pepper grasps with ease. He was on flawless form on this date. He is still "at home on the Coast" and still a miniaturist but one of the best; there is no faking or bare formalism. We may note in passing the lower register work on *Popo*, the elegant scurrying over the keys in *Apropos* and generally his varied distribution and note values contrasted with the less agile Rogers and Giuffre. His use of note values—viz. in agogic accents—resembles his use of rests (a more dramatic method).

Turning now to his best work here—*Sam and the Lady*—a fine arrangement creates a suspended sensation by way of continually interlacing lines and the altoist solos beautifully with a rich lower register and dancing pointillist ascents. Rogers plays some fine ideas and battles gamely against superior odds in the four bar breaks where at the climax he produces a strong if slightly mishandled melody only to see it capped by his sideman's scooping variant which is also a logical outcome of what he had been suggesting throughout the exchange. The altoist's solo piece, almost a miniature concerto, *Over the Rainbow* is a fully reticent performance reproducing the exquisite sensitivity of Konitz. It has beautifully performed filigree, refreshingly cool but enhanced by Pepper's dancing rhythms that breathe life into the type of decoration that has often become in other hands merely examples of an icy baroque. This solo stands as one of the peaks of his achievement in the cool mode and as near greatness as the hermetic form can achieve, equalled by only the best of the two other white saxophonists. The tune has a remarkable sense of completeness and, it must be mentioned, benefits from Rogers's caressing backgrounds. The high range of the alto is used particularly poignantly and the perfectly executed smears and general poise indicate that he was even then amongst the most instrumentally gifted of all saxophonists yet to have taken breath.

Personal difficulties must to some extent explain the fall from the pre-eminence on the Coast predicted by this early session;

coupled with the developing solo power and pretensions and commercial potential of his colleagues this may have reduced him to the role he plays in the later Giants' recordings. Certainly we hear much less from him in the big band sides of 1953 and the music suffers. Some of the items are merely dull as, for example, *The Sweetheart of Sigmund Freud* with a neo-Lesterish tenor solo of no great achievement (said to be Pepper, who appearing as Art Salt may also have played baritone on this piece), and some excruciating to these ears; *Contours* with depressing Milt Bernhart trombone and atrocious thumping from Manne, and *Tale of an African Lobster* complete with pretentious Kentonish intro leading to a sick ballad trombone solo (the blank mindless trombone flutterings will ever stand as an indictment of the Kenton influence). The latter, by the way, contains a few bars of Pepper's fading Konitz influence. Having said this it is well to point out that the remaining tracks (they were released on "The Big Shorty Rogers Express" album Am. Vic. LPM1350, HMV DLP1030) have moments worthy of attention. *Coop de Graas* is a pleasant duet for Bob and John; *Infinity Promenade* with a short light-toned tenor solo from Art concludes with high trumpets on tuba and Maynard Ferguson shrieking the harmonic parallel (it is a comment on the advance in percussion technique that Manne's "semi-pitched" cymbal line, adventurous then I suppose, is laughable today), *Boar-Jibu*, a four brothers voicing, has some fine tenor and baritone exchanges, the first tenor spars the line well and may be the altoist doubling once more, while the final tenor (Giuffre?) finds some nice crushed Pres-like phrases. *Short Stop*, a riff blues, includes an excellent Pepper solo on some Parker-ish rhythms, some rough tenor and pleasing trumpet.

Despite the occasionally impressive arrangements and odd solo of worth by Rogers et al. it seems that the real justifications for remembering these performances are Pepper's solos and the fiery ensembles. *Chiquito Loco*, the remaining title, is sufficient evidence for these claims. This item recalls in form the Rogers-Pepper duet on *Sam and the Lady* but in addition enables us to view clearly the latter's affinity for Latin rhythms. His habitual division of the beat and pent-up phrasing gives him a natural ease with the metre which has inspired some of his greatest work. Shorty too is on exceptional form, his tone sweet and with a firm edge lacking the meandering fluffiness he would later affect. The trumpet states the theme which the alto repeats serenely, the power picking up with brass shouts over full ensemble. After a brief improvised passage (using the same line as the fourth tenor solo on *Jibu*) the trumpet returns to the theme, there is a break, then Latin rhythms usher in the marvellous down-trailing figures of the jubilant alto. In the following exchange, the men striking fire off each other's phrases, Pepper again exhibits the "joie de vivre" vibrating through the space surrounding his lines. Yet as before it is staggering to realise that this "spontaneity" is subject to a formal design itself of considerable expression power. For as the lines trail down in the first break the second finds them begging ascent but clipped back before finally being set free to ascend in the last. The horn exchange finally resolves in a tightly knit duet of considerable beauty. This is a clear example of Pepper suddenly transcending what was otherwise an unremarkable session.

In February 1953, a month after the above recordings, the artist was arrested. He was released in May of the following year but found himself divorced and unable to find steady work. He was brought into the prison hospital for treatment in December, not to be released until mid-'56. Rogers must have immediately engaged him for the July 5th date for Victor. The three titles issued on HMV EG8250 are the best from Pepper's point of view, the fourth, *Pay the Piper*, contains an unadventurous solo lacking rhythmic or tonal tension. This cannot be said of his work on the fast *Blues Express* where the phrases come crackling out and set the scene for the revelation of the completely developed style now in his hands. He is more forthright, confirming the trends of '53, and he is clearly aware of his unique handling of space—note particularly his second full chorus; to gauge his originality compare this with the heavily Parkerised Mariano solo on the same piece to realise how most alto men were thinking. Also indicated is the developing predilection for rhythmic variations on a single note or small intervals which will reach a peak on *Rhythm-a-ning* and *A Bit of Basie,* and are used to create tension by making the repetition prolong the melodic element unnaturally, the melodic stream damming up to release with added impetus in a flowing line or a polarised sequence of scattered fragments. Another property is shown in the fine *At Home with Sweets* solo in which we clearly see melodic elements compressed in time and thrown almost vertically across the rhythmic flow; this is a source of asymmetry in Pepper's constructivist style, his personal sense of the contemporary vertigo.

PACIFIC JAZZ

1956–57 was a period of considerable recording activity for the altoist both as leader and sideman. Much of this activity was for World Pacific sessions and that company has captured much of his finest work of the middle period. In general it confirms the maturity and increased intensity of this phase which represents the stylistic norm discussed in the first part of this study. Pacific seems to have recorded many snippets by various musicians as part of normal album sessions and has released these in the Jazz West Coast series. Amongst these are Pepper's first small group recordings to be made after his release. *Old Croix* from July has a quartet with Pete Jolly, Leroy Vinnegar and Stan Levey and is a beautifully driving piece based on *Cherokee.* Art only has the opening and closing choruses but the sparkling pointillism of his work, each note sounding with perfect articulation and crystal tone, make this one of his best performances. As usual these brilliant fragments are brought to order like glinting filings in a magnetic field. He was able to practise during his absence and the mastery is clear from the start in the way each point of the introduction is touched in with absolute dynamic proportion.

Again, despite the medium bounce tempo, a sad lyricism pene-
trates the vibrant closing chorus.

Unfortunately *I Can't Give You Anything But Love* which has
Jolly dropping out is, despite the greater space available, somewhat listless. Some of his harmonic anticipations are cunning but
particularly towards the close his thoughts seem to be elsewhere
and the solo is bereft of the usual urgency.

The recordings with Bill Perkins are to my mind among the
most enchanting made on the Coast and this because they are
not spineless or twee although the saxophonists are well aware
of the beauty of two such timbres as they blend and entwine. And
What Is This Thing Called Love, nearly all alto, is one of the most
moving things he's done; completely formal and with Perkins's
sensitive solo and modest foil to Art's passionate breaks, with the
inevitable return to the ensemble, this I think is a great performance. *A Foggy Day* is a bland sequence and invariably inhibits
exploration in depth; Mingus, Carter et al. have failed and this
version also can only present a surface however polished. *Diana
Flow*, a gentle bounce theme by Pepper, is performed quietly
with the alto moving in angular lines through a static space, a
most personal analogue to the Konitz flowing stasis. *Zenobia*
(Pepper) is well played with effective enriching of the ensemble
with the lower register of the alto which goes on to make a most
passionate statement; at his best the emotion rings through the
construction like shock through a Waterford vase.

Report has it that the nonet session of August '57 was abortive.
This seems strange as the published results are of considerably
greater interest than the Baker sextet sides of the same year.
They are modelled on the 'classic' Rogers's items, having Red
Callender playing tuba. It would be useful to have further sam-
ples from the session if they lie tucked away in the vaults, for
though the swinging *Popo* cannot claim greatness (it certainly
claims skill) the ballad *Bunny* in a fine arrangement has majestic alto.

The tracks discussed above have been collated on "The

Artistry of Pepper" (Pacific Jazz PJ60) and the British outlet would be performing a service to jazz fans to release the LP here.

If I have cast some slight on the Chet Baker–Art Pepper sextet sides it is because they provide so little time or inspiration for the soloists to achieve anything, devolving as they do to a quick run through of all concerned sandwiched between a couple of mechanical theme statements. Baker is often stilted, Phil Urso swings but doesn't dig in, while Pepper sounds much as he does on the well-known "Meets the Rhythm Section" album for Contemporary, but only really makes ground on *For Minors Only,* his second chorus on *Resonant Emotions* where one feels a rawness amongst the glossy surroundings. His work on *For Miles and Miles* and *Minor Yours* is bright and finely wrought but the classically constructed blues solo on *The Route* by a similar group with Richie Kamuca (tenor) the preceding year is superior to the majority from this session.

THE TAMPA QUARTET

I have delayed discussing these sides, although they were recorded soon after his release, for I think they form a pinnacle amongst the achievements of his maturity. With his own quartet we see the full range of the man we glimpsed in *Old Croix,* including some work to rank with that piece, *What is* and one or two others are arguably great music. The first Tampa date however was with the Marty Paich Quartet (London LZ-U14040). Here he is closer to the mood of *I Can't* rather than the more expressive *Old Croix,* the result being a pleasant if not outstanding set. The inevitable consistency of performance is there but he is generally uninvolved and the new version of *Over The Rainbow* is no match for the classic performance of '51. He does catch fire at odd moments though, as in his second solo on *All The Things You Are,* the first having shirked the tune's potential entirely, in gentle undertone to *Melancholy Madeline* and perhaps *You and the Night and the Music.* Still, there's abundant evidence throughout of his original conception which one feels now needs broader scope.

This was given him on his own quartet LP (London LZ-U14038). Here the rhythm section was ideal to his needs; Russ Freeman, Ben Tucker and Gary Frommer offer exactly the self-effacing support demanded by his attitude to improvisation at the time. It certainly reveals him as a West Coaster but he is the best of them and as always need only look to himself for strength and without finicky intervention such as that by Paich on *Rainbow* he finds it. The white aesthetic of self-exploration dominates but here is no self-indulgence, at times crippling to Getz and Konitz, each nuance of feeling is tested for strength; sometimes it gives and both listener and player feel the pain, and against this the sheer pleasure of blowing. As a collection only the later "Smack Up" LP (Contemporary) can equal this unique set, which is one of the most well-known albums in my library (some similar sessions for more obscure companies will be discussed later). Indeed it is difficult to be objective about solos which I have come to believe rank with the classic recordings of the last decade.

Art's Opus, with its closely argued structure, moves quietly from point to point inevitably drawing us to the crux, the smeared fanfare (cf. Parker), and holding us transfixed. *I Surrender Dear* is a deep exploration: the inevitability of the restless theme statement rises in a reiterated and modulated motive variant that merges with the final theme phrase which in turn is decorated with a brief recapitulation of this shape. The movement passes naturally to the beautifully spaced break that sets his solo lines stalking freely over the harmonies. These are marvellous ascensions from a crushed lower register and countless rhythmic shifts, suspensions, reiterations. Indeed expressive formations abound in the solo (each have the solidity of a theme) and one wonders how he has been thought to be merely another altoist.

Martin Williams and reportedly Pepper himself to the contrary, this version of his melodic balled *Diane* is the finer, aided as it is by the absence of the extraneous variations of others. It is an austere and rigorously restrained performance; it moves as a piece neither too short nor too long, nothing stands out for it has quiet implacable unity, theme and variation are one. On the other hand *Blues at Twilight* is strangely less moving, sounding inhibited despite the magnificent tone. *Val's Pal*, an ultra-fast blues, is too brief but the altoist's ease and brilliant construction (note how the theme motive flowers out through the length of the opening improvised chorus) can be heard.

Two masterpieces remain. *Pepper Pot* has the quintessential ambiguity of his artistry, a bounce tune beginning apparently as a set of excellent swinging variations, say open to a Sims for example, but developing with startling logic to a totally new world of courage and pain; beautifully underpinned by the section we are in Pepper's own organic world; it is coherent, there are laws we are in no position to understand, the rhythm and register shift by discontinuity but no loose end sets us free. The timbral control and articulation are staggering and the rhythmic development toward the close of his solo is worthy of Young or Monk. The breaks along with those on *I Surrender Dear* are simply amongst the highest examples of the genre and are intensely moving in themselves. Only Navarro I think equals Art Pepper on this ground of structured tragedy, the heart of Lester Young and the mind of Benny Carter.

Besame Mucho, alto all the way, is for me possibly the greatest solo he has ever recorded; although I often turn to it for pure enjoyment I nevertheless end by being moved by its fusion of invention, élan and passion. It is full of mastery—the staggering doubletime near the opening of the even metre section; passion—the gleaming tone and lyrical paraphrase; and tragic insight, the whole nervous fabric pierced with desire for a transcendent serenity, ascensions that soar above the kaleidoscopic rhythms and spaces of his underworld analogous to the bold and equally tragic gestures on *Parker's Mood, Billie's Bounce* and *Chi Chi* reflecting back to *West End, Potato Head* and beyond; almost "style beyond style."

7

PEPPER, ART

Max Harrison

PEPPER, ART (1925)
alto and tenor saxophones

Pepper was one of the few high quality soloists associated with the West Coast school of the mid-fifties, but his commitment to jazz goes back at least ten years before that. He was also, indeed, among the few authentic jazz musicians to work for Stan Kenton, the earliest of his several periods of service beginning in 1943. Despite such connections, for his best recorded work Pepper has required a good rhythm section only, and his finest LPs so far—the last four listed below—benefit from superb bass and drum contributions by players like Paul Chambers, Philly Joe Jones and Frank Butler. The presence of other horns such as Chet Baker and Phil Urso, on the *Playboys* set (3) serves only to show how far Pepper has advanced beyond their kind of derivative competence. *C.T.A.* (3) is a good illustration, though it should be added that this session also features Carl Perkins, the most sympathetic pianist with whom Pepper has recorded.

If Pepper's solos have a character all their own it is because he is one of the outstanding melodists of jazz—though not widely recognised as such. The quality of his music has depended on a fairly unusual interaction of lyricism and rhythmic inventiveness. And despite his consistency he has been a constantly developing improvisor. Comparison between, say, his two versions of *Diane*, (2, 5), made in 1956 and 1960, will give an idea of how Pepper's work deepened its emotional impact and diversified its imaginative resource even during those few years. The many transformations of popular ballads Pepper has recorded throughout his career are naturally revealing of the melodic and lyrical aspects of his art, several of these—on the *Intensity* LP (7), for example—being classic demonstrations of this standard jazz procedure. With an outward casualness that is deceptive, the phrases are redistributed in a more musical way, the whole pace of the melody being altered and its inner tension heightened while bogus romantic overtones vanish. Better still is the insight with which Pepper explores the expressive potential of these modified thematic phrases, and his melodic powers are such that he rarely falls back on mechanically running the changes. And his methods vary. With *Long ago and far away* (7), for instance, the ideas seem to grow out of each other while, in contrast, on *Whims of Chambers* (5) much of his solo is developed from its opening phrase. In the latter, and also on *Bijou the poodle* (5) and *Rhythm-a-ning* (5), Pepper makes a striking use of short, detached phrases and of space (rests). It is unimportant whether this linear discontinuity is due to Charlie Parker's example—an influence that may be detected in earlier Pepper solos like *Blues at twilight* (2)—or whether the use of space echoes Thelonious Monk's practice. What does matter is that these devices are fully integrated into Pepper's own idiom, the melodic shapes being juxtaposed with a skill and sensitivity that produces solos of subtle yet definite balance and unity. The fresh, distinctive emotional climate which this music has possessed from the beginning has been progressively enriched by the fusion of lyrical expression and rhythmic assertiveness.

47

Such qualities cut across the artificial—almost arbitrary—divisions of style or school, and it is apt that for the *Smack Up* collection (6) Pepper chose, among other pieces, Benny Carter's *How can you lose?*, Ornette Coleman's *Tears inside*, Duane Tatro's *Maybe next year* and Buddy Collette's *Bit of Basie*. That he can meet the quite diverse challenges of these items and build a personal statement out of each is an encouraging sign of the strength of Pepper's own sensibility and of the essential unity of jazz.

(1) ART PEPPER QUARTET
     Vogue(E) LDE067, Discovery(A) LP-3019
(2) ART PEPPER QUARTET
     London(E) LZ-U14038, Tampa(A) TP-20
(3) PLAYBOYS
     Vogue(E) LAE12183, World Pacific(A)1234
(4) ART PEPPER MEETS THE RHYTHM SECTION
     Vogue(E) LAC12066, Contemporary(A)C3532
(5) GETTIN' TOGETHER
     Vogue(E) LAC12262, Contemporary(A)M3573
(6) SMACK UP
     Vogue(E) LAC12316, Contemporary(A)M3602
(7) INTENSITY
     Vogue(E) LAC553, Contemporary(A)M3607

8

OF DOPE & DEATH:
The Saga of Art Pepper

Grover Lewis

On a lambent, semi-smogless Los Angeles Sunday in March, Art Pepper is taking his first day off from work in over a month. A highly-regarded alto saxophonist back in the era when Bird ruled the jazz roost, Pepper earns his bed and board these days as a bookkeeper and all-around handyman at an organic bakery out in Venice, a thriving new business venture that's owned and operated exclusively by ex-Synanon gamesters. Laurie, the fetching young lady friend Pepper met during his recent 33-month stay at the Santa Monica Synanon facility, says it isn't uncommon for Pepper to work 12–15 hour shifts at the bakery without complaint. Flashing a smile radiant enough to draw bids at a Sotheby auction, Laurie also tells people that Art "talks like Gertrude Stein would have written if Gertrude Stein had been a junkie jazz musician."

Sprawled out on a rump-sprung sofa in an artist friend's comfortably cluttered apartment near the MGM Records building on Sunset Boulevard, Pepper sips an early-afternoon glass of cold duck, chain-smokes Winstons, and dispassionately shows off his prison tattoos to a visitor from San Francisco. On his left arm, there's a likeness of Pan, and above that, Snoopy and Linus. On the right arm, comedy and tragedy masks, and above those, a bearded skeleton smoking an opium pipe. "Like death," he explains with a weary shrug of the shoulders. "Like dope and death, you understand."

Frowning, Pepper rolls down the sleeves of his Hawaiian-patterned shirt and reaches for his wineglass. A trim, fastidious man of 46 with olive skin and hooded, watchful eyes, he speaks in a voice with a graveled edge to it, but a hint of music, too.

"I was always purely a sensualist, all of my life," he says, drumming his fingers at full-chase tempo on the coffee table in front of him. "All I ever lived for was just the pleasures, you see what I mean? Immediate gratification—every second was spent in trying to fulfill that hunger. And not just from week to week or day to day—I mean from minute to minute. My whole life was spent waking up in the morning and getting loaded like on whatever was around. You know, just never stopping till I fell out someplace. Then I'd start all over again. Every day was like a lifetime. At the age of 15, I was a complete alcoholic, and by the time I was 22, I was as strung out on shit as you can get.

Yeah, sensuality . . . And narcissism—is that the right word? Narcissism, yeah—that has to do with the reason I got myself tattooed while I was in the joint. When I was young, dig, I used to look at myself in the mirror for hours. I was like totally caught up in the outer beauty of myself and the things around me. So when I went to the penitentiary for the first time and saw all those down cons with tattoos, I thought, my God, can they be kidding? I couldn't imagine marking up my beautiful arms and chest and all with those fucking things.

"But then I started getting into the life of like boosting and burglaries and armed holdups and fucking around with whores and all those other junkie dope fiends—and I kept going back to prison. By the time I was doing my stretch in Quentin, I realized I'd changed—my values had changed. I felt defiant. In places like

Quentin, there are very few acts of defiance open to you. The total act of defiance is to kill some asshole screw and get away with it—to test your manhood, to let the real down cons know you did it, but not to get caught. I even planned to do that for awhile, but fortunately I got out before I carried it through. I was at that point, though.

"See, tattooing is against the law in jail. Like they can put you in the hole for doing it, put you naked into solitary confinement. The whole procedure of getting tattooed was very difficult, the equivalent, almost, to somebody hijacking a plane on the outside. And it was fucking painful, too, man. I can tell you. Well, I wanted to see if I could stand the pain, and I wanted to show my defiance of the joint. I did both, I guess. It seems fucking rotten to me, though, when a man's last resort to expressing his manhood calls for self-mutilation, messing up his own body."

With an irritable grunt, Pepper lights a fresh Winston from the butt of the one before.

"I guess I was born defiant," he mutters, tracing a finger along the intricate Chinese figures embossed on the face of the coffee table. "Like my parents, who lived in Gardena, California, they didn't really want me from in front, and I was born very sickly. When I was five, they shipped me off to my father's mother, an old German lady who had a little farm in Paris, California. They frankly wanted to get rid of me, see. My parents were both alcoholics, and I was just too much bother.

"So I went with my grandmother, and she never showed me any love or affection or anything; you know. She was like from that old German stock—very cold and orderly, very clinical, very reserved. I had my own room. She had her own room. I could never get in bed with her when I was scared. I felt that I wasn't loved or wanted, that I wasn't worthy of anything.

"So what happened was, I started living in a fantasy world. I wanted my father and mother to love me, but they didn't, maybe couldn't for all I know. So I became very imaginative, and everything I did, I did by myself. Like games—I played games by myself, played all the parts. Somewhere along in there, I just naturally gravitated to music."

For the first time of the afternoon, Pepper smiles, a fleeting alteration of facial planes that makes him appear ten years younger. He leans forward to poise the bottle of cold duck over the visitor's glass.

"More juice?" he asks. "No? You sure? Anyway . . . I just always wanted to play music. Very early on, I knew that that's what I was supposed to do. I kept talking to my dad about it when he'd come to visit. He wanted me to be a draftsman or an engineer instead because I was pretty good at math. But I just kept after him and kept after him, and finally he brought this music teacher around to talk to me. I was nine years old, and I wanted to play trumpet more than anything, but I'd just gotten my front teeth broken in a fight. The teacher looked into my mouth and said it wouldn't be cool for me to play trumpet because I'd never have the chops for it, you know, so he suggested that I play clarinet first, and then later on, saxophone. I didn't really dig either instrument, but I figured I'd better grab something—anything—while I had the chance. So I took lessons from the guy for awhile. The music was just there—it was natural. I never had to practice or anything. Like it was almost automatic. The teacher'd assign me a lesson, and a half hour before he'd come the next week, I'd run through it and then play it for him. He was always knocked out.

"It all came so easy for me that by the time I was around 11, I was like ad libbing, you know—improvising. Listening to jazz records, I found that I could play along and keep up and so on. I was living with my grandmother in San Pedro by that time, and I forget exactly how, but I ran into this guitar player named Johnny Martisia, who was about ten years older than me. I took my clarinet over to his place one night and we jammed the blues. That first time, I was able to play along without really knowing what I was doing. I just felt it and heard it. By then, I felt I was like destined, you know, to be a great musician. I *knew* that I was gifted. It was almost as if it was pre-ordained or something. I just accepted that. It was easy.

"But I have to say my head was totally messed, too. Pretty soon, I got in tight with some friends of Johnny's and we started going out jamming, and that led to my starting to drink. We drank Burgie ale, I remember, and Gilbey's gin—that was our one-two kick. But, shit, man, I mean, there I was—an unloved 11 year-old lush-head kid hanging out with cats twice my age, trying to escape into music and private games. I was totally alone because I couldn't relate to the older guys other than musically. So my fantasy movie just kept unreeling, and my craving to be loved, and at the same time, the feeling was building in me that I wasn't worthy of love because I was no good, you know? I remember wondering, if I'm no good, then how come I'm so talented? To save my life I couldn't figure out how I could be such a genius musically and at the same time be such a worthless bastard that nobody would love me. I was in trouble, man. I was 11 years old, and I was in hell."

Looking pale and shaken by the memories he's reviewing, Pepper clasps his hands tightly together between his legs and rocks forward and backward, forward and backward.

"Well, uh . . . I started to, uh, you know, get around," Pepper falters in a voice dry as raked leaves. "There were, uh, a lot of open jams back in those days . . . . That was down on Central Avenue, the big black street in L.A., just before World War II. I used to go down there and the spade cats would all say, 'Hey, now, here comes that little white boy.' I first got turned on to weed down on Central. All the people were very friendly back then. If you did something well, everybody let you know about it.

"Finally, at some session or other, I ran into Dexter Gordon, the tenor player. Like me, he was also very young, and we started like jamming together regularly. We jammed with Charlie Mingus, who was born around there, and Gerald Wiggins, the piano player, and Slick Jones, a drummer who'd played with Fats Waller, and, oh, just all kinds of cats. Then I got a gig at the Club

Alabam with Lee Young, Lester Young's brother who played drums. When there was an opening in Benny Carter's band I got the job. I had to drop out of high school to swing it, but I later got a diploma while I was serving two years for smuggling at the U.S. Public Health Service Hospital in Fort Worth. It was 1941 when I joined Benny, and I was like 16.

"I stayed with Benny for quite a while, and then he got booked to do a tour of the South. I couldn't go because I was the only white guy in the band—it was like that back in those days, all that color bullshit. Anyway, right away I joined Stan Kenton, who needed an alto player. It was just that easy.

"I was with Kenton, I guess, for about a year. During that time, I got married to my first wife, Patty, the most beautiful woman I've ever known. Then, in February of '44, I got drafted. A total drag, man—like I tried everything I could think of to stay out, but I couldn't cut it. I was in the field artillery and the combat engineers, and then I was an MP in London for a long time. I didn't play much music while I was in the Army, but I did one or two things. I gigged with George Shearing and two or three other guys whose names I don't remember.

"I got out of the service in '46 and went back to Kenton. I stayed with him until '51, which was about my peak year in terms of musical acceptance. I was cutting a lot of albums on my own by then—must've been 20 or 25 in all with me billed as leader—and in '51 I finished just 16 votes behind Charlie Parker in the Down Beat poll. I never played with the cat, man, but I finished like 16 votes behind him."

Again, Pepper rocks backward and forward, this time with hoarse laughter. A light breeze stirs the curtains at the window, carrying in faint trills of bird-song from the palm trees.

"At first, things were really cool when I got back with Kenton," Pepper says, winding a corkscrew into a second bottle of cold duck. "Patty had had my daughter—her name is Patricia—while I was overseas, and I really, really like loved them both. I was making lots of bread, you know, and winning recognition. I was a stone alcoholic, sure, but I was a *happy* alcoholic. For the first few months, Patty and the baby traveled with me on the road, but—" Pepper grimaces at both the corkscrew and the recollection— "Patty finally decided it was too hard on the kid, and she stopped coming along. I was devastated, I was so lonely. I got wrecked every night on booze, pills, pot—everything except stuff. And I'd always ball some chick or other, and I'd feel guilty afterwards, you know? I would get ill. I would actually get sick at my stomach because I felt so evil and rotten.

"Well, like this happened once too often in '48. The band was playing the Civic Opera House in Chicago, and I was sharing a room at the Croydon Hotel with Shorty Rogers, the trumpet player. I spent the whole night after the gig in the hotel bar, but they closed the joint down around five o'clock. Well, I was all fucked up, you know, with nowhere to go, so I headed up to the room. There were some people up there . . . uh, you know, getting loaded. Like I'd been around shit for years, man, but I'd never taken it before because I knew if I ever did I'd really get strung out. Well, hell, I don't know—it was just one of those moments.

"So I horned some shit—you know, sniffed it—and that was it for me from that instant on. Curtains. I was hooked from the time of that first snort. Afterwards, I'd stay loaded all the time and it was a cure-all for everything. I had no worries. I didn't have to feel guilty about balling chicks anymore because shit killed my sex drive. I was like able to function. It was great until I got to the point where I became so hooked that it started to work the other way. And you know something weird? It was pointless, all for nothing, all of it. I hadn't like allowed myself to realize it, but my marriage was already over before I got hooked. I'd lost my wife and kid the day they stopped traveling with me on the road."

Pepper rakes a hand through his short-cropped hair and takes a long swallow of wine. Beads of perspiration glisten on his temples, and he's perched on the very edge of the sofa, as if he might bolt at any instant.

"I finally got busted by the feds in '53 for smuggling heroin," he mutters into the palm of his hand. "I was living in a hotel on the Strip with this girl, and we'd gone to East L.A. to cop, and when we got back to the room the feds were waiting. A friend of mine had gotten busted, you know; and like he wasn't man enough to pay his dues, so he ratted on me. I got busted with one gram of shit—ten caps—and got two years in Fort Worth. That was a pretty stiff sentence at that time, considering that I didn't have any previous arrest record.

"When I got out, I was put on CR—conditional release—which means like your good time. Then I got busted for marks and possession of codeine and spent a year in the old L.A. County jail. When I was released, the feds violated me on my previous sentence and sent me to Terminal Island to do the remainder of my time, which was 414 days.

"Then, in '60, the state busted me with two quarter ounces—a half piece of heroin. I drew two-to-20 in Quentin. I did about three and a half years, and they let me out on five years' probation. What happened then was like a series of returns to Quentin. I'd be out for maybe a couple of months and I'd start using and hang up the parole, and they'd haul my ass back to the joint. In all, I did about six years in Quentin, nine years total, for possession of a gram and a half-ounce of shit.

"Yeah, I would sometimes play on record dates during the time I spent outside. Strictly, for the bread to score, you dig, which I'm kind of ashamed of now. If I got a chance to make an album, I'd sign away my royalty rights, whatever, just to get the cash—maybe $500—to cop a piece of heroin. That's really all that mattered to me. I'd go into a session cold. Like I made two different albums with two different Miles Davis rhythm sections. We'd never played together before, which was typical. For one of those sessions, I scribbled off a couple of little charts, you know, and gave them to Wynton Kelly and Paul Chambers, and that was it, man. We just played. After we ran through those few set things, I asked the producer how many minutes we needed to finish off the album. Then we played the blues in F or something like that for the remaining time, and I watched the clock, and when the time was up, I said, 'Let's take it out. Let's go home.' And we went home. Or off to score, in my case. There were some good moments on all my records, you know, but nowhere as many as there like should have been.

"I never had any real friends among musicians, when I stop to think about it. Oh, you know, there was like the common ground of dope, like scoring together, stuff like that. Otherwise, it was pretty much that thing of buddying up to a guy or having him buddy up to you out of self-interest—getting each other gigs or record sessions, like that. The only close friend I think I ever made in the music business was Les Koenig, who owns Contemporary Records."

Pepper rubs his nose pensively and falls silent for a minute. When he speaks again, his voice is faint and muffled, as if he's talking through a surgical mask.

"During those times when I was in and out of Quentin, I uh . . . like I pulled a couple of armed robberies, you now. No nobody got hurt, but I probably would've shot anybody who endangered me. I don't know, it's a hard question. I might've— I'll put it that way. I might've. There was, I guess, a double motivation for the robberies. Obviously, I needed the bread to score, because I couldn't make enough through playing music to satisfy my habit. But there was a deeper reason, too. I wanted to test myself. I wanted to see if I had the nerve to do it. I wanted to see if I could measure up to the down characters I was hanging around with. Same thing with boosting, which I also did—a test of nerve, a test of your manhood. This other guy and I used to walk into some filling station or other right in broad daylight. He'd distract the attendants and I'd wheel off down the street with a battery charger. You know, one of those big old jobs on wheels? I wanted to know if I had the courage to do stuff like that, and I proved to myself that I did.

"Maybe another reason I went to such extremes to prove

myself had to do with my second wife. She died in prison while I was still up in Quentin. Yeah, she was an addict, but she died of cancer. She died in prison, though, and that was my fault, at least indirectly. I felt like a lot of guilt about that. She'd left a husband and two children to marry me, and after we got together, in order to get me to stop using shit, she started using it herself. There was nothing I could do to stop her, you know? If she hadn't found me, she probably would've found somebody else just like me.

"Anyway, I kept on boosting and pulling burglaries and stuff like that, off and on, until '69, when I went into Synanon. When I got out of Quentin in '66, I shacked up with a chick named Daphne, the sister of a con I'd known in the joint. She played piano, you know, and guitar and the tambourine, and she sang pretty well. I didn't have any bread, naturally, so she helped me get a horn—she cosigned for it, because by then I didn't have any credit or anything. I could only get one horn—it cost over $500, which was like a fortune to us—so I got a tenor instead of an alto. I figured with the way music was going, the kind of rock-jazz thing that was doing down, a tenor might be more appropriate. Well, I fell in love with it, man, played nothing else for three years."

With a lopsided grin, Pepper pantomimes honking on an imaginary horn.

"Actually, there wasn't all that much work for me in Southern California. There're like just a few clubs, you know, where jazz is welcome, and the terms of my parole prohibited me from traveling very far. To get around that, I went on two years of Naline testing. I was supposed to like stay clean the whole time, but I didn't. In that program, the time sequence changes, see. First, you take the test once a week, then every two weeks, then finally once a month. So I used to fix like maybe three days straight, then kick and clean up for four days. I had this friend who belonged to the Beverly Hills Health Club, and I'd go there and take steam baths until I felt like my skin was going to fall off. I'd also drink wine and take uppers.

"Another dodge was shooting crystal. While I was playing the Jazz Workshop in San Francisco, I found out that shooting crystal tends to change your metabolism, so even if you're using shit very strongly, a shot of crystal just before the Naline test will put you in the clear. I did that pretty regularly for a while, and it really fucked me up physically. Methedrine is like about a million times more harmful than heroin, you know. Anyway, I passed the test for two years, but I stayed loaded at least half that time.

"Daphne was kind of a street freak, you know, so I got into that trip for a while. Like I had my ears pierced and wore an earring and grew my hair and beard, and Daphne and I would just wander from place to place along the Strip. I got to where I'd sit in with any kind of group—western bands, rock and roll groups, whatever. I even started playing insanity music like Pharoah Sanders and Archie Shepp, all those guys. I was really good at it—I was playing extremely well. But it put people off. I worked at Shelley's Manne-Hole and various gigs like that, and people would come up to me and say, 'Wow, it sounds great, but what happened to the old Art Pepper who used to play so pretty?' Well, that dragged me because I was like playing the way I felt. I'd try to tell them that I couldn't play like the old Art Pepper because I *wasn't* the old Art Pepper—things move on, times change. Those kinds of hassles left me very bitter, people wanting to categorize me and all that shit. I felt that what I was doing was right, but it didn't seem right to anybody else."

Pepper fumbles for a cigarette, but his pack is empty. Accepting one of the visitor's, he expels a fog of smoke and scowls darkly into his wineglass.

"Things got very spooky in '69. I was playing very little, and almost never for any substantial bread. Daphne was delivering auto parts for $1.70 an hour or something to support us, and we were constantly scuffling. I'd started taking acid to try to figure out why I used heroin. I was very messed up as far as being together and facing any kind of reality or responsibility. While Daphne was at work, I'd like wander around the streets, muttering to myself, cussing people out. I was into like total withdrawal from any kind of personal contact except with Daphne. Finally, the two of us more or less just hid. We lived here in Hollywood in a little house on Virginia Avenue, and like the blinds would be drawn all the time, and the doors all locked. Sometimes the phone would ring and I'd be too afraid to answer it. Some days, I wouldn't answer the phone or the door or anything.

"Then I got a call from Buddy Rich's manager, asking me to join Buddy's band as lead alto. Oh, fuck, man, I about panicked. A job like that, you're the leader of the section, and you have to be in very good shape. It's a loud band, and you have to play loud. You have to read all the charts, and they're very tricky charts. I'd never met Buddy, but I'd heard that he was a really severe taskmaster, like a perfectionist. On top of all that, I didn't have an alto. Buddy's manager said not to worry about it, that I could use Don Menza's alto. Don was one of the tenor players in the band, and I'd never met him, either. Well, you know, everything considered, I didn't want any part of the gig, but I realized that if I turned it down, there wouldn't be any hope at all for me. I would have really been lost.

"Two days later, I walked into this ballroom at Caesar's Palace in Vegas, and I was scared shitless. Buddy was sitting there behind his traps, all the guys in the band milling around getting ready for a rehearsal, and the manager spotted me and pointed toward the horn. I walked over to the alto like it was my own and took a seat in the middle of the sax section and Buddy said, 'OK, let's go.' Fortunately, the horn played well, and I did too."

Splashing more wine in his glass, Pepper allows himself a faint smile.

"When I went with Buddy, see, I stopped doing shit because he doesn't approve of it and he's very wise to who's using and who isn't. I drank a lot instead. Then I started swelling up and having terrible stomach pains. By the time we left Vegas and opened at Basin Street West in San Francisco, I was in such pain that I couldn't sort out the charts on my stand. Joe Romano, the guy who sat next to me, had to get my music out for me. At the end of the first night, Buddy took me to a hospital. I had exploratory surgery, and the doctors discovered I had a ruptured spleen. I stayed in the hospital for three months. It was a miracle that I lived.

"They had a big benefit for me at some club in Oakland. Roland Kirk played for it, and a lot of others, and that gave me enough bread to recuperate for awhile back here in Hollywood. Then, before I really had my strength back, I rejoined Buddy's band at the Riverboat Club in New York. It was a mistake, and a bad one. My incision ruptured, and I had to fly back to the Veteran's Hospital here for more surgery.

"When I finally got out of there, I was really in bad shape. Instead of cooling it, I started using neo-morphine, a very strong new drug that's a little like a speedball, you know—a combination of heroin and coke. Also, I was drinking a lot. My body just gave up on me. I was helpless. I couldn't play. I couldn't get around to like boost or pull a burglary or anything. I was to the point where I couldn't even try to con anybody out of anything.

"Finally, Daphne couldn't take it anymore—couldn't bear, you know, to watch me like killing myself, which was what I was doing. She called this guy I knew, a trumpet player I'd done time with at Terminal Island. He was at Synanon, and he'd told me several times that if I ever needed any help to come down there. So Daphne explained to the guy what the deal was, and he told her to bring me on down."

Pepper frowns and rubs his palms together with a dry, scraping sound.

"It was a bring-down, all right. See, before, I'd always felt that I was like a king, that I could do anything and survive anything. I was the master of dopefiendmanship. Like I could always shoot more shit than anybody else, take more pills, ball more broads.

I was the cat who could always fix a junkie whore with bad veins. I had whores who'd have me score for them because I could fix them when nobody else could. I was really good at stuff like that, so that like made me think I was good at everything else.

"Synanon set me straight about that. Once I moved in, all of a sudden there was no shooting dope, no playing music, no fixing chicks, no hiding. Synanon like saved my life, or I would've physically expired. I had to be there, and they won't allow you to escape, you know—they don't give out weekend passes. And right away, the whole community knows everything about you. You're totally exposed. *Totally.* Playing The Game, you reveal everything about yourself—your hatred, your prejudices, all the shit you've always tried to conceal behind a super-cool front. It all comes out because the Synanon people are masters at The Game, and pretty soon you've exposed yourself—your real true self—and you think, oh, my God, what am I going to do now? They *know.*

"At first, I tried to play my same role, the one I'd played all my life, but I wasn't able to keep it up. They break you down, you know. It was a fascinating learning experience, but after almost three years, I'd reached the end. I was tired of hearing how I was no good and rotten, that I was a scumbag and the most disgusting, slimy being who ever lived. It was either leave or become like a Synanon soldier, which is a lifetime thing. There's no worries if you go into that—you don't have to bother about the phone bill or the police or income tax or doctors and dentists, nothing. But you also start losing the will and desire to create or to do anything that's real because there's no reason to.

"Laurie, my girlfriend, and I decided it was time to leave around last Christmas. It seemed to me like the only way that I could salvage anything and stay alive and stay young and have any sort of inner happiness. But I was like terrified, because I'd been brainwashed by all those stories about how if you left Synanon, you'd die.

"I stayed the first couple of weeks on the outside with a guy who was on the methadone program. He had a job, and he was getting his dosage every morning, and he kept telling me, 'You have to get on methadone, man. There's no other way for people like you and me to make it.' Well, fuck that, I couldn't accept the fact that I had to act like some kind of vegetable and scurry off somewhere every morning and drink down my medicine, standing in a line like in some nuthouse or something. It really turned my stomach to think about it. Methadone's the same thing as shit, except it's legal. I've taken it, and it gets me off about as good as heroin. It doesn't do that for everybody, but it does for me.

"Well, I saw where that guy was at and I thought, uh-uh, man, that's not for me. Also, I began wondering whether I should've left Synanon, because you can't ever go back once you cut out, you know—you leave Synanon just once. Then, at a gathering of ex-Synanon people I ran into this dude I'd known before who'd started out baking bread for friends. He had this little thing where he baked it in coffee cans, you know, from stone-ground wholewheat flour, rolled oats, honey, and sea salt. Finally, there was such a demand for his bread that he and a partner opened a little store-front bakery in Venice. He offered me a job there and a place to stay.

"At first, I didn't want to take it, because I wanted to like leave open the avenue of failure, you know. I knew that if I accepted the job I'd be trapped into trying to do good. Anyway, I thought it over and finally went to work. At the start, I was like picking up and delivering things, washing pots and trays, all kinds of stuff like that. But I'd worked in the paymaster's office in Quentin and in the bookkeeping department at Synanon, and gradually I began to keep the bakery's business ledger. I enjoy that—It's a little like writing music. It fits in with my personality, too. I'm extremely rigid, you know, compulsively neat—I'm a Virgo and a German, which is really all the same trip."

Cocking his head at an angle to avoid the spume of smoke from the cigarette in the corner of his mouth, Pepper leans forward intently, his elbows planted on his knees.

"It's a great job, man. The guys who own the business have really been good to me. There's not much bread yet, but I don't need a lot. I want to be comfortable, you know—I want to be like content. I keep busy enough that I don't have time to think about other things. I've got a beautiful room in the boss' house. I have my horns, a clarinet and an alto, set up on my sax stand. I've got earphones, and I listen to the jazz station. Sometimes, yeah, I play along. Laurie lives just a block away, and I see her every day. I still have a contract with Contemporary Records, and I've got plans to write and record an album right away. And I just entered into negotiations to write a book about all that's happened to me.

"Like maybe it's just getting older, but I feel more relaxed, you know? I feel more comfortable with myself. I'm still clean, and I intend to stay that way. I feel very good about the future. Like I want to stay out of that sick fantasy world from before and try to live within the realm of real possibility. Like from here on out, man, I intend to pursue art for art's sake and Art for Art's sake."

By August, six months later, Pepper has undergone a drastic sea-change in attitude. Sitting slumped on the sofa-bed in Laurie's pin-neat walk-up apartment in Venice where he now lives, wearing chinos and scuffed black shoes with broken laces and looking maybe just a trifle wired, Pepper sullenly recites his grievances to a couple of visitors while Laurie pours glasses of the champagne Pepper had "liberated" from the bar the night before after playing a pickup bar mitzvah gig. In a bitter mood, Pepper says that he's recently quit his job at the bakery, because his boss was a "greedy asshole." In a flat, weary voice, he goes on to reveal that he's just applied for and been granted ATD—Aid to the Totally Disabled—which means that he has a guaranteed lifetime income of $177 a month from the State of California, but is prohibited from playing engagements or making records or otherwise earning any taxable income. Art Pepper, in effect, has become an ex-jazz star.

"I'm also like going to try to get on the methadone program," he mutters, draining off a tumbler of champagne as if it were water. "Shit, man, methadone is almost as good as stuff and it's free besides. I guess I'll go to a VA shrink about that right away."

"Shrinks," Laurie sniffs from her perch on a floral-printed pillow on the floor. "The best advice I ever got from one of those assholes was to get an alarm clock."

"What the fucking shrinks should do," Pepper growls, "is prescribe junk to anybody who needs it. There's nothing in the world to compare with good shit, man. I'd like to have some right now."

"Oh, Art," Laurie says, mildly reproving, "don't start thinking about it or you'll want to go out and cop. You know we can't afford it."

Pepper scowls and shrugs. "Yeah, you're right. Methadone is where it's at, I guess."

Laurie, who has never used drugs, peers at Pepper closely. "You know, I've only seen you loaded once," she muses. "I remember you looked so . . . happy."

Closing his eyes, clasping his hands tightly together between his legs, Pepper rocks forward and backward," forward and backward, "I was," he sighs. "I was."

9

SOME INTERESTING CONTEMPORARIES

Michael James

To those of us for whom, once Parker died, jazz's future seemed to rest with the East Coast players who trod in his footsteps, the recordings then being done in California held limited interest. The first wave of bop stylists, players like Teddy Edwards, Sonny Criss, Wardell Gray and Roy Porter, had receded, and the Western scene, so far as one could judge from records, was dominated by Shorty Rogers, Shelly Manne, Bob Cooper and other Kenton alumni. Consummate technicians to a man, these players nonetheless largely eschewed the rhythmic density and ferocity of attack that distinguished such New York-based groups as Art Blakey's Jazz Messengers and the Max Roach-Clifford Brown ensemble. Consequently, as the decade progressed and the popularity amongst collectors of the music which Rogers and his colleagues represented began to fade, the attention of many enthusiasts swung away from a company such as Contemporary, which had been to the fore in documenting their activities. With the benefit of some fifteen years' hindsight it is now clear that this was not an unmixed blessing, though at the time it seemed a

"Some Interesting Contemporaries" by Michael James originally appeared in the January 1973 issue of *Jazz and Blues* magazine.

healthy reaction, a righting of the balance after an unfortunate phase which had seen players like Dorham and Davis temporarily in the wilderness. This essay, however, is not conceived as an enquiry into the excesses of critical response, but as a summary of some Contemporary albums which are at present available as E.M.I. imports and constitute an extremely interesting body of music: less consistently brilliant, perhaps, than that recorded by the short-lived Signal concern, but still attaining an aesthetic standard comparable with the mass of Blue Note or Prestige recordings, two companies that fell sharply away from their previous high standards once Hard Bop began to founder in the slough of funk and so-called soul jazz.

If the reader turns back to the list of available imports published in our April 1971 issue and which, I am assured, has changed hardly at all since then, he will be struck by a feature which, in the light of my introductory remarks, may seem strange; namely, that of these records, only a few are by musicians one would readily associate with the men who dominated Californian jazz recording in the mid-'50s. The explanation is that the label's character itself evolved once the highwater mark of the West Coast school, around 1955, had been reached. Its director, Lester Koenig, as the several volumes done by Howard Rumsey's Lighthouse All-Stars attest (C3501 and C3508 are currently available here), had never been averse to more extrovert improvisatory styles, and now he began to take advantage of the resurgence in his area of principles, and also of the arrival of younger men whose curiosity led them to defy harmonic guidelines to which their elders almost invariably conformed.

Whilst it is tempting to view as a turning point in his company's policy Koenig's success in capturing in this one album much of the musical strength that made Rollins so pervasive an influence in the late '50s, the situation was more complex. For that matter, Koenig clearly had too much respect for the stylists he had hitherto featured to drop them overnight, and in any case one or two of them, previously associated with the Californian school, were now developing in more personal ways, exploring new improvisatory methods. Art Pepper is an outstanding example. The five albums he recorded for Contemporary between early 1957 and late 1960 cover a very interesting stage in his musical development. Already in the late '40s his was a recognisably personal talent, his approach embodying rhythmic and melodic elements drawn from both Benny Carter and Charlie Parker, whilst his harmonic palette was quite as broad as any of his colleagues in the Kenton band, one of whose leading soloists he was throughout those years. When he left Kenton in 1951 to settle in California, his native state, his musical growth seemed to accelerate. In company where the accent was placed firmly upon technical perfection rather than emotional passion he swam steadily against the prevailing tide, so that some five or six years later he began to figure as a most uncharacteristic product of the Hollywood locale. The decision to record him, in January 1957, with the rhythm section then employed by Miles Davis may now be seen as an acknowledgment of the surprising trend his career was taking, a recognition of his increasing affinity with Monk, Rollins, and even, in his probing into harmonic areas new to him, John Coltrane.

Art Pepper meets the rhythm section (S7018) makes it clear that the saxophonist's espousal of methods associated with these men was not the upshot of cold and clinical assessment, but rather the outcome of a consistent impulse to attain deeper levels of emotional intensity. *Imagination,* for instance, is stripped of all specious sentimentality to emerge as a raw and tender statement, whilst the blues items find him adopting a jagged, jolting phraseology that couples with his very individual manipulations of sound to convey those impressions of private grief and isolation we associate, irrespective of period, with the finest practitioners of the 12-bar form. These characteristics gain in effect from his use of a wide register, and indeed he occasionally juxtaposes forays into the bottom of the alto's range with piercing high note work to disturbing effect. The new elements in his playing are most apparent at medium tempo, and are less obvious in a fast item like *Straight life*, where he tends to revert to the running, more obviously symmetrical patterns of earlier items like *Brown gold* or *Surf ride*.

On theoretical grounds one might have jibbed at Pepper's being recorded with an ostensibly alien rhythm team comprising Red Garland, Paul Chambers and Philly Joe Jones, but they all worked together most effectively. Conversely it might have been expected that presenting Pepper in a big band context prepared by Marty Paich, with whom he had worked many times before, would have resulted in consistently vital, or, at the very least, strongly integrated performances. Yet *Art Pepper plus eleven* (S7568), done in 1959, is a disappointment. Paich's scores are workmanlike rather than inspired, and the accompanying group only occasionally seems to catch fire, but to my mind the basic weakness consists in the unduly rigid programme, which comprises well-known jazz compositions of the '40s and '50s. Tunes like *Four brothers*, *Bernie's tune* or *Walkin' shoes*, which familiars of Pepper's earlier career might have adjudged ideal material for him, turned out to constrict his thinking. He fares much better in such time-honoured bop items as *Move*, *Shaw 'nuff*, *Donna Lee* or *Groovin' high*, maybe because these melodies carried within themselves the germ of the rhythmic dislocations he was by then exploiting. It is also instructive to note how well he plays in such neo-bop compositions as Silver's *Opus de funk*, where he unleashes a harsh yet curiously plaintive emotional energy, Rollins's *Airegin*, or, possibly most affecting of all, Richard Carpenter's *Walkin'*. His tenor also in this familiar blues, fraught, it seems, with an overwhelming sorrow, achieves this effect through broken phrasing, bent notes, flurries of double time and a tonal colouring which by this stage of his career was Pepper's private and unalienable domain.

It is tempting to examine in detail the three Contemporary albums with which he followed these two, but the exigencies of space and the general intentions of the present article make this impossible. Suffice it to say that *Gettin' together* (S 7573), *Smack up* (S7602) and *Intensity* (S7607) rank with the most intriguing saxophone jazz of the decade. If the trumpet and piano solos are of inconsistent value, this is but a trifling criticism in view of the substantial nature of Pepper's contributions, and as a counter-weight to such shortcomings the bassists and drummers react with genuine insight to their leader's handling of each musical situation, whatever the tempo or mood may be. In these three sets Pepper developed still further those vocalised tonal shifts, the fragmented melodies, the use of space, the arhythmic phrasing, and the occasional surprising harmonic departures that had distinguished those first two albums, if in less marked a degree. An article by Grover Lewis which appeared in the September 14th, 1972, issue of the magazine *Rolling Stone* casts an interesting sidelight on his approach to at least a couple of these Contemporary dates, besides going into considerable detail on his chaotic life, his recurrent addiction problems, and the gaol sentences this sickness and its concomitant pressures brought him. "I'd go into a session cold. Like I made two different albums with two different Miles Davis rhythm sections. We'd never played together before, which was typical. For one of those sessions, I scribbled off a couple of little charts, you know, and gave them to Wynton Kelly and Paul Chambers, and that was it, man, we just played." If it were not for the fact that every jazz improviser's performance is in one sense a protracted course of musical study, it would be fair to describe Pepper's attitude as purely intuitive. Yet he is far from complacent about these albums, gripping as the music they contain is: "There were some good moments on all my records, you know, but nowhere as many as there should have been." On the evidence of these recordings, most listeners would deliver a far more charitable verdict.

10

ART IS THE ART

Pete Welding

Of all the musicians to have emerged from what has been called the West Coast jazz movement of the 1950s, alto saxophonist Art Pepper is unquestionably the single most important, the one whose strong, intense and always compelling music—from every stage of his troubled, frequently interrupted career—is most likely to withstand the test of time. Unlike most of his contemporaries on the Los Angeles scene of those days, Pepper has been one of jazz's true originals, possessed of an instantly recognizable sound and style that are his alone, the hard-won results of years of dedicated, constant effort to not only master his instrument and the art of playing jazz but to retain while doing so a sense of self—that is, to find and maintain a strong personal identity. He has been conspicuously successful in this goal and, along with Lee Konitz, Paul Desmond and perhaps one or two others, has become one of the major individualistic voices on alto saxophone in post-Charlie Parker jazz.

It was no easy task he set himself. In the 1940s when Pepper was first setting out in music, jazz, through the accelerating, increasingly important activities of the beboppers, and Parker in

"Art Is the Art" (liner notes excerpt) by Pete Welding, originally from *Art Is the Art*, Nadja Records, 1976.

particular, was in the midst of a major reshaping of its technical and expressive means. By the middle of the decade these efforts had borne fruit and most of the parameters of the new musical approach had been fully established, although as a result of a two-year ban on recording imposed on its members by the American Federation of Musicians law, musicians no less than listeners, were aware of the full extent of these developments. When shortly before the end of World War II the ban was lifted, increasing numbers of recordings in the mature bop idiom were produced, among the most notable of which were Parker's Savoy recordings of late 1945 and the even more important Dial recording series that commenced in March of the following year, through which were disseminated ever more widely the innovations of the chief architects of the new music.

Incontestably Parker was the foremost influence on younger, forward-looking musicians of the time, and they eagerly devoured every recorded scrap of his to which they had access. By 1946 when, following two years of military service, Pepper returned to Los Angeles to resume his musical career, Parker's spellbindingly original alto saxophone had become the dominant sound in postwar jazz; few young musicians were able to escape the pull of its influence. Pepper, however, was one who did—the result, he explained, of a conscious decision. While he unreservedly admired Parker's daring, imaginative music, he had no wish to imitate it—certainly not as slavishly as he had witnessed a number of others who had come under Parker's spell then doing. He had observed that as a result of this, such Parker imitators "gave up their identity to sound like him. They gave up their own thing completely. They copied solos off the records and played them note for note. They'd practice them and practice them."

Such was not for Pepper; it never had been his way. From the start he recognized that the path to genuinely creative, personal expression was to be found only in one's self and that while one might learn from a study of the music of others, Parker included, who had achieved the kind of individualized expression he sought, imitation of such approaches was not the way to go about it. Imitation would not free the latent self but would, rather, lead it down blind alleys and might eventually imprison it. One, however, easily can understand its attraction for the young musician yet to find a strong personal identity; imitation at least allowed him to perform with a measure of competence, confidence and an illusion of creative strength, albeit borrowed from another, stronger voice.

Art Pepper recognized, such a procedure finally was frustrating, self-defeating and more than probably harmful to the young musicians. Not only did imitation not lead to personal growth but often in fact inhibited the proper development of a musician's natural gifts; it stifled or at the very least muted his own voice. What it took many players to discover only after years of working in the shadows of others Pepper knew instinctively: that one must always strive for a sense of self in one's music and, no matter what the dictates of current fashion, continually persevere in this goal.

This does not mean, of course, that the altoist was without his own influences. He had a number of them, as he is quick to acknowledge, but it should be emphasized that they were of a more generalized nature than was the case with those who chose to imitate the styles of such specific players as Parker, Dizzy Gillespie, Miles Davis, and so on. Part of the process of attaining mastery in any art form always entails a study of its past to the extent of one's choosing, if only unconsciously, models to admire and emulate. In this Pepper was no exception, although he chose a tenor saxophonist, Lester Young, as his model, to which he added a few others—none of them alto saxophonists, it should be noted.

"Even though I play alto," Pepper observed of his admiration of Young, "he was the man who influenced me more than anybody else—he and Zoot Sims. Before that I liked Joe Thomas, who played tenor with the old Jimmie Lunceford band. Naturally I liked the way Charlie Parker played, but I never imitated him like almost all the other alto players did. He ruined a lot of alto players who were so taken by him that they became nothing more than imitations, and they lost their individuality. I loved his playing but not to the point where I wanted to copy him. The players I liked most were tenor men."

Pepper elaborated: "You know, Bird had a great sound, a great sound for him and for jazz. But it wasn't pure 'legitimate' sound. It was *his* sound. It was real, and it was beautiful the way *he* played it. A lot of other guys had worked to get a pure sound. But they tried to destroy the beauty of their own sound in an effort to sound like Bird! Where Bird sounded *beautiful* playing his sound, their playing cost them all their individuality completely. There were a few people, however, who really stayed and played themselves—Paul Desmond, Lee Konitz and myself. I couldn't see copying someone else. I've never, ever taken anything off a record or memorized somebody else's solo—never, ever. I wouldn't even look at them.

"Of course," he added, "I got put down by a lot of other people, because if you didn't play Birdlicks, you weren't nothing. But I kept developing and playing myself throughout that whole period, say from 1946 to 1951, through that whole time I was with Stan Kenton's band." Such single-mindedness eventually paid off, the altoist feels. "In the early '50s, I started a group, recorded, and everyone knew who I was. They could immediately tell that it was Art Pepper playing, which was great. All I had to play was alto."

Since this was all he ever wanted to do, Pepper was exultant when it occurred. Its attainment had taken him the greater part of a decade during which he had remained steadfast in his commitment to a goal that, for whatever reasons, had eluded to many others. He wanted only—but not, as it turns out, simply—to become a jazz musician. For Pepper this meant not only absorbing all the technical and conceptual mechanisms of jazz performance (many, after all, have accomplished this) but marshaling all his inner resources to the achievement of total mastery in what he viewed as the essential, unique nature of jazz: its goal of immediate, spontaneous, totally creative music making, an exhilarating discipline which at all times demanded the very utmost of its practitioners.

Now, one may find such a view of jazz naive, unrealistic, unfounded or simply romantic, but all of the music's great players, those who have given it, and us as well, its greatest moments, seem to share this view. Most in fact have dedicated themselves so wholeheartedly to its pursuit that it has become, in effect, their life's work and its mastery something to be sought, maintained, and extended constantly, often over decades of a professional activity. Many jazz musicians—Louis Armstrong, Duke Ellington, Benny Goodman, Coleman Hawkins, Barney Bigard, Joe Venuti, Jack Teagarden, Red Norvo, Count Basie and Earl Hines by no means exhaust the list—have had significant, productive careers of five or more decades distinguished by consistent, high levels of creative achievement. And each, it should be added, continually sought to, in Pepper's apt phrase, "play himself"—to project in his music that compelling, powerful sense of personal identity that always has marked the work of the truly original artist.

It is a characteristic that has distinguished Pepper's approach to music as well. Certainly it was a major factor in his decision not to follow in the footsteps of Parker or of any other player, and to eschew as well any form of conscious imitation: appropriating another's ideas, solos, licks or even, for that matter, developing a body of stock phrases of one's own. These were not for him. Instantaneous creation of the sort he desired demanded that Pepper free himself of reliance on anything other than his own inner resources, which alone would permit a truly spontaneous response to the materials with which his art dealt. He has pursued this goal with clearsighted, singleminded determination since his very earliest years, as in fact he continues to do even now. Pepper will settle for nothing less.

"Jazz is so beautiful," he has stated. "So many feelings can be expressed, and it's immediate, and each work is a total finished piece." Pepper's goals are embodied in this simple phrase, yet their fulfillment has required a lifetime of the closest, most demanding husbandry.

11

A NIGHT AT DONTE'S

Dan Morgenstern

As another fringe benefit of going on the road for *Jazz People* (and thanks to Stanley Dance for his review in the February issue) I got to hear and see the great Art Pepper in Los Angeles. It was a stroke of luck, since Art was subbing for Pete Christlieb in what usually is a two-tenor group led by Warne Marsh, with a rhythm team of Lou Levy, piano; Monte Budwig, bass; and Nick Ceroli, drums.

Warne I'd last seen at Newport time, with Lee Konitz. Those collaborations between the two ex-Tristanoites are always something special, but Warne sounded stronger and more relaxed in the familiar surrounding of Donte's, a pleasant North Hollywood hangout for LA's studio jazzers and their fans. I understand that Warne is getting ready to leave the somewhat rarefied California climate for another stab at New York, where, no doubt, he'll be teaming up with Lee. He certainly sounds ready.

With Art, there was less intricate interplay than with Konitz, but nonetheless quite a bit of collective improvisation, of a kind too seldom heard. Art, who looks fine and is in full command of his horn, seems to have found his true form once more. There is

"A Night at Donte's" by Dan Morgenstern originally appeared in the June 1977 issue of *Jazz Journal International*. Reprinted by permission of the author and *Jazz Journal*.

clear evidence of his love for Coltrane, but the Parker roots are still (or again) showing, and so is that fine, classic sense of form and construction.

I'd never heard Art live before and his true sound was a revelation. He projects strongly and clearly, with a nice hard edge on his full tone—a blues tinge. And he takes charge when he comes to bat, with the kind of authority that only real players have. Art is Californian-born and bred, but there is nothing "west coastish" about his music.

He was at his best on a way-up *I'll Remember April;* on the blues (*Billie's Bounce*), and on his solo feature, *You Go To My Head,* where he showed that he can go "outside" with the best of the free players. Warne, too, shone on his feature, *Easy Living,* evoking the spirit (not the letter) of Lester Young.

Levy was a delight. On *Lady Be Good,* his feature, he opened with some imaginative rubato passages, then moved into a swinging middle tempo that gave the tune a new dimension. Elsewhere, he showed his mastery of the Bud Powell idiom, and his comping was just right. Budwig and Ceroli kept things moving, and the closing *All God's Children* truly took wings. By this time, Art and Warne had found each other, and their interplay was no longer tentative. Both men have gone through considerable changes since *The Way It Was,* recorded in 1956. It would be interesting to get them together again, for the record.

12

THE WHITENESS OF THE WAIL

Gary Giddins

In alto saxophonist Art Pepper, the jazz mythographer finds not only a prototype for the psychoses and guilts, the triumphs and losses of the white hipster jazz musician, but a colleague as well. For Pepper is one living legend who takes his status seriously, like Sarah Vaughan, who, when asked by a sycophantic Sammy Davis how it felt to be a legend, replied, "Well, I get up in the morning, look in the mirror, and shout, Hey, I'm a legend!"—only Pepper means it for real, and with something like astonishment at having survived to tell the tale. He's eager to tell, to provide an iconography of the talent and the waste, the music and the junk (which he calls "a kind of cultural tradition"), the scuffling for work and the shuffling in prison yards (for more than a decade), the despair and the eventual rainbow sign: "It looks for me like life begins at fifty," he's written, "and I never thought I'd live to see fifty, let alone start a new life at this age."

Pepper has outlived his own worst fantasies and is looking back at them boldly but cautiously, fearful perhaps that they'll overwhelm him after all. He's no longer the handsome Pepper

who once adorned record jackets like a late '50s movie star—
Steve Cochran about to metamorphose into Warren Beatty; he
looks diminished, staring through a fog on the cover of the 1976
release *Living Legend,* his first album in sixteen years (as he
mused several times during a heralded Village Vanguard engagement, seemingly awed by the fact). In the picture he wears a
Texas Lutheran College sweatshirt with the arms cut off, revealing four fearsome tattoos, one of which looks like a skull with a
toupee. His hair is slicked down, framing a less certain face than
the one we knew from the classic + *Eleven* album, glassy eyed and
worn. His gossipy liner notes avidly recount his tribulations. In
the notes to a subsequent album, *The Trip,* he compares the bull
sessions at San Quentin to the process of making a jazz solo—in
both instances, one takes the improvised "trip" of an imaginative
storyteller. In the '50s, you were discreet about "personal problems" like serving time and taking junk, but junk finds its victims
outside of jazz today, so the survivor's song recalls another age.

And it's comforting to find in Art Pepper the Homeric muse.
Part of the myth of the hipster musician is that he makes it to the
other side but, like Orpheus, can't or won't return. Or at least this
is the myth of the white fan who seeks in jazz the intimacy of
blackness, fearing it all the same. In the Midwest during the '60s,
I heard several stories about the pilgrims who made the journey
to Charlie Parker's Kansas City neighborhood or gravesite and
never lived to tell about it. For some reason, the stories seemed
believable then and were accepted for their cautionary value,
i.e., get as close to the music as you can, white boy, but don't go
beyond the music. Terry Southern may have understood this
aspect of the white Negro as well as Norman Mailer when he
wrote a story about a cornball Charlie who wants to meet the
only Charlie who counts and gets bopped on the head in an alley.
A couple of years ago, Allen D. Coleman, who has written widely
on photography, published a little book called *Confirmation.* It
consists of twelve pictures of a tombstone: "Son Charles Parker
Jr. August 29, 1920–March 23, 1955." There's also a page of text

describing his trip to Kansas City to see the confirmation of Parker's death, and therefore of his life. For a touch of local color, one "young and limping" black is quoted as saying to another, "Char-l-e-e-e Parker! Dat man could make his hawn talk!" It doesn't matter that no one on earth speaks like that: the point is the otherness of that dark and inviolable world. (Of course, the tombstone may not be a confirmation after all, since Bird really died March 12.)

Our fascination with the great white bebopper—of whom there is none greater than Art Pepper—is part envy and part admiration because he got close to the secret world of black culture—that world of genius and fire and bared emotion that promised salvation. He could speak Bird's language; moreover, he could make from it his own language. Pepper speaks much about the cry in his music, the happiness in the sadness, or the sadness in the happiness: it is the gift of swinging with melancholy that the best white jazz musicians have offered (Beiderbecke, Teagarden, Russell, the Four Brothers reed section in Woody Herman's Second Herd, Gil and Bill Evans) and that helps explain why the black musician who cloned the most white players was Lester Young, the most melancholy and secretive of swingers. The important thing about the good white jazzmen is not that they appropriated the black American's music—a narrow and paranoid sentiment that denies the individuality of all jazzmen, white and black—but that so many of them chose a black aesthetic as the best possible source for self-examination. Those who dug deepest avoided minstrelsy and went beyond mere technique. They offered the jazz listener the only quality no black jazzmen can offer—the pursuit of the white wail, a revelation of Caucasian inwit through the black idiom of the blues: a personal search fraught with peril. For in mastering a foreign musical syntax, they have straddled the racial division of American life, crafting a music that is not only of itself, but about itself. The fan's guilt-ridden correlative is the folk story in which the white yokel timidly trespasses in the dark culture, armed with a collection of hip records and a sentimental love for blacks. Oh, what did I do to be so white and blue?

For some, the musical route was not sufficient. Junk provided a keener initiation; it was another step in the excommunication from home that had begun with the original commitment to what James Jones liked to call "an outlaw music." Here, finally, the pathology of the white musician seems to attain equal footing with that of the black musician, who also took junk to get closer to an illusory "cultural tradition," though some blacks must have felt it was a cultural imperative. Billie Holiday once said that in her youth whorehouses were the only places where whites and blacks got together—the shooting gallery was another. Pepper's legend encompasses that hipster's myth of black-white contentment as well. He made his first record twenty-five years ago with Hampton Hawes, the funky bebop pianist who, like Pepper, contradicted most generalizations about West Coast jazz; they were reunited for Pepper's resurgence on *Living Legend.* Here was a salt-and-pepper team with so much blues in common, even racial pedigrees could be discounted. (Hawes, a smart and funny man who died in 1977, gave us his own mythography in a remarkable book, *Raise Up Off Me,* and Pepper is about to do the same. His liner notes and nightclub patter reveal a man who can't stop talking.*)

What a shock it must have been for white musicians when the racial/junkie/musical brotherhood fell apart. By the mid-'50s, it was no longer enough to share the music or a needle. Pedigree won out after all. If the white musicians could accede to the studios, those lucrative Muzak factories into which paleface dilettante jazz artists frequently passed, then at least the black artists would maintain the purity of the race in the jazz world. Suddenly, white musicians were poor relations, and many of them, who could have handled any adversity but rejection from their

---

*Just how eager Pepper was to tell all became clear in late 1979, when his autobiography, *Straight Life,* was published. It is almost fanatically confessional, and one of the finest of all jazz autobiographies.

adopted family, gave up and went back to the sticks.

Many have expressed the dismay of disenfranchisement. Here's Pepper, in the notes to *Early Art:* "musicians were starting to be afraid to let you sit in, afraid you'd steal their jobs. The warmth and beauty left jazz. It became more difficult to play. It was less enjoyable. And then mistrust showed up in the music. There used to be a healthy spirit of competition. You'd go up on the stand with, say, Sonny Stitt, and you'd try to outplay him, and he'd try to outplay you, but it would all be done with good feelings, in the right spirit. Around the mid-'50s, it got to be more like a battle to the death." Even Europe was no help here: In the '60s, famous black musicians reluctantly fired white sidemen because the European promoters wanted "authenticity." Ted Curson paid dues throughout the '60s for carrying an integrated band. Maybe that's why the mutual testimonies by the four musicians on the jacket of *Living Legend* (Pepper, Hawes, Charlie Haden, and Shelly Manne) are so moving; everybody loves everybody again and it's cool to worry about the music first and later about the politics.

It used to be said of Pepper that his direct source material was Charlie Parker and Lee Konitz, a sensible blend of insuperable black brilliance and soul with undeniable white originality. Parker's breathtaking facility was in the immediate service of his emotions, while Konitz, comparatively timorous though resolute, seemed to be thinking out loud, maintaining a cooler temperature for swing. To have combined those two into yet another original voice was to accomplish the most pressing task of the white hipster musician, the balance of both objective (black) authenticity and personal (white) sincerity. In Leonard Feather and Ira Gitler's *The Encyclopedia of Jazz in the Seventies,* we learn that Pepper now considers his real models to have been Lester Young and Zoot Sims, a similar combination, though swing rather than bop oriented. It's a revealing admission, I think, for part of the originality of his sound may reside in his transference of tenor stylings to the lighter horn—this seems especially true of his early recordings (now on Blue Note and Savoy). Even now, many of his ideas suggest Young's and Sims's phrasing grafted to Parker's rhythms. The third influence he mentions, the one that accounts for his present style, is John Coltrane, proving that the most cognizant players (black or white: think of Dexter Gordon and Jackie McLean) are best tuned into the evolving lexicon of the art. His present work is alive with splintered tones, modal arpeggios, furious double-timing, and acerbic wit. He continues to play from deep inside.

What do fan mythologies have to do with Art Pepper, whose appearance at the Vanguard was his first solo flight ever in New York (he has been here previously only as a sideman with Stan Kenton and Buddy Rich)? Probably not very much, and I wouldn't bring it up if Pepper could restrain himself from fashioning his own myth. He talks constantly at the gig, assuming our intimacy with his problems, assuring us of his gratefulness; and since he's right, of course (we do know all about him and are rooting for him for reasons that can never again be *entirely* musical, even if our interest in what he says stems from his immersion in music), we respond in kind. Ornette Coleman, who had played with him in L.A., came in on opening night and noted, "Art sounds good and the audience is making him feel good and that's important." It's reassuring to know that behind the legend is the substance that prompted the sentimentality and admiration that fostered the identification. He refers to his past with a tale-spinner's wonder, like someone amazed he could have experienced it and survived; but he plays like a knowing athlete, trained and poised. Jazz legends never die; they become self-fulfilling prophecies.

13

BARING A WHITE MAN'S BURDENS
Art Pepper Perseveres

Bob Blumenthal

Art Pepper. The name may be no more than a vague memory—one of the several California musicians who were most prolific in the late '50s and recorded for the Contemporary label. Art Pepper is too important to be relegated to a West Coast footnote, but his uncommonly consistent playing on alto saxophone is often forgotten. Largely as a result of his almost obsessive honesty, most people think of Pepper as jazz's most notorious surviving junkie, the man who fought—and lost—battle after battle with heroin, the three-time loser who spent ten potentially productive years in prison.

In 1960, at the time of Pepper's third drug bust, *Down Beat* declared in an article of rare (for the time) and brutal detail that he was at "The End of the Road." His image was fixed. A talented, attractive and sensitive man, he was triply displaced: a white master in a black idiom, a passionate, "hard" player based on the "cool" West Coast, and a jazz artist in a society which considered him just another lowlife player. Heroin promised release

"Baring a White Man's Burdens" by Bob Blumenthal originally appeared in the July 26, 1977 issue of *The Boston Phoenix*. Reprinted by permission of the author.

from his dilemmas, and Pepper the musician became Pepper the criminal.

Pepper left prison in 1966, but life on the outside proved almost as painful. Except for rare Los Angeles nightclub appearances and two stints as lead alto in Buddy Rich's band, he has performed little until recently. But somehow Pepper has managed to survive, with the aid of his wife, Laurie. In fact, the past year has seen something of a Pepper boom, what with two strong new albums on Contemporary, *Living Legend* and *The Trip*, plus reissues of important early material on Blue Note, Savoy and Xanadu, and gigs in New York, Chicago, and, a couple of weeks ago, Boston. The deceptively wholesome good looks of his youth have worn down to a gaunt severity which can come as a shock to those familiar with the clean-cut image of Pepper's early album photos, yet Pepper doesn't look like a 51-year-old veteran either.

Much has been written about Pepper's extra-musical significance (See Gary Giddins's brilliant examination of Pepper as the archetypal white jazzman/junkie in the July 4 *Village Voice*). "Art feels he's been discriminated against because he's white," Laurie admits. When someone mentions McCoy Tyner, Pepper quickly asks, "He's not into black power, is he? He's not into hating white musicians?" The questions arise from bitter experiences. According to Pepper, Wayne Dockery, his black bass player, once called the late Jimmy Garrison about getting a bass fixed, and Garrison asked, "Is the cat you're working for black or white, Wayne? Because I don't want to send you out to my repairman for no honky motherfucker." Such attitudes have driven many of Pepper's old associates, like pianist Russ Freeman, out of jazz entirely.

Racism is a source of much anguish for Pepper, who proudly recounts how bebop gadfly Babs Gonzales recently upset a Los Angeles club by bellowing, "Art, you white nigger nigger nigger, you motherfucker you! You the only white nigger who can play jazz, you white nigger nigger, you motherfucker you!" Savoy

Records expressed Gonzales's sentiment with greater subtlety by including Pepper's first session under his own name on its *Black California* anthology. "When I was 14 or 15," Pepper says, "I started going to Central Avenue (the main musical drag of black Los Angeles) on the streetcar alone. I'd be the only white guy for three or four blocks, and somebody would always say, 'Here's that white boy! Come on, get that horn out and blow now.' Everyone encouraged you—it was beautiful. If you didn't know a song they'd say, 'Go on, man just blow what you hear.'"

The Gardena, California schoolboy, who describes his father as "a real redneck," made his way to Central Avenue after visits to the Trianon Ballroom. "Jimmie Lunceford's band would come there—that was my inspiration. It was the greatest band I ever heard in my life. The trumpet section would flip their horns in the air, catch them and immediately hit a note. What showmanship! And the saxophone section was so rich and beautiful and big! Joe Thomas, on tenor, was a monster. He had that big, big tenor sound." Pepper demonstrated by blowing some wide-vibrato, lower-registration blues on his alto. "Willie Smith played alto just like Joe Thomas's tenor, and he was so loud!" He played more blues, this time at the top of the alto's range. "And Earl Carruthers was the best baritone player I ever heard."

Few established musicians rave as enthusiastically about their peers as Pepper, who, unprompted and punctuating his encomiums with the phrase, "I swear to God," began listing his influences. "I love Zoot [Sims]. He's the greatest player in the world outside of Trane and Miles. Louis Jordan was a favorite, too, but the tenor players were the people I really liked. They really shaped my style. First Pres [Lester Young] with all those augmented chords he was into, and guys like Allen Eager and Buddy Wise—all the white, Pres-school tenor players. As soon as I started hearing the black cats, though, I dug them more. Dexter [Gordon] was so loose, and Illinois Jacquet and Wardell Gray. I loved the way they ran through bridges, those changes they used [Pepper sang chord progressions] those whole-step, half-step bridges [he sang "Well, You Needn't"]. The black cats seemed to have that down, but Zoot played the shit out of that stuff, too. So did Stan Getz and Al Cohn. I have it, too . . . not many of the cats had it."

Charlie Parker is conspicuously absent from Pepper's reminiscences. "Bird never affected me like that. I'm too much of a perfectionist and Bird wasn't—he was too rough and out of tune. When people hear you say that, they want to kill you. In fact, I had a fight once with Joe Maini, the alto player. He said I was prejudiced because I didn't like Bird. But I like Bird—he just wasn't the greatest player in the world."

Much of Pepper's attitude undoubtedly stems from the frustration felt by all of Parker's alto-playing contemporaries. Between 1947 and '51, while Parker was at his peak, Pepper was receiving his first important exposure, with Stan Kenton. He admits, "I think I was jealous of Bird. Al Porcino and all the guys I admired in the band would take out their tape recorders after the gig, and all they had was Bird and classical music—that's all they talked about. I was like nothing. No one ever said I sounded good. And I swore to God I would never fall into the trap of playing like Bird. So I made a conscious effort: I never once played a transcribed Bird solo, and I listened to him as little as possible. I would only listen to him when I was alone, just me and him, and then I could really love him."

Blotting out Bird totally was impossible, however, and Pepper concedes that Parker made an impression. On tracks like "All the Things You Are" from *The Early Show* (Xanadu), Pepper and pianist Hampton Hawes playfully lead each other through Parker quotations. Yet more successfully than most, Pepper avoided the emulative rut. But his frustration during his Kenton years led Pepper to heroin, another trap which Parker knew much about. "Kenton didn't like the way I played, but as soon as I left he hired Lee Konitz, Zoot, Frank Rosolino, all the guys who played subtly the way I liked to. When I was there, he had people like Maynard Ferguson and it was screaming."

His work with Kenton and some 1951 appearances with trumpeter Shorty Rogers did enhance Pepper's reputation to the point where he could wrangle some club and record dates of his own. His work from 1952 to '54, documented on *Early Show* and *Black California* as well as on *Discoveries* (Savoy), suggests that only Parker was playing more inspired alto at the time. I'm particularly fond of *The Early Show,* a non-professional tape made at Hollywood's Surf Club. Much of the melodic and harmonic material is associated with Parker, but aside from an occasional quotation ("Don't Blame Me," one of Parker's favorite ballads, drifts into another, "My Old Flame") there are few of Bird's licks. While most alto players were repeating Parker *verbatim,* Pepper had already learned his lessons from the master and arrived at a personal style. Tracks like "Easy Steppin'" and "Tickle Toe" emphasize Pepper's tenor-based tendencies and feature a relaxed sound reminiscent (but not simply imitative) of Lester Young. His blues are hard yet limber (the cry would become more pronounced as the years passed) and the constant musical dialogue, (phrases traded with Hawes, unaccompanied unisons, simultaneous improvisation with Jack Montrose's tenor on *Discoveries*), is substantial, not merely flashy. Then there are moments of frenzy, especially on the alternate take of "Chili Pepper" (*Discoveries*), where Pepper gives us a glimpse of jazz's future.

But heroin was beginning to impede Pepper's career. Between 1953 and early '56 he was arrested twice on drug charges, serving a sentence of over a year each time. It was an era during which many musicians disappeared. "I played with Sonny Clark a lot," Pepper said. "What happened to him—did he die?" What made Pepper unusual was that he never denied his addiction. In Leonard Feather's *Encyclopedia of Jazz,* compiled at the end of that decade, Hampton Hawes, who was in a Texas prison at the time, was said to be "off the scene as a result of personal problems," and there was no mention of drugs or even "personal problems" in the entries on Dexter Gordon and Stan Getz. Yet one read that Art Pepper had "narcotics problems."

"Why lie about it?" Pepper says now. "It happened. It's there. Besides, I'm very open and I love to talk to people. If I get the opportunity, if somebody gives me an opening, they've had it. What I've gone through accounts for how I play. I know that tonight, for instance, I'll play great because I've paid all these dues."

Yet, as Pepper knows full well, artistry is more than simply a matter of paying dues. *Early Art* (Blue Note) and *The Way It Was* (Contemporary), both dating back to his 1956 "return," and the 1958 *Omega Man* (Onyx) chronicle the growth of a musician inspired by much more than heroin. His execution here is impeccable, and he commands a variety of attacks. Sometimes his lines dart and rip at the time. Elsewhere he settles into a groove while still discovering and probing new melodies. Able to encompass both the linear mazes of the Lennie Tristano school (especially on *The Way It Was*) and the funk of the hard boppers (the quintet session on *Early Art*), Pepper played for keeps.

In 1956, Pepper began his association with producer Lester Koenig and Contemporary Records. Three albums recorded between 1957 and early 1960 solidified his reputation: *Art Pepper Meets the Rhythm Section* (with Red Garland, Paul Chambers and Philly Joe Jones—Miles Davis's rhythm section of the time), *Art Pepper Plus Eleven: A Treasury of Modern Jazz Classics* (arrangements by Marty Paich), and *Gettin' Together* (with trumpeter Conte Candoli and Davis's later rhythm section of Chambers, Wynton Kelly and Jimmie Cobb). All three are currently out of print (Contemporary has told Pepper they plan to reissue them), but two outtakes from the combo sessions (on *The Way It Was*) prove that Pepper could rise to the challenge of the East Coast's finest rhythm players.

To judge from the music, the late '50s should have been Pepper's heyday, but the old frustrations remained, exacerbated by increasing racial animosity, diminishing jobs, police informers and general mistrust. The spirit within the musical community was souring, as illustrated by the following story (which Pepper was anxious to see into print):

"Miles Davis is my favorite player today. He's my idol. I've recorded with two of his rhythm sections, and I met him five, or six times while he was playing at a club where my second—or was it my third—wife worked. Every time he's acted like he doesn't know who I am, and he's got to know because his sidemen had to tell him what they were doing. Yet I don't know how many Miles records I've worn out. *Kind of Blue, Sketches of Spain* and *Miles Ahead* are probably the three favorite records I've heard in my life. Plus *Blue Trane* and *Ole,* but just for 'Trane—the other cats sound ridiculous, like little children after 'Trane's solos. He was so cruel on *Blue Trane!* He should have let the rest of the band play *before* him."

Coltrane became a friend of Pepper's. "When Miles would play on Sunset Strip my wife would sneak me into the club's kitchen so I could listen to 'Trane practice during intermission. I didn't want to bug him, so I hid out of the way, but I listened to every note, thinking 'Oh my God!' I wanted to kiss him every night. He was the greatest thing that ever lived. When it came time to play, he's the one horn player who would stay on the stand when he wasn't soloing, listening to the piano and what was happening with the time. His fingers would be moving—you could feel them vibrating over the keys. You know, that 'mind practice'?

"I would talk to 'Trane in the parking lot every night after the gig. The other cats would say 'Come on, 'Trane, let's go. We've got some crazy chicks.' And 'Trane would say, 'Aw man, I'm talking to Art Pepper about music. I'll see you at the hotel.' We'd talk and talk. 'Do I sound OK, Art? Is my tone alright? I don't think I'm playing good anymore.' That's the way the greatest player in the world would talk to me. This was at the time of *Giant Steps,* yet 'Trane would say, 'What should I do? All these young cats come up to me and they've heard Ornette, and they say, "Hey baby, you better watch out."'" (Pepper was well aware of the challenge presented by the young Ornette Coleman, and was one of the few Californians to encourage him.)

Coltrane also tried to persuade Pepper to break the heroin habit. "'Trane would say, 'Art, man, when are you going to straighten up? God gave you a gift. Don't destroy it. When I see you it makes me so sad I feel like crying. I went through the same thing and I know it's hard, but you can do it.' He was like a preacher, he'd say it so soft."

"But," Laurie Pepper adds, "that approach didn't work either." He was busted again in 1960, served in San Quentin until he was paroled in '64, then broke parole and was incarcerated for another two years. During his 1960 trial, Koenig recorded him twice. *Intensity*, a quartet date, is a straight-ahead sampler of popular songs, a companion piece to Jackie McLean's *Swing, Swang, Swingin'* (Blue Note) from the same period. *Smack Up*, cut with a quintet, is one of Pepper's best records and an even better indication of the increasing angularity and toughness of his approach. What had been among the most flowing of styles had splintered, and cries, honks and grunts became more prominent. Frank Butler, the drummer on both sessions, added the kind of charge Pepper no doubt appreciated and most California drummers of the time couldn't supply. But with Pepper in jail and the accelerating rejection of anything labeled "West Coast," these albums were neglected.

After leaving prison for good, Pepper, as he puts is, "almost got destroyed by 'Trane. When I got out of the joint I had no horn and could only get one on credit, so I got a tenor instead of an alto. I told myself it was because the jazz-rock thing was coming in and I could get more work, but the main reason was 'Trane. I loved him so much I couldn't imagine playing another instrument. Shelly (Manne) and a lot of people put me down, but many others said I was the only guy who could play outside and still be beautiful.

"In June of '68 I got a call to go with Buddy Rich's band playing lead alto. I hadn't played alto for ages, so I borrowed Don

Menza's. I'll never forget going back to the hotel after the first rehearsal. I took that alto out, stood in front of the mirror and started playing, and I just went crazy: 'Man, this is me! Where have I been?' I realized what I had almost done and made up my mind right there to only play *me*, the way I feel."

Pepper's trials and tribulations were far from over, however. A ruptured spleen almost killed him, and rejoining Rich before fully recovering, he suffered a ventral hernia. "Here's my stomach," he says, revealing a swollen knot on his abdomen. "That's what I play with. No belly button, pain all the time. I wear a belt when I perform." Three years in Synanon followed, then two more as a bookkeeper while he fought once again with his heroin habit and eventually went on methadone maintenance.

What finally worked? "Her," Pepper pointed to Laurie, "Synanon, and age is probably the most important thing. When I turned 45 I realized that if I got busted with a cap of heroin, I could go to the joint and with three prior felonies as a habitual criminal. The least I would get was 15 years."

His resolve has already given us two important albums. *Living Legend,* a 1975 session with Hampton Hawes, Charlie Haden and Shelly Manne, extends still further the fragmentation of lines (his operations may have played a part here), and the new, starker sound echoes the change in Pepper's physical appearance. The constants are strength, agility, and the total conviction of his blues playing (especially on the long-metered, "What Laurie Likes"). Melancholy has become persuasive: "Ophelia" slowly unfolds with a bristling sadness, and "Lost Life" is a down alto soliloquy. *The Trip,* recorded last August with George Cables, David Williams, and Elvin Jones in the rhythm section, is more redolent of Pepper's idols. There's a superb, mid-period Coltrane feel to the rhythm section (though Jones is relatively subdued), and the title piece finds Pepper borrowing licks directly from Coltrane. Miles Davis is also invoked in the introduction to "The Summer Knows," which recalls "Flamenco Sketches." But it is the repeated progression at the close of "Junior Cat" which best summarizes Pepper's current mood. Like so many pieces on both albums, it moves from an extended vamp to an unaccompanied coda instead of fading out. Pepper seems to be fighting against conclusions here, always coming up with something more. The effect suggests desperation, yet even after so many years in limbo, Pepper is incapable of making less than very good music.

At the Jazz Workshop three weeks ago, Pepper delved still deeper into the Coltrane vernacular. His playing was more fragmented and genuinely funkier than ever. The rhythm section could have stood improvement, but the accompanists were only a minor deterrent. "I hope the band's all right tonight," Pepper had said earlier. "But it really doesn't matter, because I play through the band. That may sound boastful, but nothing stops me."

Looking at Art Pepper as he sat in his hotel room, and realizing that a few bookings in jazz clubs are a far cry from proper recognition or economic security, I wondered whether Pepper's 30-year struggle could be called a victory. "The main thing is to swing and be honest," Pepper concludes in his notes to *Living Legend:* He might have added that merely surviving is the best revenge.

"After Miles's band would go off to party, 'Trane would look at me, standing there in that parking lot, and he'd say, 'Wow, those cats are on a bum trip. They aren't going to be around very long.' And most of them weren't—and 'Trane isn't either." Art, of course, lives.

14

SUDDENLY, ART PEPPER IS RED HOT

John B. Litweiler

Some observations on alto saxist Art Pepper's week at the Jazz Showcase:

- For nearly fifteen years prior to August 1975, Pepper had recorded only once: three solos on a Buddy Rich date in 1968. Through most of the '70s he's kept active playing in California, but the journey that recently brought him to Chicago is probably his first ever to the east as a leader. He's recorded four new lps since *Living Legend* (*Reader*, February 4, 1977), and he wants to do a live recording date as soon as possible. Suddenly, following jail and then a loss of faith in music, Art Pepper's career is taking off.
- He last appeared here in June '74, representing Buffet saxophones ("I work for Selmer, now—I'm moving up in the world"). This was at a music industry convention, and his long blues and "I Got Rhythm" solos with a pickup group partly verifies the publicity about "a new Art Pepper." The performance was less a surprise than a revelation: he organized new

harmonic and tone qualities in a most coherent way with procedures he established in the early '50s.

- Pepper's current tour has him fronting local rhythm sections wherever he plays. This invites catastrophe in any place other than New York, Los Angeles, here, and perhaps three or four other cities. His effusive praise for his Chicago accompanists (Willie Pickens, piano; Steve Rodby, bass; Wilbur Campbell, drums) was justified, even his favorable comparison of Rodby to Charlie Haden. Rodby's decisive lines completely avoided the acrobatics that young players so often present in music like Pepper's; Pepper himself was sufficiently impressed to invite Rodby to New York, where this week they're recording a live album at the Village Vanguard. Even more importantly, Wilbur Campbell was on fire the three nights I attended. This happens often enough with the drummer; even so, something in Pepper seemed to touch Campbell's most subtle and emphatic responses.

- Pepper brought a book of "fifteen or twenty" arrangements with him, and 75 percent of each show was material from the last three record sessions he led. Thus modal and jazz-rock pieces were included with the blues that are so close to him. Some jazzmen of Pepper's generation tend to shrug off original themes as "something I made up on the way to the session," a bit of disguised bragging that Art has indulged in, too. Pepper themes that surfaced this time, were new ("Lost Life," "Ophelia," "Valse Triste") and old ("Pepper Pot" and "Straight Life"), and they included perfect distillations of his thought. He recorded "Straight Life" at three critical points in his career in the '50s, and each version is a striking contrast to the others; his Thursday "Straight Life" was the best and most exotic performance of it that I've heard. As is true of soloists like Rollins, Coltrane, Monk, certain themes by Pepper call for re-examination over the years; I hope he records "Straight Life" again soon.

SUDDENLY, ART PEPPER IS RED HOT

Pepper began his week with a blues on a cold horn and did not conclude his set until his new alto was long warm and he'd sipped 24 ounces of water. In fact, the water supply served as a clock all week, for he took long solos in long sets, and seemed able to continue till infinity at a fabulous creative pace. Part of the crowd's interest derived from the publicity about "the new Art Pepper": he was one of the very first to record an Ornette Coleman piece, and in one of his rambling monologues he repeated his story about once nearly losing himself in John Coltrane's style. In fact, though, only a single passage in Sunday's "The Trip," which he'd composed for Coltrane, clearly suggested a Coltrane influence. Surely Pepper's sense of timing and space is too personal to admit more than the occasional sheet of sound or repeated sixteenth-note scale fragment. His sax sound, though, fairly often demonstrated the impact of the most advanced recent developments.

This requires a bit of information. In a 1964 series of *Jazz Monthly* articles, Terry Martin pointed to swing saxophonists and early Lee Konitz as the inspirations for Pepper's mature style. While it's true that harmonic adventure has added increasingly to his style at crucial points, he is unusual among modernists in his general rejection of chromaticism. Recurringly, flatted or sharped notes are placed as stresses in his lines, and as his art has grown in sophistication, altered sound and off-pitch tones have had the same effect. This tonal shading is all the more notable for its appearance in Pepper's thoroughly precise lines: without added coloring, his sound is nearly as pure as Konitz's once was. His sonic effects can be as broad as the high overtones and low chord tones (including harmonics) that appeared most prominently in three versions of "The Trip." They can be as subtle as the top edges of the tones in "Here's That Rainy Day," now warm, now jagged. I suppose the most striking kind of virtuosity is mastery of the alto sax's extreme ranges, an expertise represented in Eric Dolphy and Joseph Jarman. But Pepper's virtuosity lies in the exact delineation of timbral variety within his middle register, and his tonal precision throughout the sax's normal range. And his virtuosity is of no less a kind.

At no time was the extent of Pepper's total mastery clearer than in one of his performances of "Straight Life." Pepper had been bummed out by some customers who talked through his preceding ballad; he unloaded by choosing an incredibly fast tempo and then, as his solo progressed, *speeding* it. He managed to lose each of his accompanists, however briefly, in the absolutely vicious solo, and its most stunning feature was the perfect clarity of every note, even the smallest-valued passing ones. The theme of "Straight Life" is made of broken phrases, and these served as the model for asymmetric, angular lines in a cathartic fury. Beyond the wealth of invention here, the demarcation of note values, line, and space was surely an ultimate answer to any possible questions about Pepper's powers.

These matters of technique are important, because Pepper's lines can bear a rare weight of communication. Other major saxophonists who represent the white aesthetic in jazz—and the white jazzmen were an especially distinctive current in the '50s mainstream—did not project the emotionalism that is so deep, varied, and, again, well-defined a part of Pepper's expression: next to such admirable artists as Konitz, Stan Getz, and Warne Marsh, Art Pepper is an outsider. Terry Martin's discussion illuminates the opposite pulls of Konitz and black models such as Benny Carter, and Carter-inspired players, on Pepper's youthful, evolving sensibility. But Carter has always been foremost an architect and artificer; I'm not sure that Pepper is a greater artist, but he's advanced the method in the most illuminating way.

For Pepper is above all an architect of emotion. This is implicit in the above discussion of "Straight Life," and two performances of "No Limit" approached the matter another way. The theme was offered in a middle register, and the opening choruses of improvisation were generally contained within the range outlined by the theme. In one solo, Pepper's line grew gradually more "outside" after the pianist was signaled to enter the open-

ing trio's work; in the other a phrase began and ended in time
with the rhythm section, but Pepper's internal tempo was in no
other way related. Performances of "Girl From Ipanema,"
"Cherokee," and "Caravan" found minimal theme statement,
because to Pepper the main points were the changes (in "Caravan," the introductory vamp solo was as long as the solo based
on the chords). One version of "Red Car" moved through the
heavy contrast of staccato-legato accented notes within phrases,
another incorporated sheets of sound and high-register squeals.
A "Rita-San" and a "Mr. Yohe" included truly raunchy sections,
while the pain engendered in one "Lost Life" could only be
resolved fiercely a cappella.

In every solo Pepper began within small confines—of key, register, rhythm, sound—and developed through accent and phrase-
spacing. Polytonal phrases or intervallic extremes or "outside"
sonorities presented themselves either early or late in solos, as
their development demanded. Thus, dramatic points were made
in a context determined foremost by rhythm, the particular fac-
tors being phrase length and spacing. At one point in his career,
Pepper's vocabulary included much less variety, so his sense of
tragedy could be contained in vignette. By now his techniques
have expanded so that only long solos such as he offered here
can realize the extent of his message. More than ever, the perfect rhythmic definition (almost no long note values or rests
beyond three to five beats) determines Pepper's communication.
The immensely subtle containment of Pepper's early work is lost
forever; in its place are evolving media that, at present need this
kind of architecture to complete their message. The longer forms
are a necessity, and we might well fear that the usual lp confines
may be too restricting to adequately represent his present art—
except that Pepper's skill and intelligence promise further
refinement.

Especially on Thursday night, the terrific tension of his developing structures found release in false register squeals and "outside" sounds that recalled an altoist who is Pepper's emotive

equal and whom no one would usually consider in the same sentence: Jackie McLean. Both were urgently taken with the Coleman-Coltrane advances in the '60s, too, and apart from recordings both have pursued quasi-academic, quasi-professional careers in recent years. They'd make a wild team for a record or a night club gig, given the contrasts of their structural notions and the passionate intensity they both communicate. McLean has recently been active in public and recording, too, and Chicago could be an ideal place for a meeting of minds. But Art Pepper has proven the best show of 1977 in jazz (this has been an unusually pleasing year, too), and, since he's indicated he'll return, you who missed a wonderful trip have something to look forward to.

15

STRAIGHT LIFE

Brian Case

Few among the congregation who rose to their feet and applauded before a note was played at St. Paul's Church, Hammersmith, could have had much idea of what that ovation meant to the performer. They wouldn't have learned much from his face, but they were to hear it in his music. It was one of those spontaneous exchanges of gifts that achieve a rare fulfilling parity, a love for a love, and not the love-all of those exchange & mart comebacks with the bombardiering boxed orchids.

The tribute to Art Pepper was compounded of respect for his endurance, his artistry, and—for those who understood the shifting symmetry of anguish and elegance in his playing—an acknowledgement of the toll of that equation. Real music costs.

"Before Art went to Japan the second time," said Laurie Pepper, "he went through a period of what the doctors diagnosed as—"

—"Oh boy!" sighed Art—

—"clinical depression. He couldn't get out of bed—"

—"couldn't drive the car or anything," Art intercepted. They're very close, Mr. and Mrs. Pepper, won't travel apart, interview together, which makes sense since his memory lapses are

"Straight Life" by Brian Case originally appeared in the June 9, 1979 issue of *Melody Maker*. Reprinted by permission of IPC Magazines Limited.

redressed by her total recall. After all, she coaxed him through his autobiography, *Straight Life*, to be published by Macmillan. "My mouth was all numb. I couldn't talk. I couldn't remember anything. What fear! I think that's why I so seldom work."

Last here in improbable white army gaiters and a sawn-off shotgun guarding Marlborough Street Jail during the Blitz, Art hasn't been anywhere too much in the intervening 30 years: Japan twice, New York once. It's a difficult temperament, the creative resilience way ahead of the metabolism. On a ballad, you can hear him test it for its supportive strengths, find them wanting and invent his own. His life has taken longer.

"I play this little club in Los Angeles coupla times a month, and I get nervous there. First, it's the fear that the people won't be there, and the club-owner won't be happy because he won't be making money, then after that, I'll be afraid I won't play good enough—"

"—and then when he does play good enough," said Laurie, "and gets big rave reviews in the newspapers he's afraid that the next performance won't justify all that."

A serpent with its tail in its mouth, this circuit; something he has to live with, and nothing like the darting expansiveness it fuels in his music.

"I'm getting a lot better than I was," said Art, at rest on the hotel bed, bare feet, Levis, grey track-top. "I think being sober has a lot to do with it." And methadone. You don't get far into conversation with the Peppers without tribute being paid to the methadone cure: addicts had a shaky one per cent chance of cure before the institution of the methadone programme. Art, a three-time loser who has spent years of his life in Chino, Folsom, Terminal Island, Synanon and San Quentin, knows that this time the cure has to be for keeps.

"If I get busted again in California, I'd get 15 to life. Murder is going seven. I could have one cap of heroin and do more than if I'd murdered five or six people. It just doesn't make sense. It's still so archaic, you know, I can't imagine how they passed this law. They made out every killing and rape was someone crazed on heroin. People who're on heroin, that's the last thing they wanna do, have anything to do with. They can't make love to their wives, let alone a rape."

Like Stan Getz or Chet Baker, Art gained recognition for his craft before he was mature enough to handle it. Sensitive, anxious, he found life on the road with the Stan Kenton orchestra, the nightly showcasing of his talents, and the separation from his wife and home an intolerable strain. He turned to dope. From then on, his life was divided between prison and the recording studios.

He placed second to Bird in the Down Beat Poll in 1951 and 1952 and third in 1952 and 1953, while in February of 1953, he took his first narcotics fall. Released in May 1954, he was back in prison by December. In despair by 1957, he gave up playing to sell accordions, and again in 1972, retired to become a book-keeper, but he couldn't stay away.

Even a six-year stretch in San Quentin—the prison that made its gas-chamber debut with a rabbit and ended with a deranged black who believed he was Christ—couldn't destroy the urge to create music.

"When I first got to San Quentin, you couldn't play, but after a certain length of time the restrictions lighten up a little bit. You go from the South Block to another block, and if you can find an instrument anywhere, you can play it on a weekend. If you get to the West Block, which is an honour block, you can play it of an evening until eight o'clock, till the lights, you know—till they lock you in your cell. I played a lot with Dupree Bolton on the week-end. We used to play down the lower yard. That was nice . . .

"A lifer had sent for an alto out of the catalogue. See, lifers can send for things and they're delivered from the company. Only way you can get something is if it comes from the factory, packed where no one can get at it and put any dope in it—but even so, they shake it down, take all the pads off. I didn't have a saxo-phone to be sent, and I don't think I could have had one any-way, being a narcotics addict."

Had they been curious about these things, California's penitentiary authorities might have been interested to hear that they had thrown the bolt on California's most unique musical sensibility. Born in Gardena in 1925 of an Italian mother and a German father, Arthur Edward Pepper was the only white West Coast saxophone player to avoid the local academicism and the ubiquitous Birdimitations, and to fashion a style of his own.

He has the sort of rhythmic freedom—a stretched tight, pent-up surface of alternating rests and twisting timbres—that is rare among white musicians, and his thematic improvisational approach finds parallel only on the East Coast in the work of Monk and Rollins.

"At the beginning, when I was very young, playing on Central Avenue and everything, I asked someone about Willie Smith and that he looked so white, and they told me that he was a seventh-grain negro, and I remember wishing that I was. I wanted to be black because I felt such an affinity to the music. It's been a very difficult thing, because I had no prejudice at all until I started into the prison thing, and then the whole thing was changed. The prejudice in prison is beyond description. The hatred is just unbounded."

It wasn't that way in the Forties on Central Avenue, not among musicians, although outside the shared craft—and Chandler's *Farewell My Lovely*, which Art had open on the bed, paints a different picture in the straight world—the barriers were up. The teenage altoman sat in with Dexter Gordon and Sonny Criss and Charles Mingus, worked with Lee Young's nine-piece and the Benny Carter bands and enjoyed the healthy competition and free flow of ideas.

At 18, he joined Kenton—an apprenticeship which culminated in the Innovations In Modern Music Orchestra, using charts by Pete Rugolo, Johnny Richards, Bob Graettinger, Bill Russo and Shorty Rogers. In 1951, Art was featured on the historic "Cool & Crazy" session with Shorty Rogers, appearing for contractual reasons as Art Salt.

"Yeah. It's so obvious, but I actually had several people ask me, 'Have you heard of this guy, Art Salt?' I looked at them because I thought they were just putting me on, real subtle I said, Oh yeah—I've heard of him a little bit. I'm waiting for a joke, you know. Well, they finally say, 'He sure plays a lot like you—but he's black.' I can't believe they're serious! See, a long time ago, they all thought I was black."

Pepper apart, one of the few white schools of originality in the Forties was the ascetic and hermetic Tristano Cool School, but despite an early Konitz influence and some fine collaborations with Warne March, a deeper entente proved incompatible.

"I had the feeling that that was the avant-garde of the music world, an outside type of playing—but as much as it seemed avant-garde, it wasn't. I enjoyed it very much, but I didn't want those boundaries. All the boundaries were placed. It was very narrow. I thought it was kinda cute to do it in a certain setting, just like if I sit in with Zoot Sims and play like him. Proving your musicianship, you know."

As a result of the belated release of the Pepper-Marsh Contemporary album, "The Way It Was," the two musicians got together for a Sunday afternoon concert, their first meeting in 20 years. Laurie Pepper had been so impressed by Marsh that, braving the celebrated remote and patrician manner, she had rushed backstage to congratulate him.

"I just want to tell you that I think you're wonderful," she said, adding, to disassociate herself from the bobbysox faction, "and I don't go around saying this to musicians very often." Warne's reply was typically succinct. "You wouldn't, being married to Art Pepper."

Ornette Coleman, active in the Los Angeles area in the late Fifties, offered a similar challenge to Pepper's musicianship, and he was one of the few musicians who was open at the start to the fellow altoman's radical departure.

"I played standards with him and Don Cherry several times, before he became famous. Their approach was so different, and finally I was able to see exactly what they were doing. I didn't want to do that either, but it was interesting. See, I just like the melodic way of playing so much. That's why I like Miles. I admire Ornette for what he does, but if I was gonna play outside, I'd have stayed in my Coltrane bag."

In tribute, he recorded Ornette's "Tears Inside" on his "Smack Up" album. "I enjoy that tune very much. I love his tunes. He wrote this tune called 'Lorraine' for Herb Geller's wife—it was so beautiful. What they did was they played the melody together, but instead of doing it exactly together, they would be just a fraction behind, and that's what gave it that sound. I noticed that on a couple of Gil Evans things from 'Sketches of Spain', but it was written that way and that's hard to do. It had that thing.

"That's what I heard in Ornette's playing—the sound of a human voice crying out for acceptance and for love and understanding—and people just couldn't understand. It was really a shame—I really felt sad about that—and I think Ornette could feel that in our contact."

In fact, Ornette acknowledged Pepper's early support by asking him to come up out of the audience at Newport, and play with him.

Pepper puts a lot of store by recognition from fellow saxophonists. Sonny Criss, who shared his anxiety about playing, and killed himself in 1977 rather than face a tour of Japan, once made a gesture of support that Pepper will never forget.

"He made a trip all the way to Shelly's Manne-Hole to hear me play. I was playing tenor at the time, and he came in alone with this great big dog. He had to go through something to get there, bring this dog in, you know. He didn't go there for any reason, to get anything—just to listen. Afterwards, he said, 'You sound great on tenor, but alto is our instrument.'"

Untypically, having withstood the influence of Bird and Ornette, he fell for a period under the spell of Coltrane. It started with "Kind of Blue," and came to a head in the mid-Sixties during a period of scuffling typified in a syndrome known as The L.A. Slows.

"It was the first time I'd ever succumbed to anything like that. For a little while it was like that with Coltrane, because he was so marvellous. Everything about the way he played—his tone, his approach—was just so incredibly right. A master! Being a saxophone player, it was like, so challenging. I didn't have a horn at that time, and I knew this girl and she was able to get credit for one horn, either alto or what, so I got a tenor because I liked Coltrane so much.

"I play differently on tenor. I feel more harsh, more power, more frantic, more outside. It's easy to move on, to play fast. After a while I got a call to join Buddy Rich's band on alto, and I had to borrow one—and then I realized that's what I should be playing, and I worked through that thing of Coltrane's. I just learned from it and then discarded it and after that I just became myself again."

Why not Rollins and the thematic approach?

"I agree with what you say about how he makes things as a whole—I didn't like his sound. That's the way it was years ago—a player would play and the whole thing would be a composition with a beginning, a middle, and an end. People don't play that way any more, as a rule. I think the people that were listening to Coltrane and Ornette Coleman—not them themselves—had something to do with it. They were too much interested in doing something that was far out than thematic-type things, creation as a whole."

He wasn't interested in the extended solo possibilities that followed in the wake of "Chasin' the Trane"?

"It's hard. The only time I've ever found myself doing that is if I'm not able to say what I want to say because of the rhythm section, or because of my pre-occupation with the people or something. Sometimes I'll continue playing because I don't want to admit defeat—and finally I end up with I should've stopped long ago. If it isn't gonna happen, it isn't gonna happen.

"Sometimes I have that feeling—and when I start out, I realize I was wrong. If I feel sure about the rhythm section and there's a lot of people, then the adrenalin starts pumping and I know something good's gonna happen. Sometimes I'll do it and think it was fine, and I won't get the response, and I'll play bad, and get the response, and not be able to figure it out. It's very frustrating.

"But I do have times when I start warming up on the horn—I just have a certain feel in my consciousness and going to my fingers. There's just a directional thing that happens from the brain to the muscles—you know, like running or dancing or a basketball player—where the horn just becomes an extension of myself, and I'm not aware of the saxophone, the metal, the reed, fingers, the technical aspects of music. It's just an extension of me as a being, using that as a form of communication . . .

"Shapes? Yeah. At the beginning it should be real subtle and really beautiful—even a fast tune can be like that—but a ballad, that's where I really have the thing happening. It starts out and it forms patterns. I'm consciously aware of that sometimes, other times I'm not. If there's something wrong with the rhythm section or the crowd, that blocks it.

His latest album for Galaxy, "Art Pepper Today," contains a version of "Patricia," first recorded for his daughter in 1957, that Art believes represents the pinnacle of his playing. He had taken it into the studio along with a sheaf of other old originals, and didn't even recognize it when Stanley Cowell began to pick it out on the piano. They cut it in one take.

"Up until the ending, it was just really happy, and when I'd done that I knew that was really it. This is really a composition, because at the end it goes completely outside and then comes back in, starts from just beautiful crying to total insanity like in the middle—but a controlled insanity." He made a tapering and belling gesture between his fingers. "It's just like that. Every time I play it from now on will be just an anti-climax, you know."

"When it was all over," said Laurie, "Roy Haynes said to Art 'Where did you say you were from?' and Art said, Gardena, California. Roy Haynes said, 'SOUTH Gardena?' He couldn't believe a white guy was playing with that much soul."

Pepper is so pleased with it, that it is going on a single to be enclosed with the autobiography: same thing, really. "If you got that, and you weren't a jazz-liker, you'd play the thing anyway just to see what it was, wouldn't you?" he asked, innocent in the face of commerce. "They might throw it on accidentally, and if they listened to it, it might change their thoughts, mightn't it?"

"Gettin' Together" remains his personal favorite from the astonishing year that also produced "Intensity" and "Smack Up," only to bury him alive with a two-to-20 sentence despite an open letter from the music establishment to the American State Department pleading for clemency.

"At that time I was just really together musically. I'd been playing a lot at the Lighthouse with Conte Candoli—working every night, which has been a rarity for me. I'd just gotten out of prison, and I was able to play. I don't know if it was that, or what I was saying. Mostly the fact that I was able to do what I wanted to do. And Jimmie Cobb? I loved playing with him because he was so sincere. He'd just listen to what you were doing and he was just perfect."

Art recalled an earlier session with a Miles Davis rhythm section: "Art Pepper Meets The Rhythm Section." "Philly Joe? Uh—he sometimes intimidates you a little bit, Jimmie Cobb never does. Frank Butler is subtle, too. I hope everything works out for him because it's getting to that point, you know—like with me. If I hadn't started making it now, probably it'd never happen. Frank's in the same boat."

The death of Lester Koenig ended the classic association with Contemporary, the best of the West Coast labels, but Art's new contract with Galaxy is free from commercial pressures and has a life-long dream built into the quota in the shape of a ballad album with strings.

Endearingly enough, the only demands upon him are from the small Japanese labels, which want him to recreate 1956, same tunes, same sidemen. He has also attracted publicity for his soundtrack work on the Clint Eastwood movies, *The Enforcer*, and *The Gauntlet*, scores by Jerry Fielding.

Laurie Pepper laughed, "Jerry called Art up and said, 'Art do you play baritone?' Art said, Uh . . . yeah. Art had played baritone in prison one time because that was the only available horn. Jerry said great, because Gerry Mulligan wanted too much money. Art went in, and there were all these studio guys who are ex-Kentonites—all old jazz players, all sitting round the studio—and Art walks in with his baritone. Everybody BUT Jerry Fielding knew Art Pepper was NOT a baritone player!'"

"He asked someone if I could read music too," said Art, a tower of resignation.

He has recently had footage of a solo saxophone improvisation for *Heartbeat*, a movie about Jack Kerouac, and has hopes of further studio offers.

"That might mean an opening for me, because otherwise I never get any kind of a studio phone. That'll be it. Three calls in ten years."

To anyone in that audience at St. Paul's, it was incomprehensible that the world at large was not beating a path to Pepper's door.

The biting silver of his alto flashed among the gilt crucifixes, the lyrical ache at the core of his soul rushed upwards along the massive granite aspiration of the nave. Architectures locked like fists, the one a frozen perfection of forgotten quarries, hoists and blueprints, the other living, precarious, transient.

"If you could build highest church tower in the world." said Hilde in *The Master Builder*, "I thought you must surely be able to produce a kingdom too, of some sort or other . . . "

No, but getting nearer.

16

ART PEPPER
Living the Straight Life

Mark Leviton

"The Hole" at San Quentin is a completely dark, horribly damp cell where cockroaches and rats roam free. Twice a day the heavy steel door is opened briefly, and the prisoner unfortunate enough to be confined there sees a little light before he's sealed up again. If there is any music in The Hole, it is the sound of solitary, lonely human voice weeping or singing. Art Pepper knows The Hole from the inside.

"I went through as much as anybody can go through without being killed," the famed alto saxophonist grimly says. At 53 years of age, Pepper is about to publish his lengthy autobiography, *Straight Life*, letting us all in on the details of his difficult past—the ten years in prison, the back alleys of severe heroin addiction, the sexual exploits, the glories of L.A.'s Central Avenue scene in the '40s, and how he's managed to emerge healthy, full of musical ideas, and somehow playing better than ever. "I don't want to bury the past." Art says, sipping iced tea from a beer mug that exists as a reminder of the days when he used to drink more than his share of booze. "I want people to read about what I've

"Art Pepper: Living the Straight Life" by Mark Leviton originally appeared in the August 17, 1979 issue of *BAM* magazine.

gone through. It's a very unique life, and I tell the exact truth. Maybe some people can learn from it." New York City publishers Macmillan have the book on their fall schedule. If Art's life story, prepared in collaboration with his editor-wife Laurie, is as influential and discussed as his music, he may have the best-selling jazz book of all time to add to his collection of achievements. And as his just-released album, *Today*, suggests, his fourth decade in music may be his best.

Pepper was born in 1925 in Gardena, California, and was raised by his grandmother after his parents split up when Art was 5 years old. As detailed in *Straight Life*, Art found solace in his own fantasy world where his cold-hearted grandmother couldn't penetrate. Working on his own, he began playing clarinet at 9, picking up scraps of information from the occasional book or teacher, and by the time he was in his teens he had switched to alto sax and was jamming at the thriving Central Avenue clubs along with other youngsters like Dexter Gordon, Charles Mingus, Zoot Sims, and Lester Young's younger brother Lee, who gave Art his first professional job.

"A lot of white musicians around L.A. had their roots in records, just in listening to records," says Laurie, "But people like Art and Zoot were on Central Avenue playing live music alongside black musicians. They spent their childhood down there." Although Art became identified with the so-called "L.A. cool school," his playing was far more passionate and deep than that label might suggest. He had, as Mingus recognized, "soul."

"It's happened so many times that people think I'm black if they've only heard my records," says Art. "I learned my music in the same place. I never really thought about the race thing in jazz until it was sort of foisted upon me, in the Army and when I started going to prison. I didn't even *know* about prejudice, and then I saw it and went through it. It's on both sides.

Art was an impressive, fiery saxophonist from the start, and in the '50s, when he wasn't in prison, he made a series of spectacular recordings for the Contemporary label. His technique and tone are still impeccable, and the years haven't slowed him down or hurt his wind. He is a pure, supple improviser and a fine composer whose life is encapsulated in his many original titles, such as "Lost Life," "What Laurie Likes," and "The Trip." Recently he played a few quartet dates at Donte's in preparation for a Japanese tour, and blazed through the hectic, ironically-named original "Straight Life" of 15 years ago with the same verve he brought to his most recent masterpiece, "Patricia," a tune that appears on *Today* in a performance Art feels is his greatest recording.

"Jazz for me is instant gratification, instant genius I call it," he comments. People sometimes say there's no such thing as really *new* improvisation. You do get to a point where it's all happened before, but as in 'Patricia' you can go beyond that to something that just hasn't been done, not the way I did it. I'm not even aware the alto is a different part of my body," Art adds in an intriguingly-phrased statement. "I'm out of a musical context—what chords and such—and it's all coming from my soul.

"I used to play when I was a heavy heroin user, and sometimes I'd be sick because I couldn't score. I was so miserable when I'd play a ballad I'd just cry through the horn. I'd feel awful and the other guys in the band would say, 'Wow, you ought to be sick all the time.' It was terrible for me. Now I'm in great shape physically. I quit smoking at the Schick Center, and my love for Laurie is a new beginning. Everything in my life has been building toward this. It's all so much *righter*."

When Art got out of prison for the last time in 1966, he couldn't afford instruments and found that with the rock boom on, everyone working seemed to be playing tenor sax. There was little room for a traditional alto player with a history of drugs and drink, no matter how "straight" he'd gone.

"Coltrane was the only person I listened to then. I almost got immersed in his genius. The first time I heard him I'd just come out of prison. I didn't have a horn, but had a chance to get one, with a chick signing for it, and I got a tenor. I figured I could get more gigs because I could play rock jobs—it's more suitable for making money. But that wasn't the real reason. I was hung up on Coltrane. I finally got an offer from Buddy Rich to play lead alto, and I had to borrow one from Don Menza. As soon as I started warming up on it I realized the alto was *me*. Alto is harder to play technically—if you play alto you really have to be saying something, you can't just be bullshitting. So many people have started on alto and been unable to master it. In fact, Coltrane started off on lead alto in Dizzy Gillespie's band, years ago."

Unfortunately, Art's past life caught up with him again. His spleen ruptured and he had to quit Rich, and in continuing ill health he entered Synanon, where he spent three years, leaving well before the institution got into its well-known legal problems. From 1972 on, Art has been working on his autobiography with Laurie, doing jazz clinics and playing when and where he can.

"I never try to get a job," Art says, pointedly, "I just wait for someone to call. I won't get down and lick somebody's shoes, or go in the studios and degrade myself. I've stopped doing those casuals I used to have to do to eat—the weddings and Bar Mitzvahs. There are so many white musicians in L.A. who do studio work, play several instruments, arrive on time—they've sold out, they hardly play jazz anymore. Now, a lot of black guys are coming out here from New York to sell out. I won't do things where someone tells me what to play. I don't want to be a servant."

"You can see where we live," adds Laurie, gesturing to the front door of their tiny house on a dingy industrial block in Van Nuys. "People who play in studios feel there are things they want to have, things more important than artistic integrity, and they have to keep playing to keep them. They like to sit around the pool and drink; drive big cars. It means more to Art to have Elvin Jones call him up for a show—which recently happened—to get *that* kind of respect. He's proud of himself and his work. In the book, Art tells everything. He's like an emotional exhibitionist, and it gets real scary, it's all so real."

"My playing is all involved with love, jealousy, frustration, being in prison—all my life experiences." Art says." In the book I tell things no one would *think* of telling about themselves— things I've thought or done. It's honesty. I feel the same way about music—the truth can't be wrong."

17

THE CONTEMPORARY ART OF PEPPER

Chris Sheridan

Arthur Edward Pepper, whose style has been glimpsed over the years with the regularity of the sun at an English cricket match, finally stepped into the suffused orange light of the bandstand at this Gothic memorial to Victorian enterprise after an absence of 35 years. The atmosphere that greeted him was an electric combination of religious fervour, awed disbelief and fascinated anticipation.

Taken as a whole, the first set presented, in microcosm, and in no particular order, some details of Pepper's evolution. It was identical—in content at least—to that played at Hammersmith the previous evening, starting, as so often in the studio, with the blues, this time *Whims of Chambers*. A mercurial *Scrapple From The Apple* reflected not only his much surer grasp than most other Californians of Parker's innovations, but also his individual interpretation of them. And, in trading fours with bassist Peter Ind, he introduced novel textural variation.

In the second set, for which Pepper first thought his left lung would fail him, a glowing, loping *Ophelia* (from 1975) was succeeded by a punchy *Mambo Koyama* from his soon-to-be-released

"The Contemporary Art of Pepper" by Chris Sheridan originally appeared in the September 1979 issue of *Jazz Journal*. Reprinted by permission of *Jazz Journal*.

Galaxy LP. *Straight No Chaser* swayed and weaved compellingly before he reached the lyrical peak of the night—*Here's That Rainy Day*, "a tune my wife asked me to play." It was a consummate performance, rich in textural variation as sweeping phrases which sang through the length of the saxophone were juxtaposed cunningly by flurries and interjections. It was, however, his rollicking version of the late Kenny Dorham's *Blue Bossa* that brought the four hundred members of the audience to their feet for a lengthy and exceptionally well-deserved standing ovation.

This is a man whose playing vividly reflects his emotions, whose playing is concentrated through his saxophone so that he stands virtually motionless, his alto gripped firmly in the left hand side of his mouth so that his head is turned slightly to the right. Only the occasional bending of the knees betrays the intensity of his feeling outside the natural milieu of the music.

Yet, in conversation, he is among the most candid of musicians, equally happy to discuss instrumental problems as personal ones.

Born in Gardena, near Los Angeles in California in 1925, Art was a professional musician by the age of 17. He played with Benny Carter's band in the early '40s—and Benny gave him a large share of the spotlight—before a proposed tour of Southern states forced a move (he was the band's sole white member). Art then joined Stan Kenton, with whom he remained—apart from the War service which brought him to the UK in 1944—until 1951. Separation from his wife and family had already caused the itch for which drugs were seen as a palliative, and the frequent gaps in his discography thereafter tell their own tragic tale. Altogether, he reckons to have spent eleven years of his life in penal institutions or hospitals or convalescent institutions, including Synanon.

This partly explains why he has remained on the West Coast, making his first appearance as a leader in New York—at the Village Vanguard—only two years ago. "For a long time, I didn't have to think about it, because I was with Stan Kenton. Then, after that, I started going to jail and there was no question of leaving the West Coast! When I did finally make it to New York, I loved it and decided that's where I wanted to live. I called everybody that we were moving there but, when we got home, I suddenly felt the 'safety' of being in Los Angeles and decided against the move."

On a happier note, Art remembered easily the highspots of his career: "Playing *Art Pepper* with Stan Kenton at Carnegie Hall, making *Art Pepper Plus 11* and *Gettin' Together* for Contemporary, going to Japan, and then the reception last night in London and here tonight. But by far my most gratifying moment, musically, was making this side *Patricia* that is coming out soon on Galaxy."

Altogether, the contract he has just signed with Galaxy—a Fantasy/Prestige/Milestone subsidiary—calls for four albums, including one with strings. "That was one of the conditions of the contract. Also I'll do a side on the second album with clarinet."

Art is probably the most individual contemporary performer on this difficult instrument (outside the New Music) and prefers it to soprano. "At one time I only had a real old beat soprano that belonged to some chick's brother. It had a nice tone, which is unusual, so I played it for a while and got to like it. But, in the end, I realised it's too close to the alto in tone and range to give good contrast. The clarinet, though, I enjoy if I'm really practiced up on it. It's the hardest of all the reeds—going through the middle fingertips, for D and C and G-sharp, is incredibly hard. You have to plan ahead because, if you get it wrong, you have to change your whole idea. You can see how difficult the instrument is by how few people play it."

He did use it most recently during his tenure at the Vanguard, which was recorded by Contemporary. The sessions will be released although Art feels that, at times, "I was too nervous and got too experimental. I would rather have done them over."

Of influences, apart from Benny Carter, he named Lester Young, Joe Thomas (Jimmie Lunceford's tenor man) and Louis Jordan. Charlie Parker? "I really loved the way Bird played, but he didn't influence me, you know. When I got out of the army, everybody was imitating Parker and they just ruined themselves. All kinds of guys that really had original styles destroyed their playing entirely. The only person that really affected me that way was John Coltrane. The way he played on Miles Davis's *Kind of Blue* album really turned me round. I even bought a tenor, but, once I got the lead alto job with Buddy Rich's band, I realised alto was my horn, so I tried to get away from that influence.

"I feel it was something I just grew through, technically—just a stepping-stone. I really feel I'm far better now than I've been at any time before."

The whole Art Pepper story, though, will appear in print in October, when the biography written by his second wife, Laurie, is published. He did though add one revealing note to explain how he has survived all the tribulations. " I felt I'd gotten the bad end of the stick so many times that I should start getting rewarded. I'd paid so many bad dues that it was time to get the good things, and it's starting now. All of a sudden, with Laurie hounding people, I'm getting royalties, so I don't have to play casuals or corny TV things. I can play jazz and survive without working myself to death. I'm thankful that's happening, but I feel it's my due because I never purposely tried to harm anybody."

On the contrary, what he has done is to bring a great deal of love to people through his music, as evidenced most strongly at Birmingham and, by all accounts, at London the day before.

18

NO LIMIT/AMONG FRIENDS/ART PEPPER TODAY

Terry Martin

Pepper returns! Again! And these three albums apart from heralding that most recent resurrection appear to foreshadow a significant transition in the style of one of the most gifted altoists in jazz history. His change of direction involves a rediscovery of and identification with his first mature style (achieved in the 1955–1957 period, and now reasonably represented on the excellent Blue Note collection BN-LA 591-H2); the coincident return to the public ear and to a former esthetic incarnation may imply discoveries for both audience and artist.

Contrary to his personal life, apparently a disordered array of self-questing and frequently self-destructive gambits, Pepper's musical world has from the very first evidence (1940 recordings with Kenton) revealed the presence of a finely discriminating taste and natural ease of construction. True, these remarkably coherent self-assemblies also displayed marked internal tension; they were made to bear considerable emotional weight as efficiently and as elegantly as possible. Pepper's success in that amalgam of form and passion makes him a rare jazz artist, one whose contributions rank with those of Beiderbecke, Teagarden,

"No Limit/Among Friends/Art Pepper Today" by Terry Martin originally appeared in the September 6, 1979 issue of *Down Beat*. Reprinted by permission of the author.

Warne Marsh and very few others, as natural both to their own integrity and to the stream of a predominantly black music. Not an innovator, he has nonetheless created an inimitable fusion of the finest natural alto saxophone techniques, Benny Carter-like grace of form and Parker/Konitz modernity, with his own deep rooted angst.

In the 1960s Pepper (like his counterpart, Jackie McLean) made some stylistic modifications to accommodate the new esthetic worlds of John Coltrane and Ornette Coleman. Unfortunately that period of transition and new achievements is not documented on commercially available recordings. Now we can only hear what appears, from the present point of view, to be the tail end of this phase of his creative life. The examples are contained on the first albums arising from the current Pepper revival: Contemporary's *Living Legend, The Trip* and now the March 1977 *No Limit* session. The intentional "disordering of the senses" and acquisition of more recent expressive devices, including "sheets of sound" and high harmonics, have not always achieved Art's self-alleged goal of greater emotional honesty—his passion had been so perfectly contained within organized nets of shifting phrase patterns, acutely articulated rhythms and subtle Lesterian timbral effects. Still, the Contemporary albums do reveal many fresh insights and the period has clearly expanded the altoist's armament for use in the future.

No Limit, in fact, is less successful than its predecessors, but nonetheless will remain an essential item for Pepper devotees. The reasons for this are both found on the second side of the album. To take the less esthetically significant of these first, there is the novelty of hearing the Pepper alto and the Pepper tenor duet (by overdubbing) on his old composition *Mambo De La Pinta* (a fine orthodox quintet version from '56 is on the Blue Note two-fer). The value of this performance is reduced by the long, and uncharacteristically meandering, tenor solo. The highpoint of the record is attained on the modal ballad *My Laurie*, which is a superb example of the dialectics of grace and pain typical of his post-1960 style. The sober line is broken by McLean-like shrieks (Jackie of *Let Freedom Ring* and *Right Now*); there are also of course those entirely distinctive marks of Art's personality in the abundance of timbral alterations, provocative silences and control of time. The closing alto statement begins in meditation but breaks into glimpses of rock-blues and internal fires to complete a complex, multilayered portrait of the artist's wife. The rhythm section is merely a presence rather than a contributor to these explorations, and Art's is the only solo voice of substance to be heard on the album. A positive feature of the production is Pepper's own liner notes, which pay tribute to his friend Lester Koenig of Contemporary Records, who died shortly after this session.

In September 1978 the altoist was indeed *Among Friends,* of whom Russ Freeman and Frank Butler had been longtime musical associates. It is also pleasant for the rest of us to encounter Freeman again after the years of his interment in West Coast music factories and he contributes some typically brittle solos to the proceedings. Butler also plays well, although neither he nor the pianist is sufficiently forceful on this occasion to completely overcome the lugubrious artifices of Magnusson, who as yet lacks the maturity to provide sympathetic support and instead is frequently quite distracting in his role of "contemporary hip bassist." The lack of integration of the rhythm section is thrown into further relief by the extreme isolation of the instruments in the recorded sound; this sort of clarity is counterproductive. Perhaps in view of these introductory remarks it will surprise the reader to be told that the major virtues of *Among Friends* are a mellow relaxation and general good spirits. The songs are, of course, old friends too, and a number of them have been the subjects for some of Pepper's finest recordings (particularly the '56–'57 *What Is This Thing* and *Besame Mucho* should be sought out). While the revisitations lack the urgency of the vintage performances, they are very fine and there are some new offerings of real substance. *Blue Bossa* receives a stimulating treatment; it moves at a good clip and Art enters stabbing and prancing around the Latin meter in typically indigenous fashion, then develops his solo with a tense momentum that projects an impression of continuously expanding musical horizons. Indeed, it is on the faster pieces that the album's finest moments are found, the tempos lending urgency to the otherwise pervasive mellow mood.

In isolation one might have felt that the Interplay recording was the product of a dedicated but nostalgic Pepper enthusiast, an attempt to recreate the aura of the artist's past achievements. The nature of the Galaxy album however, suggests that the return is of the altoist's own choosing. And, whereas there are moments on *Among Friends* when a relaxed objectivity towards the material threatens to become a lack of involvement, *Art Pepper Today* finds the artist completely emotionally engaged with the themes and style of yesterday, and they leap to life with joyous urgency.

The December '78 sessions have probably produced the finest album yet under the banner of the slow starting Galaxy label. Certainly it is one of Pepper's most satisfying recordings of recent years. The rhythm section, apart from a few of those seemingly ubiquitous bass cliches McBee allows to slip into his work on the heads, is a fiery unity and the recording quality is a reasonable reflection of that integrated spirit. Given the flying carpet his colleagues lay down, Art needs no urging to swashbuckle his way through some familiar changes. *Miss Who?* is an excellent start to affairs, as he glides over Sweet Georgia's shapely progressions with exemplary phrasing and beautifully judged tonal effects, before giving way to Stanley Cowell's flowing, almost neo-Wilsonish solo. The alto breaks have more than enough spark to leap across the drum sections; Haynes plays well, and it is no disgrace that Pepper outswings him, for no one in the music can touch the altoist in such exchanges when he is fully engaged in the battle. *Mambo Koyama* is a wittily sketched Latin piece with Art coming up from below the belt in another of those continuously opening structures which gain power from the skill and emotion so obviously held in reserve. The performance does wind down a bit during the piano and percussion outing, but the alto soon returns with the line, then sails free into a coda which the musicians allow to fade gracefully away.

The engineers fade (arbitrarily) the end of the lightning paced *Lover Come Back* wherein Art's jagged phrasing finds a natural home; he leaps and tumbles with fine edged abandon in the solo, the jousts with Haynes and that unfortunately attenuated coda. Some faulty programming is also apparent on the second side of the album where adjacent ballads of similar formal outline diminish their separate effects. *Patricia*, incidentally, is a beautiful melody with passing resemblance to *Old Folks* and can be heard in a fine early version on the Blue Note Collection. *Chris's Blues* is a stablemate of *Val's Pal* (for those who remember the remarkable '56 Tampa album, now Vintage Jazz 111453), a tear-up riff blues in which its author jumps right out of the head, as comfortable as ever at breakneck tempo (or double it), and his warm timbre burrows through the lower register with tremendous ease. This brief piece is an exciting coda to an exciting record, and perhaps the introduction to a time when Art Pepper will bring his old and new skills together in some new conjunction of form and feeling.

19

ADDICT

Whitney Balliett

In Henry Mayhew's great nineteenth-century oral history "London Labour and the London Poor," a boy with "long and rather fair hair" speaks of the rigors of his childhood:

> I'm a native of Wisbeach, in Cambridgeshire, and am sixteen. My father was a shoe-maker, and my mother died when I was five years old, and my father married again. I was sent to school, and can read and write well. My father and step-mother were kind enough to me. I was apprenticed to a tailor three years ago, but I wasn't long with him; I runned away. I think it was three months I was with him when I first runned away . . . I stopped in lodging-houses until my money was gone, and then I slept anywhere—under the hedges, or anywhere. . . . I had to beg my way back . . . but was very awkward at first. I lived on turnips mainly. My reason for running off was because my master ill-used me so; he beat me, and kept me from my meals, and made me sit up working late at nights for a punishment.

And here, a hundred and twenty years later, in the autobiography "Straight Life" (Schirmer; $12.95), is the alto saxophonist Art Pepper speaking of his childhood:

One time when my father had been at sea for quite a while he came home and found the house locked and me sitting on the front porch, freezing cold and hungry. She [Pepper's mother] was out somewhere. She didn't know he was coming. He was drunk. He broke the door down and took me inside and cooked me some food. She finally came home, drunk, and he cussed her out. We went to bed, I had a little crib in the corner, and my dad wanted to get into bed with me. He didn't want to sleep with her. She kept pulling on him, but he pushed her away and called her names. He started beating her up. He broke her nose. He broke a couple of ribs. Blood poured all over the floor. I remember the next day I was scrubbing up blood, trying to get the blood up for ages.

Most of Mayhew's four-volume work consists of interviews he conducted with London street people—prostitutes, beggars, flower girls, pickpockets, sweeps, peddlers. Pepper's book is largely a self-interview. He is a drug addict, and seven years ago, after he had finished three years in Synanon, he began talking his life into a tape recorder as an act of catharsis and stabilization, and this letting loose continued for several years. There is a plethora of tape-recorded books—books set down in a false prose, whose authors have sidestepped the hard, distillative act of writing. But "Straight Life" demonstrates again and again that Pepper has the ear and memory and interpretative lyricism of a first-rate novelist. He describes what happened to the tenor saxophonist John Coltrane:

He got on that treadmill and ran himself ragged trying to be new and to change. It destroyed him. It was too wearing, too draining. And he became frustrated and worried. Then he started hurting, getting pains, and he got scared. He got these pains and he got scared. He got these pains in his back, and he got terrified. He was afraid of doctors, afraid of hospitals, afraid of audiences, afraid of bandstands. He lost his teeth. He was afraid that his sound wasn't strong enough, afraid that the new, young black kids wouldn't think he was the greatest thing that ever lived anymore. And the pains got worse and worse: they got so bad he couldn't stand the pain. So they carried him to a hospital but he was too far gone. He had cirrhosis, and he died that night.

Here is the sort of subterranean soul Mayhew relished:

I looked around the club and saw this guy there, Blinky, that I knew. He was a short, squat guy with a square face, blue eyes; he squinted all the time; when he walked he bounced; and he was always going "Tchk! Tchk!"—moving his head in jerky little motions like he was playing the drums. Sometimes when he walked he even looked like a drum set: you could see the sock cymbal bouncing up and down and the foot pedal going and the cymbals shaking and his eyes would be moving. But it wasn't his eyes; it was that his whole body kind of blinked.

Pepper was born in 1925, in Gardena, California. His father was a tall, tough, handsome merchant seaman and labor organizer, and his mother, raised by an aunt and uncle, never knew her parents. Pepper's parents were twenty-nine, and fifteen when they were married, and he was born with rickets and jaundice. There was little to the marriage. Pepper's father was at sea, and his mother was irresponsible and dissolute, and the relationship soon broke up. Pepper was sent to his paternal grandmother in the California countryside when he was five. He was a lorn, fearful child. "I'd wander around alone, and it seemed that the wind was always blowing and I was always cold," he recalls. "I was afraid of everything. Clouds scared me; it was as if they were living things that were going to harm me. Lightning and thunder frightened me beyond words. But when it was beautiful and sunny out my feelings were even more horrible because there was nothing in it for me." His grandmother was a cold German woman who had her own sorrows, and when his father, who paid her to raise the child, visited between sea trips, Pepper was caught in a cross fire:

My grandmother cooked a lot of vegetables, things I couldn't stand—spinach, cauliflower, beets, parsnips. And [my father would] come and sit across from me in this little wooden breakfast nook, and my grandmother would tell me to eat this stuff, and I would-n't eat it, couldn't eat it. He'd say, "Eat it!" My grandmother would say, "Don't be a baby!" He'd say, "Eat it! You gotta eat it to grow up and be strong!" That made me feel like a real weakling, so I'd put it in my mouth and then gag at the table and vomit into my plate. And my dad was able, in one motion, to unbuckle his belt and pull it out of the rungs, and he'd hit me across the table with the belt. It got to the point where I couldn't eat anything at all like that without gagging, and he'd just keep hitting at me and hitting the wooden wall behind me.

Pepper took up the clarinet at nine, and his father would sit him in bars in San Pedro and make him play "Nola" and "The Music Goes 'Round and 'Round" while his friends nodded approvingly and said, "That's Art's boy. He plays nice music." Pepper switched to the alto saxophone when he was twelve, and by the time he was seventeen he was married and working for Stan Kenton. He was in the Army from 1944 to 1946, and then spent five more years with Kenton and made his name as an orig-inal and graceful alto saxophonist. But his true career, the weight and heat of this book, began in 1950, when he became addicted to heroin. He was already an alcoholic, and he had long popped pills and smoked pot. None of these gave him surcease from the demons of loneliness and self-hatred. The heroin did—particu-larly the first time he tried it: "I could feel it start in my stomach. From the whole inside of my body I felt the tranquility . . . Sheila [a singer] said, 'Look at yourself in the mirror! Look in the mir-ror!' And that's what I'd always done: I'd stood and looked at myself in the mirror and I'd talk to myself and say how rotten I was . . . I thought, 'Oh, no! I don't want to do that! I don't want to spoil this feeling that's coming up in me.' . . . But she kept say-ing, 'Look at yourself! Look how beautiful you are!' . . . I looked in the mirror and I looked like an angel." In 1953, Pepper was arrested and sent to jail for possession of narcotics. During the next thirteen years, he spent more time in jail than out of it. He did five years in San Quentin, and his descriptions of life there are relentless and brilliant.

Pepper hit bottom just before he put himself in Synanon. He was an alcoholic and a junkie, and his career as a musician was in abeyance. His girlfriend had thrown him out, and he found himself, aged forty-four, sitting on his mother's porch, surrounded by his few belongings, and drinking brandy in the midday sun:

> My mother had changed a lot over the years. She had found God. She had accepted Christ as her personal savior, and she'd stopped drinking and smoking . . . She said, "What happened? Where's Christine?" I said, "Christine's gone. She's gone. She's finished. She's gone. She left me here." My mother said, "Oh, Junior, you can't stay here! You know that. We've tried that before. It won't work." I said, "Don't get upset. Don't start flipping out, ma! I know it isn't going to work. I'm not asking to stay with you. I'm not going to stay with you. I know you don't want me to stay with you. You'd rather have me lay in the gutter and die than have me stay with you!" She said, "You don't have to talk like that." I said, "Well, it's true, isn't it?" She said, "Oh, Junior, *please!*"

Pepper has married again, and he is playing and recording. He is in a methadone program. He has no illusions. ("And that's what I will die as—a junkie.") Nor does he have any remorse or self-pity. He has lived the inverse of the straight life, and he has lived it as well as he knows how. He does not rail against the laws that treat addicted human beings as criminals; the straight world has *its* hangups. He is an eloquent and gifted man.

20

ART PEPPER THREATENS THE GROOVE

Gary Giddins

Art Pepper, who's been recording since 1943, finally made his New York debut as a leader three years ago at the Village Vanguard. A lifelong Californian, he made the trip East alone and was confronted with a rhythm section he deemed unsuitable. When he returned a month later, he was greeted by a hand-picked band which, nonetheless, wasn't *his* band. It hardly mattered. Both engagements were attended by tremendous enthusiasm and Pepper is never more stirring than when he feels he has to prove something; his emotional willfulness would have seen him through if he'd been accompanied by the Ramones. Still, he took no chances when he opened at Fat Tuesday's last week—he brought his own musicians, and it made all the difference in the world.

From the first notes of the first blues of a first set, the groove was unmistakable. A groove can't be notated, and probably can't be disciplined, though it is often earned through practice, and occasionally achieved at an impromptu session. The effect is always the same: tranquil exhilaration, time regulated with the certainty of a juggler's pins. The montage of rhythmic accents, tones, walks, and fills generated by pianist Milcho Leviev, bassist Bob Magnusson, and drummer Carl Burnett was unequivocal. Wherever Pepper sprinted, they were always snapping at his heels or one marvelous step ahead.

One important lesson Pepper learned from Coltrane is to out-pace his audience's expectations. He was never a facile player, but the tension in his improvisations was often mitigated by his swinging, loping, bebopping proficiency. Now, after an uneasy period in which he sought to adapt Coltrane's harshness to the alto, as though that transference could satisfy his own expressive needs, he's arrived at the most demonstrative music of his career: intense, poignant, ragingly expressionistic. It's almost as though he were trying to kill the groove that bolsters him; instead of rid-ing the harmonic curves of the tunes he plays, he riddles them with short, stabbing phrases, keening tremolos, pitches just left of center, and overtones. Pepper pulls them together (much as Charlie Parker resolved the fugitive phrases of his "Klactoveed-edstene" solo), and for all his straining, he never sacrifices beauty or rhythmic strength.

A blues for the former Count Basie bassist, John Heard, was notable for Pepper's expressiveness in the saxophone's lower register without honks or dynamic shifts in volume. He followed with a blues written in Japan, called "Landscape," which has two or three 12-bar themes, a subtle chord progression that mini-mizes the subdominant change, and a percussion break; the per-formance included a driving alto-drums duet, concluding with internally counted exchanges. Pepper launched "Caravan" with a pedal-point cadenza, consisting of bent notes, fake notes, tense speech like phrases, and finished with a wickedly fervent last chorus. The high point of the evening was another tune he's been playing for decades, "Over the Rainbow." His unaccompa-nied introduction, played with a rigid embouchure to eliminate any semblance of vibrato, veered through three octaves with menacing yet oddly lyrical harmonics and elliptical arpeggios.

When the rhythm entered for the theme statement, his variations became increasingly perverse, referring more and more obliquely to the original tune.

He ended the set with "Straight Life," proving the tenacity of his bop chops. Yet his playing remained dissonant and acerbic, as deliberately disjointed one- and two-measure phrases eventually melded into light, latticework arpeggios. The rhythm section flawlessly negotiated the abrupt breaks and rushes of the piece—especially Burnett, who traded furious fours and twos with Pepper—and stopped on a dime. Another impressive accompanist was Magnusson, whose sure time and rich tone in the bottom register completed Pepper's frequently ethereal gambits; he concluded his "Caravan" solo atavistically by rapidly slapping the strings.

Pepper's newest record is on the same label as the best of his early work, Contemporary. *Thursday Night at the Village Vanguard* (C 7642), the first in a three-volume chronicle of his second New York appearance in 1977, is not as polished as his more recent Galaxy albums (*Straight Life* and *Today*), and one reason is the rhythm section. Elvin Jones has a good time on the clever "Valse Triste," partly because triple meter is his favorite stomping ground, and on the sprightly "My Friend John," but he's imperiously detached on the slower pieces; I miss the chatty responsiveness of Burnett or Billy Higgins. Pepper calls George Cables "the master" but I'm not convinced—although his comping is brisk and sensitive, I often find his solos glib (the same could be said of Leviev). Still Pepper is compelling, and two of his solos, in particular, are gems: "Blues for Les" is an earthy, carefully modulated performance, and "Goodbye," dedicated to Hampton Hawes, is a hauntingly idiosyncratic ballad recitation fraught with abrupt dynamics, mischievous silences, and barked notes. At times like this, Pepper is his own groove, and everybody else just better stay out of his way.

21

THE "STRAIGHT LIFE" OF ART PEPPER

Michael Zwerin

Art Pepper's "Straight Life" (Schirmer) is more than a jazz book. Taken together with his new record of the same name (Galaxy), it provides a remarkable insight into the creative process, and into that corner of American life where underground meets underworld. The drama is that the book redeems the "wasted" life that is its subject.

Great white talents in this black-rooted art are often casualties. Doomed originals similar to Pepper could be found in every major American city in the '40s and '50s—Tony Fruscella in New York, Ronnie Singer in Chicago, Charlie Leeds in Miami. Alienated from both white and black cultures, angelic improvisers who never entered or were quickly dropped from the reference books, they made one record or none, died young or went directly to jail without ever passing go.

In those days anybody but a dope fiend was considered square. Jazz and heroin often went together because jazz was the only art where the artist had to create anew six nights a week and he worked in an environment where heroin was available. The antidote was there for the stress and besides the hero of the day,

"The 'Straight Life' of Art Pepper" by Michael Zwerin originally appeared in the July 8, 1980 issue of *The International Herald Tribune*. Reprinted by permission of The New York Times Syndicate.

Charlie Parker, was a junkie and if he shot up it must be hip. Heroin and jazz began to part company when the latter went into the concert hall and pay rates were raised so that a musician could afford to pace himself.

Twice Pepper finished second behind Charlie Parker in the *Down Beat* magazine readers' poll. He was featured on alto saxophone with the Stan Kenton band. He recorded with Miles Davis' rhythm section. He had solos on Henry Mancini records and played on soundtracks of Clint Eastwood films. His style was melodic, lyrical, it danced, you could tell he played from the heart. Everybody loved Art Pepper, even Easterners for whom "West Coast Jazz" was a euphemism for flab.

He was born in Gardena, Calif., grew up in the Los Angeles area and still lives there, belying the old dictum: "It's hard to play the blues looking at a palm tree." He makes it sound easy.

His father and mother separated when he was 5. He describes his father's mother, who raised him, as "old and cold." It was all downhill from there, between peaks of fame, fortune and partying. He ingested wave after wave of uppers and downers and infinite gradations and mixtures on the scale between them. This was a life dedicated to chemicals. Even the music came second. How often he pawned his horn, how many times he went to prison to pay for the parties.

There were records between stretches, and tours with Buddy Rich and his own band, but nothing near the volume of work his talent should have produced. He loved nothing better than to be in bed totally zonked with the next fix in reach. You could call it a classic wasted life, thrown out like so many cigarette butts until, at the age of 54, "Straight Life" makes sense of it all.

His current wife, Laurie, cowrote the biography. She seems to have had a large part in shaping what otherwise might have been just one more boring tragedy into something that can be compared to the novels of Jack Kerouac.

The record reveals a spare Pepper leaving more holes than in his heydey. He knows about holes. His veins are full of them, he

November 9, 1947 in Lamoni, Iowa
Eddie Bert, copyright © 1999

With wife Patti and Eddie Bert, November 9, 1947, in Cedar Rapids, Iowa

Eddie Bert, copyright © 1999

Gil Barrios, Bob Whitlock, Pepper, Alvin Stoller
and Gerry Mulligan at The Haig in Spring 1952
Photograph courtesy of Bob Whitlock, copyright © 2000 by Bob Whitlock

William Claxton

Wardell Gray, Shorty Rogers and Pepper
circa December 1952 at the Pasadena Civic Auditorium
Ray Avery

THE RETURN OF
ART PEPPER
SCORE SLP-4032

William Claxton

circa 1959
Photo by Roger Marshutz

February 29, 1960
Photo by Roger Marshutz

February 29, 1960
Photo by Roger Marshutz

February 29, 1960
Photo by Roger Marshutz

March 28, 1959, with Marty Paich and Russ Freeman
at the *Art Pepper + Eleven* session.
Photo by Roger Marshutz

March 29, 1959
Photo by Roger Marshutz

February 29, 1960, with Paul Chambers
Photo by Roger Marshutz

1977
Courtesy of Selmer

June 1979
©*Herb Nolan*

1979
Courtesy of Galaxy

has been locked in them for years. His playing is spare as a cell, this is unfurnished jazz, you can hear the silent round of needles, the clanging of cell doors, the roar of loneliness.

The music is proud, it struts despite the false starts and sputters that Pepper obviously feels are central to what he wants to communicate. A sort of limping strut. Look at me, he seems to be saying, I took all they could dish out and not only did I not crack, I can still strut.

He protests perhaps several times too often in the book that he never once informed on anybody. Except, ironically, now on himself. On himself, he is the cosmic informer. For 476 pages, he shows us every pimple, wart, and deformity in full color closeup. But it is neither sensationalized nor self-pitying. These are the facts, told with a great degree of literary grace. There is no polemic. Though he went through three years cleaning up in Synanon (where he met Laurie) there is no preaching either for or against the chemicals that sent him there.

It looks like this will be Art Pepper's year.

22

ART PEPPER TALKING

Les Tompkins

1

It's very good to play at Ronnie's; it's going very well. I was surprised that we've had the response that we have. Last night was Wednesday, and the club was packed; the same on Tuesday and Monday—and the weekend, naturally. Even the first week, we had very good crowds Monday through Thursday, but now this week it's been like a weekend every night—so that's marvellous. See, I didn't know how well I would be received by the people; I had to find out, so that people booking me would also know that I'm drawing—then they can make a more realistic tour programme.

Exceptional

This programme, the way it is now—we were on a tour in the States, before we came here, and we lost a lot of money, because of what we had to pay the guys. But I wanted to have my own band, as I have here, so that I can be heard with my music—I play mostly the music that I've written. On this trip, we'll hardly make

"Art Pepper Talking" by Les Tompkins originally appeared in the August 1980, September 1980, November 1981, and September 1982 issues of *Crescendo* magazine. Reprinted by permission of *Crescendo and Jazz Music* magazine.

any money at all, but in November we're going to Japan, and we'll make some there—that's the one place where we make money. Now, the next time we tour the United States, or come to Great Britain and to Europe, we can get money where the guys can stay in nice hotels.

It's really flattering that the people are there. The only crowd we had that wasn't really great, as far as listening, was last night. It was strange, but there were maybe three or four tables where the people were talking all the time; they didn't come to hear the music—they came just to hang out, I guess. You know, I didn't notice 'em on the faster tunes; just on the ballads, I really could tell because they were talking and everything. And rather than *say* anything, I just tried to ignore it and play—otherwise you get, like that thing of back and forth, which is very bad. People get crazy when they drink. The other people in the club were very attentive, but there were maybe three tables—and that's all it takes. Or one, actually.

Anyway, it was okay musically. The night before, I think, was really exceptional—a marvellous night. We'd had some problems—the thing of playing as a band, rather than as four individuals going for themselves. We had a little argument, on the first rehearsal we had, about where *one* was on something we were doing. Well, musicians can be very temperamental, you know. I used to be terrible—I'd really get out of line. I'd say: "I don't care about friendship, or any of that bull . . . —we're playing *music*. If you can't do it, go—I'll get someone who *can*." I was real rank, in those days. Fortunately, I was stopped doing that. I didn't do it on purpose; I would get angry—and you lose your composure. But now, I feel a lot better; I think age makes you a little more mellow.

So we've really got it together now. On Friday and Saturday night, we're going to record in the club. I've been a little worried if we should make the tunes shorter for the record; then I figured, the people like what we're doing *now*—it would spoil the record *and* the performance at the club. Of course, sometimes people play longer than they should play, it's true. But that'll help financially, too—it'll enable us to pay some of our debts off, which is nice. I certainly hope it'll be a good album.

Yes, I've worked with these guys before. I did a Japanese tour with the pianist, Carl Burnett, when the bass player was Bob Magnusson—he's a *very* strong player; he was on the "Among Friends" album. Then the last time I went to Japan, I had the present bass player, Tony Dumas, with George Cables on piano and Billy Higgins on drums. Then for this recent tour, it was Milcho, Carl and Bob again. Now, with Milcho, Carl and Tony, it's taken time, because Tony just plays different. We were rehearsing, and we had a little part on this tune, "Miss Who," that I wrote; I wanted him to play real loud on the bottom, but instead of leaving it for the bass I had to have Milcho play it on octaves also with him, to make it sound louder. Then, just jokingly, Tony really pulled, and it was just perfect; Carl said: "Wow, that's what we've been going through all this thing wanting." and I said: "Man, that's exactly what I want." Tony just laughed, like he was just goofing off—he was just playing corny. You can't do anything about that—because he has his own style, and I have to honour *his* integrity; I mean, to him, that isn't playing right. So Carl was very unhappy that we didn't sound like a band, like we did before. But things were starting to get together now.

But I've been very flattered—the different things people have said. I do feel, though, that I'm playing better than I ever have—I mean, I *know* that I am. I have more facility, more control; I can do a lot more different things, such as spreading the tone. I try not to worry about the crowd's acceptance, but it's almost impossible. I don't think anybody can just negate that; you can't overlook . . . if the people don't clap when you play a solo, then something's wrong. However, the people have been just wonderful.

Clapping

On our way, before we came here, we played a night in San Francisco, at the Great American Music Hall. It was a gigantic place, with a balcony and all that, and I thought: "Boy, what a drag. I wish it was a smaller place; it's really going to be embarrassing—there won't be enough people." So they announced us, we went out, the people started clapping—every seat was taken, and they were standing in the back. They kept on clapping, some people stood up, then everyone was on their feet—even before we played a note. That's what they did in Japan, too, the first time I went—and every time since. And it's just so wonderful—like, to be accepted even before you play.

Then you have to live up to that, too—and I have. Also being on time, being presentable; my horns are working, and I'm able to do what I'm supposed to do. And I'm sure that that's one of the things they were most interested in—you know, the clubowners, bookers and people like that. A lot of them probably didn't want to be the first ones to experiment: "Let so-and-so do it, and then, if he works out, we'll know—but we dont't want to take a chance on *our* money." Now, I'll be able to go back and make maybe twice as much money. So with me it's just proving a point, and, fortunately, my wife Laurie, who co-authored our book, realises that—and she doesn't get angry that we have to live in a second-class hotel.

Business

In Japan, it's another story. We stay at the new Otani Hotel, which is just incredible. You don't have to leave the hotel—everything that you could ever want, practically, is in there some place, with all the different shops and so on. Even medical care—everything. Well, they don't sell automobiles, but that's one of the few things they don't deal with. The first time was for six days in '77, when I had Cal Tjader with me; I went again in '78 and '79—so this year will be the fourth time. We're signed by this company—they're almost like the old American Mafia type of thing, but it's, like, business. It's a big business combine. But they don't stand for people who aren't able to live up to their obligations; if you can't do it—don't sign. The first two times; I'd walk out of my hotel room, and there would be a young guy with a suit on standing down by the elevator—a real gangster type of thing. He'd nod at me, ask me where I was going, and I'd tell him I was just going down to a shop to get something: "Oh, I'll walk along with you." It was protecting me as well as them; they didn't want anybody to try to make a name for themselves by arresting me or something. If anything happens to me, then they lose money, of course. And they lose face—especially *that*. When the Japanese make a contract, that's *it*.

As for the band they want me to take to Japan—this is the only time that I've ever made a concession: they want Tony, Carl, and George Cables instead of Milcho. It's still a great band; you've heard George Cables—he's a fine piano player. Of course, Milcho has improved so much since the time he went to Japan with me; from '78 till now, he's developed incredibly. And they don't play with me to make money; Milcho most of all—he can make a fortune in the studios. He can do anything: he can write for a symphony; he can play any style, whether it be fusion or a real old-time Teddy Wilson kind of thing—anything anybody wants. We were playing a slow blues last night, and towards the end he had a tremolo effect, on the way the chords move. It was just beautiful—you know, constant sound, and constantly changing positions—just gorgeous. And I actually heard him play two lines simultaneously before—like, one with the right hand and one with the left. He's a great player. Naturally, he feels disappointed not to be going to Japan with me, and I can't blame him; but I think he understands, that people put these pressures on you. But once I get to a point where I feel that I can ask for what I want, then I can *get* who I want. It'll be enough to carry it with just myself, without them worrying about the rhythm.

Yeah, in the past I've had some great people playing with me. I guess the first album I ever made was a quartet thing with Hampton Hawes, Joe Mondragon and Larry Bunker; then I did one with Russ Freeman, Bob Whitlock and Bobby White. Also on the same label as those, Discovery, one of the very earliest was with Jack Montrose on tenor, plus Claude Williamson, Monte Budwig and

Larry Bunker; I wrote a lot of tunes for that—like "Straight Life," which was a real fast line. The way Jack played the lines, when we played together . . . the parts that were written and the parts we played free almost sounded the same, I mean, we were so in tune with each other's musical thinking; I'd let him lead sometimes— there was no idea of *self* in it. The empathy was just beautiful. I used to do that with Warne Marsh also. But the last time I played with Warne, I found him trying to ra-ja me, you know—trying to lead most of the time, rather than it being give-and-take all the way down the line. Of course, it might just have been that night, though; you never knew—he might have not felt good or some- thing. Anyway, he's a great player—I just love the way he plays.

And I'm looking forward to the Charlie Parker Tribute concert here on July 14; I'm a late addition to that. Dizzy's on it, and Lee Konitz is going to be there; I was thinking, it'll be really fun play- ing with Lee. We only played together once. I went over to his place, when he, Warne and Jimmy Knepper, the trombone player, were all studying with Lennie Tristano. They lived in the Bronx, or toward Harlem somewhere, in one of these basement apartments, and we went and jammed there. It was just a great session—boy, if that would have been taped, it would have been marvellous; it was really excellent. But that's the only time that I played with Lee; it was so enjoyable—we really fit together, as far as our approach, and tone-wise. We both have very pretty sounds. It would be interesting some time for us to join forces.

I always wanted to do something with Paul Desmond, but unfortunately he isn't around—because he was marvellous; I really liked the way he played. As for Phil Woods—we were sup- posed to do that; we got the approval from my record company Fantasy, and I thought it was all arranged. But I think what's hap- pening with the record business hitting a slump, as of now . . . it was great for a while, and all of a sudden, when I finally get to where I'm making my move, then there's a recession. So I think that might have had something to do with it—us both wanting the same amount of money. I would think, though, that if I were a jazz collector and a record came out with me and Phil Woods on it, I would have to have that record. Everyone that follows jazz would want it—don't you think so?

Also I wanted to record with Zoot Sims—*that* would be really a pleasure—but Norman Granz wouldn't have it. Zoot was okay; he would have done it, and we would have had a *ball*. We're very similar in a lot of ways—people don't even realise it, but we are, the way we think musically. We're the closest of anyone that I can think of, as far as our styles; like, I'm a little more venturesome, but as far as the basic thing of swinging, the beauty, etc., we're very close, I think. I love the way he plays. Going to prison, you lose everything you had, unfortunately, but I have every record Zoot had ever made; which shows how I feel—if he told me that he had every record I'd ever made it would just really make me feel great. But I did, and they're all gone now; Coltrane, I had all his things, all Miles' things, and almost all the Pres things. And a few Bird things.

I tried to stay away from too many Parker things, because I didn't want to get consumed by him—like so many players did. There were all kinds of players, who were playing great . . . they were playing tenor, and really had a thing going; then he came out, and they switched from tenor to alto. They started copying his solos, and passing them around, and it just spoiled them. I'm not saying that hearing Bird would spoil 'em; it's just the idea that he was so strong, and such a great player, that he just consumed them—they lost their identity. So that's why I tried to stay as much as possible away from his influence. And I succeeded, thank God. I always tried to keep my own identity, but it's been hard at times; people have said little things, you know. When I first heard Coltrane on the "Kind of Blue" album with Miles, it was just so marvellous—and I almost got lost in him. Fortunately, I was able to drag myself through it.

2

As I'm totally convinced now, alto is my natural instrument. But at the one time, I didn't have money to buy both horns; I was able to get credit for one horn, and I picked a tenor, because I thought I would be able to get more work. Which was true, at that time—the tenor was what everyone used. But the main thing—what it really was, and I knew it deep inside—was because of 'Trane. I just loved the way he played so much that I just wanted to play the tenor, and see where I would go with it. And I had quite a few people come up to me and tell me that I was the first person playing really outside that they could understand. Right—the form was there, even through this kind of madness.

Challenge

In 1968, I had the offer to go with Buddy Rich's band, playing lead alto and alto solos. All I had was the tenor, but Don Menza had an alto and he let me use that—which was really nice of him. So I went to Las Vegas, and I made the rehearsal at Caesar's Palace on a strange alto, a strange mouthpiece, everything. When I walked in, Menza just pointed to this case; I went over, opened it, and took it out, like as if it was my horn. Then I went down and sat down to rehearse. I mean, talk about a challenge—wow! Anyway, after the rehearsal, Buddy seemed to be pleased. I returned to the motel room, took the horn out, started just blowing it and looking in the mirror. All of a sudden, I heard this sound, and I said: "Wow—that's me!" It was almost as if I'd been a genie in a bottle, and couldn't get loose, and suddenly someone rubbed the bottle and out I came. I was back home. From then on, I haven't had any doubts.

With Buddy's band I was featured on "Alfie"; also I had a short solo on the "Channel One" suite, and one of these kind of jazz waltz pieces that Woody played so well, with the solo by that excellent tenor player—yeah, Sal Nistico. I had a nice solo on that, and a couple of others, but "Alfie" was the longest one—that featured me all the way through. But I was very unhappy with the way the recording of it came out. When I heard the playback of it, it was great. It was abut four o'clock in the morning when we started it; a whole bunch of people were let in—they were digging the recording, but we were tired. We'd been working all night, with no chance to lay down and rest; we just had about an hour after the job to go back, take a shower, have a bite of food—then we had to go and start recording again. So with the professional equipment, the playback sounded wonderful—but when the record came out, and I listened to it, I was really disappointed. I had heard form Don Menza that Buddy does this: he wants the rhythm and the brass to be predominant. Stan Kenton was the same way; he wanted the brass—saxophones were like a second cousin or something; everything was lowered a little bit. Instead of sounding real big, like it was when we recorded it—the sound of the sax section and the soloist—they had cut it down, and it wasn't the same. It just should have been louder. Other than that, I thought it was a nice thing; we did it after I'd been there about a week or so, and that just reaffirmed it—the alto was *it*. I got hold of a Selmer, bought it from a guy—and I've never changed.

It was kind of like fate or something, I would have gotten back some way—I know that—but it's really amazing, the circumstances that have got me to where I'm at now. Then I got sick, had the operation, and almost died. Yeah, I was supposed to come over here with the band—but they left their altoman in San Francisco. I was really looking forward to it, too—I thought it would be so much fun, specially with that band. It was an excellent band.

Those charts were a challenge, reading and interpreting them—and I loved the way Buddy played with that band. A couple of times a trio thing came up, and he didn't sound as good to me with the small group—but with the *band*, he was phenomenal. Boy, you talk about *working* and giving your all—he pours everything into every performance; he never bull—s, man. And he won't stand for anybody in his band to mess around. He says: "I come to play. If you didn't, just tell me, and get your ass back home—I'll get somebody that *wants* to play. I want people that want to play." If you get yourself into a position where you're not physically able to play, like being too loaded, or not taking care of yourself, not eating right, you're in trouble. But it's hard—it's like a ball-player. I'd be playing up there, and the sweat's just pouring off me; it's indescribable, what that feeling is—how you work at it. I think that's one of the reasons he liked me, also—he knew that I was trying just as hard as I could to play. It was a very interesting experience.

Another interesting band came later on. After leaving Synanon and everything—not too far back—I played with Don Ellis's band. And a lot of young players around L.A. and stuff . . . I had heard from different people that guys were saying: "Man, he can't play with that band." Because everything's in nine-eight, seven-eight, five-six, five-eight, nine—eleven—just these unbelievably hard arrangements, and they said: "No, he's too old, man." And I had a solo, in five-four and seven-eight, that was just marvellous—a duet with the cello, then the strings—what a showpiece. I had to take the book home and practice—it was really hard. In this club one time, I played this solo—and the whole audience stood, which they don't usually do if you're playing with somebody's band. Michel Legrand was sitting right in front; when I got off the stand, he grabbed my arm, and he said: "Oh, superb—I had tears in my eyes when you were playing. It made me really feel great." He was real nice; I told him that I'd done "The Summer Knows," and that I would send him a copy. It's on "The Trip"; I start out playing two different minor chords for a while—the same as "Patricia." That's in a major, and then the ending is like a minor to a minor—same type of thing, but with minor chords—and it really came out nice.

Oh, you heard the soundtrack of the film *Heartbeat*, but it doesn't have the unaccompanied alto parts on it? It's in the movie—maybe they didn't put it in the album because it was just by myself. Conte Candoli was also on it, and I played alto on one swinging arrangement; then in one spot they had Bud Shank and I playing together—we didn't record it that way, but they put it together. But I guess the things that I played alone—they would just have to have a very tiny section, because they were very

145

short. Then there were some other spots where I was just with a piano, and so forth.

You enjoyed hearing me with strings on there? Well, I'll tell you—during this tour, I'm trying to figure out exactly what I want to do, and part of my contract with Fantasy was that I'd be able to make a large album. First I want to do a ballad album with strings. What I've been thinking about: it might be good to have maybe three different groups—say, a couple of ballads with strings, and then some kind of authentic Latin thing, with all those instruments, and maybe have it written by . . . there's a great Latin writer who was around the same time as Machito was, when Bird recorded with him—yeah, Chico O'Farrill, I think. Then maybe a real down-home Gospel type of group, with the fender bass—like jazz-rock, but *jazz*. So now I'm toying with that; I don't know whether to have it that way, or to have it all ballads with strings. If I were buying, I would enjoy more of a mixture of tracks, I think.

At any rate I'm going to start listening to some people's writing. I wanted to do something with Gil Evans, too; he's such a great writer, and it would just be so wonderful—I'd just *love* to play with him. I'm keeping my ears open, trying to hear some things; if I hear something that I really like, then I'm going to remember it and talk to Ed Michel, who's the producer. We did the "Art Pepper Today" and the "Straight Life" albums together, and we have a nice working relationship.

I talked to a head guy of the company—the one who decided that he would sign me. Here I was—no one had offered me a contract at all; I could have maybe stayed with Contemporary. Then Fantasy called, and I went into Hollywood to see this guy about it. We talked, and I was saying that I would like to get some kind of an initial bonus; this might have been my last chance, but I said: "Well, I want ten thousand dollars in front, without having it go on my royalties—a real bonus, that I don't have to pay back." And my wife Laurie looked at me, and she said: "Oh, *Art.*" The guy thought for a minute, and he says: "that sounds reasonable. I'll make a call." He called the director, said "Okay," and that was it. Later, Laurie said: "My God—I never dreamed that you could do that. You were so cool. I would have taken anything, if I had no other offers." But I figured; that's a shot; I'd find out right away whether they really wanted me, or it was just: "He's been a nice player—let's let him record a few songs now and then."

If I knew that I could have a string album, then a Latin album, and so on, I'd say "Okay"—but I don't want to take a chance; I want to do the best thing I can for the whole album. "Landscape" is coming out on Galaxy very soon—that's an album I made in Tokyo live. Then I'll be doing this other one, and if the Phil Woods thing comes through, I'll be doing the album with him. I'm looking forward to all of it.

3

Well, Art, the last time I saw you was when I said goodbye to you after that marvellous concert at the Festival Hall, when your version of "Over the Rainbow" was the most beautiful thing anybody's ever heard in years, I would say. Obviously, you have some very definite recollections of that concert.

That was one of the greatest thrills of my life, doing that. Like John Lewis, Slam Stewart, Roy Haynes and I had never played together or anything; I just walked out, and they misunderstood me—I wanted to play alone for a while and then have them come in, but they came on with the intro. So I thought: "I've got to do it. I'm just going to play for myself, and those that like it will like it." There wasn't a sound, and when I finished the song "Over the Rainbow," it was like a deathly silence for a few seconds. I thought: "Oh-oh"; I was shaking all over, and I had some tears in my eyes. All of a sudden this roar started—you know, people clapped and stood up. I started crying—I just couldn't believe it.

It was the first time I'd ever been in a situation where . . . before me, Freddie Hubbard was with the same rhythm section;

then Dizzy came on after me. So I was being regarded as a jazz giant, along with those guys. See, I've never really felt that I was accepted in that way, because I was never called on to do anything like that. Like, the Playboy Jazz Festival at the Hollywood Bowl—I'm not a part of that. There are many things that haven't happened. But after that, I just felt that I was really accepted. Freddie Hubbard said later: "Boy, you got the biggest hand of any of us. What are you doing, man—trying to ruin me?"

As I said in my write-up, that was the highspot, and Dizzy was almost an anti-climax afterwards. You can't necessarily define what makes a magic moment like that, but I suppose you know when you've played something particularly moving to the audience.

Yeah—I knew that was. It might have been the highest point of my life so far. There's a lot of firsts, but that was like being on the cover of an important magazine—which has never happened to me. A lot of guys say: "Oh, I don't care about winning a poll, being on a cover or anything like that"—well, I *do*. To me, it's like a tribute—you know. Like a sports figure who wins something like the Most Valuable Player award. Everyone is concerned about that—they say they're not, I think, because they think you're not really an artist unless you act like those material things have no meaning. They have all kinds of meaning to me.

You couldn't be blasé about it. Well, the point is: this is really a new lease of life for you as a player. You're now not only regaining what you had before, but you're gaining a new peak of jazz popularity. Happily, you seem to have joined the regular European touring circuit of American artists.

Right. What I'm going to do now, rather than coming too soon . . . see, when I first started recording again, I really made a lot of records—maybe too many—but I felt that I may die at any time . . . at any rate, Alexander, the guy who's booking us, feels it'd be better if we didn't come back to Europe till October of next year, something like that, so that we won't lose the drawing power. Other than maybe doing something in London around June.

Including another engagement at Ronnie Scott's, I hope.

That's what I'd like—I really enjoyed playing there last time. The people were great, the crowds were marvellous. But I've never played Montreaux; I'd love to play the Newport Festival again, and I'd love to play the Playboy Festival in Los Angeles—but I guess Jimmy Lyons doesn't care too much for me, for some reason. So as long as he's in charge of it, I guess I won't be on it—unless a lot of people start pushing for it. If they would, I'd sure appreciate it. I've never done the Monterey Jazz Festival, and I live right in California—maybe it'll happen soon. Talking about being accepted—it would be great if I was accepted *totally*; then the money wouldn't be as big of a thing as it is.

The money means that I'm able to live off what I do. I don't get studio calls usually . . . I don't play the alto flute, the bass flute, the C-flute, the oboe and the bassoon, and tap-dance and sing—you have to do all those things to be accepted. But I got tight with Jerry Fielding, and he was doing the Clint Eastwood movies; so I did the soundtrack on a couple of those—just playing solos, you know. And that was marvellous; I really enjoyed that very, very much. Then I did *Heartbeat*; Jack Nitzche was the music director, and that came out very nice. I'd love to do some more of those things. Because it's all good and well to say: "Oh, you shouldn't flood the market with records," but you have to make a living. You just hope you don't milk it dry, so that after a while people say: "Oh, no—not *him* again."

I don't think anybody's likely to say that about you. When we last talked, following my hearing you with strings on the Heartbeat *soundtrack, I said it'd be good if you could do an album with strings, and you told me that one was, in fact, planned. I now have the album—"Winter Moon." I'm sure that was a definite fulfilment for you.*

Yes, it was another big thrill, just like the Royal Festival Hall thing. I'd always wanted to play with strings, I love ballads, and I feel that I have a lot of love to give—and I give it in my playing. I was very happy; Bill Holman is a great arranger. The *Billboard* magazine is a kind of bible for the show people, and they have all these different charts. When we left Los Angeles, my "Winter Moon" album was twenty-fifth on the chart in the jazz LP section. There's fifty albums on that; it'd been on about nine weeks at that time, and it's gradually moving up. I don't know where it is right now, but I'm hoping that's continued.

Another thing about that album that is a pleasure to me is to hear you on clarinet. When you were at Ronnie's, I saw you holding the instrument backstage, but I never actually got to hear you play it.

Oh, I only played it a couple of times. Then I wanted to play it on this tour, but in the context of the way the festivals are there's a lot of people playing, you only have a certain length of time, and I don't want to hang up someone else by just staying on arbitrarily, saying: "Yeah, yeah, don't worry about it." So I really don't have the time to play it. I've been wanting to play it, though; a lot of people have asked me how come I don't play it. Because I made some records on it quite a while back. I've been practising the clarinet, and I did the "Blues in the Night" on the album—Bill Holman's arrangement was really excellent.

It's a clear indication to me that you should do it more. We don't have that many good jazz clarinet players around, and if you can make a double of it . . .

It would be a good thing. And that's what I'm going to do—keep practising on the clarinet, and hope I really get into it. Buddy De Franco is on this tour; travelling on the same bus with him, I was thinking: "Wow! What a thing to be put up against *him!*" I didn't bring it with me, because I knew we wouldn't have time. But he's an incredible clarinet player, and I would never want to compete in the area *he* plays in. Right, he's a virtuoso; with me, it's a different thing altogether—which is good. When I was a kid, I loved Artie Shaw—just worshipped him; he played so beautiful. With me—my approach is sort of like Jimmy Giuffre's style. Like, when I play the clarinet, I think of Lester Young; I have some records of him playing the instrument and boy, they are just beautiful. He only plays a few notes, but the soul is there, man. Several people, including Leonard Feather, have mentioned that they really liked the clarinet cut. So I'm hoping to use it more in the future. As I say, I'm getting better—it's a hard instrument, but I'm happy that I've at least gotten this far on it.

I hope the ballad album sells—I mean, I know that if people really listen to it, they would enjoy it. Because the musicians stayed to listen to the editing and everything; Stanley Cowell, the piano player, Cecil McBee, the bass player, Howard Roberts, who was playing guitar, and a couple of the string players—they stayed all day and all night. Stanley and Cecil said they'd never even listen to their own records the same day. They really enjoyed it. So I know people would like it, and I hope they don't think of it just as a gimmick or something. It's not—it's a real honest endeavour.

It's nice to be in Britain to play, for the first time. The last time I was here, I think I was nineteen years old; it was as a soldier during the Second World War. I played at the Palladium with Ted Heath, and Victor Feldman was on the bill—he was just a kid then. So it'll be interesting to see what the difference is between now and then.

Music was very simple for me, as far as reading was concerned. My teacher would mark a couple of pages in an exercise book, and I would play them just a few minutes before he came the following week. Having run through it once, I'd play it for him, and he'd say: "Oh, you sure have been practising." And my grandmother would say: "No he hasn't. He's just been playing jazz on the clarinet—trying to play like Artie Shaw." Anyhow, everything happened for the good—fast. Then it hit a snag, and everything became difficult after that point.

On alto, I didn't really model myself on anybody too much. I liked Johnny Hodges, the way he sounded with Duke Ellington, but that wasn't for me—I didn't want to play like him. I liked Lester Young; and Louis Jordan's Tympany Five—I liked the way he played. But there were very few. Willie Smith I appreciated, but I had no wish to model myself after him. Then I finally realised that I just wanted to play the way I play—what I heard. Because I didn't really care for any alto saxophone players that much. So that was a lucky thing for me.

If you have individuality in music, it's something to hold on to. In Lester Young's playing, there was the beauty of music; it was melodic, swinging, a beautiful sound—everything was there. Then, when he got older, with so many people telling him he should play like Ben Webster, Coleman Hawkins or something, all of a sudden he started playing louder and with a vibrato—and just destroyed himself. It was such a shame—just awful.

The period in my life of my addiction problem was a terrible one. But I don't think I could have avoided it. I mean, I tried to stay out of it for a long time, knowing what it might do. I think that, in my searching for something—for love, acceptance or whatever it is, to be a real man, to relate to my father, and all those things—going to prison was a help. It was part of my evolution, as a human being and as a musician. I feel that I have much deeper feelings now than I would have had, had I just been a musician all that time, which would have been a very dull existence. You know, I wanted something *more* than just being thought of as a musician, period. To be labelled "Art Pepper, musician," period, would just be awful—what a boring life that would be. At least I was able to go in a lot of directions—seeing how things were from another viewpoint. I got to know myself better, definitely; I was seeing what I was capable of, what my feelings were, what my morals were—all those things that are very important. What kind of strength I had— the fact of dealing with certain situations, and with a whole different type of people. People were very honest, I found, in that other thing—much more so than musicians.

23

ART PEPPER
The Living Legend Moves On

Steve Voce

When Eddie Condon had most of his pancreas removed, his doctor told Phyllis (Mrs. Condon) that Eddie would die if he ever drank again. She went to the New York branch of the AFM and asked for details of the number of jazz musicians who had actually died of Eddie's complaint. She made out a list of them and took it to the hospital and handed the list without comment to Eddie. Condon looked at it through bleary eyes and then fell back onto his pillow. 'It wouldn't work,' he told her. 'No drummer,' Condon lived, not only to record the story in his scrapbook, but to survive another 15 years hard drinking.

If Condon is indeed still organising bands in that great jazz club in the sky, then he has a new alto player to reckon with following the death on Tuesday, June 15, of Arthur Edward Pepper.

The idea of Pepper playing with a Condon group is not as far-fetched as it seems, for although Art never did play jazz with any pre-bop musicians, he was a fundamental jazz musician who spoke in a musical language that must have appealed to anyone with any kind of awareness of the music. He was notable for playing in a way distinctive from Charlie Parker's style at a time when Parker's

"Art Pepper: The Living Legend Moves On" by Steve Voce originally appeared in the August 1982 issue of *Jazz Journal*. Reprinted by permission of *Jazz Journal*.

domination of modern jazz was almost total. And yet Pepper's jazz career was very much an echo of Parker's, notably in the fact that both were gargantuan masters of the blues—again a fundamental jazz quality. It is this element in the playing of the two men that makes them differ from another great fundamental alto soloist, Pepper's fellow Angeleno Benny Carter. In an era of great originals—notably Konitz and Desmond, Pepper shared his fundamentalism with Sonny Criss, but Criss hewed closer to Parker.

Pepper had the fine jazz combination of a limitless flow of worthwhile things to say and a superb means with which to say it. In his playing he showed a consistency achieved by only a handful of greats—Johnny Hodges and Parker spring immediately to mind, and yet while Hodges was by his own standards sometimes bland and Parker did have off days, Pepper seemed to maintain an unflagging standard of improvisation which comes only to greatly gifted musicians who are prepared to live their whole lives for jazz. Humphrey Lyttelton once remarked that in this respect Lionel Hampton lived 18 feet above ground, and if this is true he was in grave danger of bumping into Pepper.

As usual Max Harrison was able to summarise Pepper's style succinctly: 'If Pepper's solos have a character all their own it is because he is one of the outstanding melodists of jazz—though not widely recognized as such. The quality of his music has depended on a fairly unusual interaction of lyricism and rhythmic inventiveness. And despite the consistency he has been a constantly developing improvisor.'

Pepper was admitted unconscious to Kaiser Hospital, Panorama City, Los Angeles on June 9, after suffering a stroke at his home in Van Nuys in the San Fernando Valley. He died without regaining consciousness. As he recalled in his celebrated and disturbing autobiography *Straight Life* (Schirmer Books), he knew that if he ever tangled with heroin he would become more dependent on it than most addicts. A reading of the book provides a picture of a man who did everything in extremes—without this quality he would not have been such an outstanding jazz player.

Though trenchant, Pepper's style was voluble, and he remained the same with the alto taken from his hands—thus his book runs to 500 pages. He was a compulsive talker, as we found out on the magical bus rides from the town to the festival at Nice last year. Those rides were full of good-humoured gossip, stories and jokes—the latter particularly in evidence when Stanley (Getz) was aboard   and Art was a great participant, his remarkable effervesence in direct contradiction of his gaunt mien. Since he began visiting Europe in his later years many of us had noticed the petrified look of his face. Illness of a typically rare intensity and general misuse of this body had surely left him on a tight-rope and he had the appearance of one who made the cliché come true by living on borrowed time. His happy dependence on his wife Laurie, a lady of tremendous strength of character, no doubt secured many extra years of life from their meeting in 1969.

Art had an early association with Benny Carter, that combination of master craftsman and exemplar human being who almost achieves the supernatural, when he worked for Benny in 1943. The same year he joined Kenton for the first time but after three months was called into the army for two years. This was a crucial time for his musical development. He'd switched from clarinet to alto when he was 13, and his main influences as he matured were Young and Parker. Late in life he claimed a profound influence from John Coltrane, whom he thought was the greatest jazz musician who ever lived.

After the army he rejoined Kenton in September 1947, gracing that band until early 1952. He recalled the pressures of early stardom, overwhelmed to see his name with special billing. 'It was very flattering to have people asking for autographs. It had never happened to me before, and I learned a lot in that band. We worked so hard and often. Sometimes, after the job, we'd have a bite to eat and the bus would leave and we wouldn't get to the next town until just before the job.

'Unfortunately at that time it seemed like almost everybody who played jazz started using heroin because of Bird and Miles.

They were like gods. I stayed away from heroin, I did everything but—I was drinking heavily, taking pills, smoking pot, but I kept away from heroin until about 21.

'I don't blame anyone for anything that's happened to me. I knew what I was doing and I wanted to do it, and I thought that I would play better.'

The horror of Pepper's subsequent years when he became demoralised, coarsened and institutionalised in prisons makes harrowing reading and one is amazed at his capacity for survival. His devotion to his music and the quality he produced seemed not to waver, and the various stages of his career have each produced a plethora of classic recorded performances. At one time recently it appeared that he was in danger of over-exposure on record, but this proved a wrong assessment, confirmed by his performance at Nice last year, when, despite the fact that he played almost the same numbers at each set, each improvisation was as fresh and inventive as though he was coming to the piece for the first time. Art Blakey's ebullient 'You can't hear the performance the same way twice to save your neck!' was ever true of Pepper.

Over the years his many quartet albums have brought about notable partnerships with great pianists, and indeed it is in the quartet that he is most potent, although there are notable collaborations with Jack Sheldon, Warne Marsh, Sonny Stitt and Shorty Rogers. His work with Kenton is well documented on the exhaustive Creative World label and it also maps out the powerful musical association that he was developing with Shorty Rogers, so notable in the stompers like *Round Robin* and *Jolly Rogers* (ST 1036), *Viva Prado* (1027) and the still under-rated *Art Pepper* (1023) recorded at length with strings in 1950. 'Portraits On Standards' (1042) has solos by Zoot and Lee Konitz as well as Art's beautiful 1951 exposition on *Street Of Dreams*, whilst an early outing is on 1034 in the 1947 *Journey To Brazil* where he shares the solos with Laurindo Almeida, Milt Bernhart and Eddie Bert. Art also solos on *How High The Moon* (1035) and *Harlem Holiday* (1036) from the same year. The Swing House and First Heard issues which have appeared since Kenton's death have their share of Art's solos. SWH-18 has him on *Unison Riff* and *Peanut Vendor*, while FH 1004 lets him loose on *Minor Riff* and *Gone With The Wind*. On FH 1006 he features on Samana and Shorty's Sambo. The Kenton band on Joyce LP 1016 has a good collection from broadcasts including *Dynaflow, Round Robin, Viva Prado* and some nice lead alto from Art in *Dancing In The Dark*.

In some ways the great 'West Coast' era began with the Shorty Rogers Giants session of October 8, 1951. Shorty, as an impending interview in these pages will show, was vastly influenced at the time by Miles Davis, and the line up of the Giants is based on Miles' 1948–49 band. Pepper is in his element on these tracks (Capitol T2025 deleted). In 1959 Dave Pell's Octet recorded a series of tracks which produced perfect copies of bands from Shaw's Gramercy Five, the John Kirby Band and groups through to Miles' 1949 band and finally Shorty's 1951 Giants. On *Popo* Art copied his original solo (Capitol ST 1309).

The classic Giants, with the amiable Kenton giving Shorty permission to borrow most of his band, began recording for Victor in early 1953, and Pepper appeared as 'Art Salt' for contractual reasons. His lithe and virile solos abound on these classic tracks and the 'Blues Express' compilation on French RCA FXL1 7234 is mandatory for any collection claiming to represent jazz. The coup de grâce (or more appropriately *Coop De Graas*) came on the March 26 session with Art soloing on alto and tenor in a string of band classics: *Short Stop, Boar-Jibu, Tale Of An African Lobster, Contours* (these two incorrectly juxtaposed on the album), *Infinity Promenade, Sweetheart Of Sigmund Freud* and *Chiquito Loco*. Pepper fluctuated not at all and the band was only slightly less potent in later sessions such as the tracks on the same album from July 5, 1956 with Art soloing on *Pay The Piper* and *Blues Express*. Art had had an even greater role in the nonet that continued the Davis influence shown in the Capitol session. There are eight tracks from January 12, 1953 on French RCA PM 43549.

From all I know Pepper never made a weak recording, and the incredible string of quartet recordings (for despite the cataclysms in his life he recorded prolifically) began with the Xanadu session of February 1952, where he was first teamed with the most under-rated of all jazz pianists, Hampton Hawes. Art recorded with Hawes in quartet again on August 9, 1975 with Charlie Haden and Shelly Manne and this session, topped off by the perfection of *Here's That Rainy Day*, is currently available on Contemporary S7633. Not too hard to find is the imported Savoy double 'Art Pepper Discoveries' on SJL 2217 with 23 tracks by the 1952 quartet with the brilliant Russ Freeman, another great original, and a quintet with Jack Montrose on tenor (some fine dialogues here) and, dare I say it again, the under-rated Claude Williamson. Hawes and Pepper again recorded on March 4, 1952 and some of the results appeared here many years ago on Vogue LDE 067 and have more recently been on Savoy 2215. Pianist (yes, you know) Sonny Clark appears with Art on the 1953 session that produced the album on Straight Ahead SAJ-1001, which is flawed only by poor recording quality, and the 1958 session on Onyx 219 is quite outstanding both for Pepper's contribution and that of the late Carl Perkins (it is not my fault if pianists are born with an 'under-rated' label in their knapsacks).

Pacific Jazz produced some particularly great Pepper, with the Johnny Mandel arrangements of Hoagy Carmichael songs (PJ1223) quite exceptional. Hoagy sings, and in an interview with Charles Fox, Art recalled that Hoagy wanted to replace all the scheduled Pepper solos with his own whistling. Fortunately Mandel prevailed. *Winter Moon* from this session has received a lot of exposure on radio lately, and the album is available on a Japanese reissue and worth whatever you have to pay for it. Also on Pacific, on PJ-LA896H are the Art Pepper Nine sessions where a band including Don Fagerquist, Stu Williamson, Bill Holman, Bud Shank and Russ Freeman re-create some of the original Shorty Rogers Capitol titles. The reverse of this album has the Art Pepper-Chet Baker Sextet with Richie Kamuca and Pete Jolly.

Pepper's fruitful association with Jack Sheldon has been mentioned, and Jack has a key role in one of the most important of Pepper's albums, 'Art Pepper Plus Eleven', originally issued here on Vogue Contemporary LAC 12229 and latterly imported on Contemporary S.7568. These virtual big band tracks use brilliant Marty Paich arrangements. Recorded in the spring of 1959 they have Art at his best on alto, clarinet and tenor. Sheldon is even better on 'Smack Up' by a quartet including Jolly from 1960 and available in stereo on Contemporary S.7602 and the same label has of course the wonderful tracks that Art made with the Miles Davis rhythm section of the time (Garland, Chambers, Philly Joe) on 'Art Pepper Meets The Rhythm Section' (S.7532) and 'Gettin' Together' (S.7573), which has Kelly and Cobb on piano and bass. Tracks from these sessions also appear on an anthology (S.7630) which has four neglected tracks by Art with Warne Marsh, another potent tandem. All of Art's later recordings are excellent, with Mole 1 and 5 being typical and an outstanding issue on Artists House AH 9412. Desperate shortage of space prohibits further mention of the great Galaxies, 'Among Friends' on Flyright 211 and the many Contemporaries, a dozen of which are usually listed in Chameleon's advertisement in our June issue.

Many people involved themselves with Pepper's tribulations, including British musicians at the time of his incarceration, but real sympathy and understanding was shown him by Buddy Rich, who took Art into his band and looked after him on his release from a long sentence. The only record of Art's work with Rich is on 'The Buddy Rich Collection' (Sunset SLD 505/6) where Art plays *Alfie*.

The best of Art's latest work and some of the finest jazz he ever played was recorded last year by BBC producer Keith Stewart and part of it was broadcast on Radio Three. It would be a fine tribute and a great bonus to the rest of us if this concert could be broadcast in full.

24

A TRIBUTE TO ART PEPPER

Arthur F. Kinney

"One strong characteristic of the way I play the horn has been that I've always tried to bring out the vocal qualities of the instruments," Art Pepper wrote in the liner notes to "No Limit" (*Contemporary* S7639). Speaking with rich depth of emotion there in a song like "Ballad Of The Sad Young Men," Pepper brought to the alto sax and to the jazz world some of its most personal and achingly heartfelt music since the late great Ben Webster played tenor. So Pepper's sudden death on June 15 of a cerebral haemorrhage in Los Angeles at the age of 56 is a signal loss.

More than many American jazz players, Pepper was especially well-received in England. Just two years ago he played a week at Ronnie Scott's to filled houses and loud ovations—and was so popular that *Mole Jazz* asked him to cut their first record.

Pepper could alternate between the lyrical and understated ballad, like "Here's That Rainy Day" on his comeback album "Living Legend" (*Contemporary* S7633) and the heavy, complicated rush of bebop in a tune like "What Laurie Likes," named for his wife and best friend on the same album. "Living Legend,"

"A Tribute to Art Pepper" by Arthur F. Kinney originally appeared in the September 1982 issue of *Crescendo* magazine. Reprinted by permission of *Crescendo and Jazz Music* magazine.

released in America in August 1975, marked the beginning of a second career for Pepper—the superstar days with Stan Kenton and the heroin days of street life in California and prison life in San Quentin, both discussed frankly in his raw autobiography "Straight Life" (1979), behind him.

Yet he continued to grow. He was doing more intricate and imaginative intros before the head, as in "There Will Never Be Another You" on "One September Afternoon" (*Galaxy* GXY-5141) or moving into competitions of fours—as with pianist George Cables and drummer Carl Burnett both on "When You're Smiling" on the new album "Roadgame" (*Galaxy* GXY-5142) released in America the week he died. On this last he was at his most joyous.

"Roadgame" is his last record, but it is not the last tape he made. That was a spontaneous duet of songs between Cables, "my favourite pianist of them all," and himself on clarinet as well as sax that was played for the first (and only) time at the memorial service held in the Chapel of the Psalms in Hollywood Memorial Park just North of the main studios of Paramount. The service opened with their lyrical, upbeat rendition of "The Sweetest Sounds"; it ended with a slower and much more sombre "Goin' Home."

Pepper cut more than a dozen records in half a dozen years once he made his comeback, insisting on acoustic instrumentation and a small quartet—only once, on, "Winter Moon" (*Galaxy* GXY-5140) did he record with a large orchestra, as he did with the Kenton big band in the early days when he was in his twenties. In all these recent records, his signature was a rich and personal tone, a genuine if sometimes soulful lyricism.

It is the honesty and passion behind such sounds that Cables praised in his eulogy. "I felt very relaxed, very free when I went to cut a record or play a date with Art," he said. "We would look at each other sometimes—not a word would pass. He was an honest man—was never cruel, never angry—but he could make you nervous because you never knew what he was going to say. I hear in his music and his tone his warmth and his humanity. When he played it wasn't an analytical thing; it was emotional, from his heart. He was eccentric, not like many of us, but he gave his love freely and we, most of us, cannot imagine what he went through. He wanted to go out roaring, and he did."

What kept him going as long as he did was his music. He took it with him to San Quentin and he practised, later, at Synanon, where he went voluntarily to kick the habit and where he met his fourth wife Laurie Miller, a professional photographer from Berkeley. What he went through, at least at Synanon, the drummer Lou Mallen recounted at the funeral, because he was there. "Art Pepper had one of the strongest physical constitutions I ever knew," he remarked. "He had a great capacity to rebound in adversity, and a great capacity for sensitivity. Still waters run deep. The one thing he showed me was that when I was in his presence and he played, he really played for keeps. He always played every note as if it was with his last breath."

That is something worth living and dying for.

25

ART PEPPER
The Legend

Hal Hill

Art Pepper: If John Coltrane were alive today, I would probably still be listening to him, or if Prez (Lester Young), or Bird were alive today. Because those are the people . . . and Miles, who is alive. So today I listen to everything. I like all kinds of music, unlike many other people I like singers, country music, rock music, all blues music, I like everything. Anything that's good; classical music. Anything that's done well, I like and appreciate. But usually I find my mood tends to direct what I listen to. I have an eight track tape in my automobile, and I have a Bill Withers tape[1] that is just marvelous, and when I am in a certain mood I put the Bill Withers tape on and listen to it over and over again. My wife (Laurie) has a tape that she had put together of some different singers. A record that I did with Melanie.[2] But if I am in a jazz mood then I'll listen to . . . sometimes I'll listen to the last album that I made. Which is "Living Legend."[3] Or "Art Pepper—The Trip"[4] with Elvin Jones. Just to learn, to try to learn what I did wrong and what I did right, as a learning experience. To see what I can cut out. The things that I liked and the things that I didn't. But it all depends on my mood. If we're talking strictly about jazz, then I will listen to Miles (Davis).

"Art Pepper: The Legend" by Hal Hill originally appeared in the June 1985 issue of *Coda* magazine. Reprinted by permission of the interviewer.

He is music to me, he *is* jazz music. He is so great that it is just beyond comprehension. I have this tape "Live/Evil";[5] the first time I played it, I didn't really like it that much, and then I played it again, and then all of a sudden I liked it more. And everytime I played it I liked it more and more. The guys in the band—Jack DeJohnette, Chick Corea and Dave Holland and John McLaughlin—the whole band was just fantastic, just beyond description! Then when Miles came in they were playing this simple little line, a kind of unison line that John McLaughlin started, just the most basic type of thing. Jack DeJohnette was just roaring behind this simple line and it was just like wild animals. It had beauty, it had swing, and then, all of a sudden Miles came in and he played one/two/three notes. He used to play the beauty of playing down low and in the middle register, when he was playing with Gil Evans, and on "Kind Of Blue." "Kind Of Blue" used to be my favorite album. I bought that album. Paid for it. Musicians don't usually pay for albums, but I bought that album, maybe three or four times, and "Sketches Of Spain"[7] or "Miles Ahead."[8] All the things with Gil Evans. I loved all those things. But now Miles just went way beyond that, and some people don't like him at all, I find. I've talked to people that *really do not* like him. The space was the thing that I really loved about him before, but now the space is even greater. He will play 2 or 3 notes, and instead of playing them in the middle register, he plays them real high. But every note is absolutely perfect, it's a gem. If you can reach the height, the epitome of anything, he has done that. He is the greatest living musician in the world. I have never heard anything like him. The way Miles plays, with the sparsity of notes, and the range that he uses. To me it's so logical, it's so beautiful. I can't think of anything more rewarding, to end my life, than to play with that group. That would be the greatest thing I could ever do in the world. Before that it was Coltrane. I loved the way he played, with the speed and the dexterity, the knowledge that he had of his horn. There's a melody in the "Live/Evil" album, this slow melody, and they play the melody just like Ornette (Coleman) and Don Cherry played melodies. The "Lorraine" record[9] from a long time ago. One horn will play the note, and the next horn will come in just a tiny bit later, a fraction of a second later; or before, and then one horn will play a little bit sharp or a little flat, on purpose, to give it that sound. That's *all* Ornette's and Don Cherry's thing. That's another thing that I really love.

On one hand I like the sparseness and the openness that Miles has, just playing an occasional note that's just a gem, and then I also love "Trane" more than anyone else. He played that speed.

So I have those two things happening, at once, in my mind. It's like a Jekyll and Hyde thing, and those are the two things I like most. And the beauty. Miles has the beauty . . . he's the most beautiful player I've ever heard, more beautiful than Prez was.

I just started the tour. It's the first time I've ever taken a tour in the east, or anywhere, as jazz musician. I find that a lot of the players, in playing the way people play nowadays, have fallen into a certain groove, tempo-wise, and when I started playing, I played with guys like Sonny Stitt and . . . well, everybody that I played with, like Zoot (Sims) and Stan Getz and Dexter Gordon, and everybody played fast; Wardell Gray. There was a certain thing. You played a medium tune, then you played a slow tune, and then you played a real, real fast tune—just a roaring tune, just a flying tune. The guys these days just don't seem to play a fast tune, I mean really fast. That's the only complaint I have against the young rhythm sections nowadays, is that they don't play fast tempos. They play fast within the context of the medium tempo, but everything is in that *certain* tempo, that certain feel, like that certain type of thing that everyone fell into; like a jazz rock feel, so the speed is in playing double or triple time, or playing certain patterns, but it's not in the tempo itself. I like to play just breakneck tempos, and I find that the rhythm sections nowadays just are not used to doing that, so they have a tendency to fall back.

Hal Hill: *Your album "Living Legend," with Shelly Manne and Charlie Haden, and the late Hampton Hawes, doesn't seem to lag anywhere at all. Is this because of long rehearsals?*

We didn't rehearse at all, not once, not for a second. We just went into the recording studio. I wrote five of the tunes, and one of the tunes was *Here's That Rainy Day*, and I just told Shelly what I wanted, and that was the end of it. Charlie Haden just followed Shelly, and Hamp followed Shelly and Charlie and that was it. Shelly is like a master. He's been around so long he can play brushes at any tempo, any speed, he can play "Cherokee" at the fastest tempo imaginable, and play it on brushes and never ever lose an instant's time, it's just a work of art. He's a great, great drummer. Anything you want to play, you just tell him what it is in a couple a words, and that's it.

But he has worked with you for many, many years—from the Kenton period right the way through to the Contemporary scene (record company).

No, I have not worked with Shelly, maybe three times in the last twenty years. Shelly was with the Kenton band for a while in the forties, and the only time I ever played with him outside of that was at a couple of record dates. But he was one of those kind of musicians who were from those days. Charlie Haden is another one of those people that is a master on his instrument, and he can play anything at any tempo. There is nothing he can't do, he is probably the greatest bass player going. I can't think of anybody playing better.

You have a new album with Elvin Jones called "The Trip."

It's the same type of thing. We went into the studio and . . . I think the first album took about six hours, and this album took about the same length of time. With Elvin I just told him what I wanted. He wanted a copy of the alto part, most of them are originals of mine, and he wanted the alto part so that he could see what was happening. So I gave him a copy of the alto part and I gave one to George Cables, a marvelous piano player who has played with Freddie Hubbard on and off for a long time. He has his own trio now, and he is another one of those musicians that can do anything that you want to do, and follows, listens, and has that sensitivity and a beauty that is just beyond description. As you notice, I really get carried away when I talk about musicians, but a good musician is like someone that has race horses—I think of them in that way. And George is one of those. That's the way the date went. I gave them the parts, they read the parts and that was it. We could have done the whole album in two and a half hours.

A lot of recording dates with musicians of your calibre don't seem to take too long. Yet you put a rock musician in a studio and they take days sometimes to just do one tune, whereas a jazz artist, people like yourself, or Sonny Stitt, or Frank Rosolino do a date in maybe 3 or 4 hours, wrap it up and that's it. It's finished. There's no overdubs, it's just a finished product.

Well I think the only thing you might take time in doing is maybe if you were using electrical instruments like synthesizers. Maybe in the "Live/Evil" album, they had to take some time in getting the sound right later on. In the mastering of the record maybe it would take some time getting the right volume out of the different instruments to make it right. In just piano, bass and drums, and horn, where the arrangement is written, and everything is written out; when I write an arrangement I write the bass part, and the piano part and the drum part. Usually with Elvin I didn't write a drum part because there is no need to write a drum part for Elvin because he knows exactly what's happening, and what you want him to do, and the same with Shelly. I had drum parts for Shelly, but I didn't even bother to give them to him because I knew he would do a better job on his own than what I could possibly write for him. Because, I'm not a drummer. Though with the bass and piano I had certain sounds that I wanted to have happen at certain points in the tune. It's just the fact that they are such good musicians, that they read the charts and that's it. There's nothing more to it, it's like eating breakfast.

Would you like to work in the electronic concept as of today?

I would like to play with the rhythm section, that I named, that Miles had. It would be interesting, I've never worked with a rhythm section like that, it would be fun. I know that I would like to work with that rhythm section. To hear the sound, to experiment and do some different things because I hear a lot of things that I want to do that are almost impossible to get out of the horn. I find myself searching, and making all kinds of different sounds with the horn and trying to spread notes, and change the notes to have a different sound to what they actually have—different timbre. So it might be interesting to see what might happen. But I would never want to get away from the basic thing of the blowing. Miles does it with just a trumpet, so I think a horn player can do it. The rhythm section is what I'm talking about. Even maybe with a saxophone there's ways of doing it—I've never tried it.

Where do you get the inspiration for most of your originals? The ballad things that you've written: one for your wife in particular, Laurie, and "Sambo Mo Mo," that you played at the club.

That's "Sambo Mom-Mom." Mom-Mom is sort of an endearing name that I have for my wife. As you notice from most of my songs, I just write a song and I can't think of anything else to name them after, some of them, so I just name them after, some of them, so I just name them after my cats, or something like that. If it's something that I really feel, I'll name it after my wife. "My Laurie"[11] is something that I wanted to write that had everything in it, that was really beautiful and different, that would show my love for her, and so I just wrote that song. I thought it was one of my best songs.

168

There's a new record that I have not heard yet ("No Limit").[12]

This album that I've made is better than either one of the other albums, I couldn't believe that. . . . Usually you make one album that is good, and one that's so-so, and another one that's fair and then the next one is good, but to make three in a row where each one is better than the other, is probably due to the fact that I realize that this is my last go-around. I've got to do it now if I'm going to do it, and I really feel that I have everything together as much as I ever had, by far more than I have ever had before.

The "No Limit" album has Carl Burnett on drums, George Cables on piano again, and a bassist named Tony Dumas, who is 21 years old and he is just marvelous. He has a special kind of bass that someone made and then gave Tony the patent on the bass (Blitz bass). I've never seen any bass that looks like it at all. There's the one guy that I think maybe I would like better than Charlie Haden, eventually. He plays like a savage. The rhythm is just so fantastically wild and frantic. I really like that sound. I think it's the fact that I like this sort of a madness. The real open thing in life and in music. Before I used to live it, and now I can't live it anymore, so the only way I can get it is through music, and I just love that kind of a sound. That's why I love "Live/Evil" so much; because it had that madness in it. That real raw sound to it, and Tony Dumas has that. We recorded "My Laurie" and it came out just really beautiful, and we recorded another tune, "Rita-San," for Laurie also. It's like one of those old time Central Avenue[13] tunes, one of those old time swinging tunes that I used to play when I was a kid, playing with Dexter Gordon. I wrote all these tunes just recently and I have no piano, I've never had a piano at home, so I write them just out of my head without anything, without a horn, without a piano, without anything. Whereas I used to, a long time ago, write tunes using the chord structure of another tune, like Bird did, like they used to a long time ago. I stopped that because the tunes had no meaning that way, they weren't mine. So now I write the tunes and the chords, the tune dictates the chord, and they have all come out right. I'm trying to do something different, not doing something different for difference sake, it's because that's what I feel inside. I have always been a very lonesome and a very sad person, and very highly emotional. I think these things are the things . . . the beautiful things I have no trouble with at all, because that's how I feel. The other things are things that are inside of me that there's no other way to get them out, but through music. And I can't get the beauty out either, because there's not enough beauty in the world. If it wasn't for my wife.

What kind of advice do you have for the young musicians that are coming up today?

I would tell them to learn how to play fast, for one thing, because music isn't always going to stay the same, everything changes and you have to be able to play for every type of person. Don't ever close yourself off. I've heard people that won't listen to acid rock at all, they won't listen to cowboy music, they won't listen to this, they won't listen to that, and they reach a certain point and they think that that's it. That's where they want to be. There is no such thing as that's where you want to be. As long as you're alive, you keep growing. I play so much differently now than I played when I made the "Living Legend" album. My playing is changing and improving, and if I would shut myself off to listening to different things I would never learn. So I think the main thing is to learn everything you can learn about everything possible there is to learn about music. You can't learn everything, but you can learn as much as possible about everything. Be open and free. Don't ever rank something because it isn't what you think is right. Play yourself—only yourself. I almost got hung up with Coltrane and bought a tenor one time, because I loved the way he played so much, and all of a sudden I realized what I was doing and I got rid of the tenor and got an alto and stopped that.

He's the only person that influenced me like that. I suppose at one time I might have bought a trumpet but it would have been too much to have done that.

Notes

1. Bill Withers is an American soul singer.
2. The album is called "Photograph." Art solos on the tune **I'm So Blue.**
3. "Living Legend"—Contemporary 7633 (Hawes, Haden, Manne).
4. "The Trip"—Contemporary 7638 (Cables, Jones, Williams).
5. "Live/Evil"—CBS CG 30954.
6. "Kind Of Blue"—CBS PC 8163.
7. "Sketches Of Spain"—CBS CK 08271.
8. "Miles Ahead"—CBS CL 1041 (Japanese CBS/Sony 25 AP 752).
9. "Lorraine" from "Tomorrow Is The Question"—Contemporary 7569.
10. "Samba Mom-Mom" from "Living Legend"—Contemporary 7633; also on "Art Lives"—Galaxy 5145; and "Goin' Home"—Galaxy 5143.
11. "My Laurie" from "No Limit"—Contemporary 7639; also on "Memorial"— Japanese Trio PAP 25037.
12. "No Limit"—Contemporary 7639.
13. A main street in Los Angeles which was the black entertainment section.

26

I WANT TO PLAY SO BAD

David Nicholson Pepperell

I met with Art Pepper during his first (and only) Australian tour in August 1981. The hotel he was staying at, the Diplomat in St. Kilda (which is right in the middle of the closest thing Melbourne has to a Red Light district), is much beloved of traveling rock bands and its chintzy sleaziness seems to make most weary travelling musicians feel right at home. He was booked into Mr. Ward's Jazz Nitespot, following Joe Henderson, had performed live on TV and had been featured heavily on the talk and variety shows. All in all the tour was going brilliantly and rightly so, for he was playing probably the best he had ever played in his chequered career.

On first seeing him I noticed the obvious fragility of his health. His skin was pale, his stomach had become paunchy, he was nervous and smoked and drank constantly through the interview. However, despite his tendency to ramble, he was lucid, thoughtful, entertaining and most of all charming. You could see underneath all the years in prison and hard times the beautiful youth who captivated men and women alike as much with his personality as his playing in the '50s.

"I Want to Play So Bad" by David Nicholson Pepperell originally appeared in the June 1986 issue of *The Wire* magazine. Reprinted by permission of *The Wire*.

His autobiography *Straight Life* had just been published in the USA and Europe to rave reviews and I could see that this was a source of great pride to him. He now saw himself as not only an articulate horn player but as an articulate speaker and writer as well and throughout our talk he answered all my questions at length and in detail. I was struck the most by the thought that what crazy kind of system would lock this gentle, brilliantly talented man up in hell holes of prisons for such long periods; and yet, as he said in the interview, each man grows by what he does and how he lives. Art Pepper was a man who grew—as an artist, a thinker and a profound human being.

DP: *I Know you've played with Richie Cole and he played with the singer Eddie Jefferson a lot. I was wondering if you liked playing with singers and if there's any singers you especially like? I do remember your famous solo with June Christy . . .*

AP: Oh yeah, "How High The Moon," that arrangement was written by Neal Hefti. Yeah, I always loved singers and I always liked playing with them—one of my favourite records is *The Genius Of Ray Charles* 'cause all of one side has the ballads like "Don't Let The Sun Catch You Crying," incredible [hums a few bars] as you can see as a singer, boy [laughs]. I really do love singers though—I did a thing on an album called *No Limit* that Roberta Flack did called "The Ballad Of The Sad Young Men"—I wanted to play it exactly the way she sang it and it's really hard to do—it being such a great ballad and her phrasing being so beautiful. I was able to more or less analyse what was happening with her—she's a great musician—she knows changes and she has a beautiful feel, like Ray Charles. I love Aretha Franklin, Barbra Streisand—this movie *The Eyes Of Laura Mars* has a theme and I've used it on my ballad album called *Winter Moon*—it's a tune called "Prisoner"—at the end of the film Barbra Streisand sings it again but this time she, like, stretches out and it knocked me out so much that I did that record. So, sure, I love singers and it's funny but I don't know the words to any song, even one. Well, maybe "America The Beautiful"—no, I don't even know that. My wife, though, she knows the words to all kinds of songs, she can sing any song I can write, y'know, sometimes I can't remember the bridge of a tune and she sings it to me. I love singers, but not their words—it's the sound, like, I try and play as if I was a singer, that's when I'm playing a ballad. That's why I don't like to play double time—they started doing that in bebop, rhythm section would go into double time. . . .

Don't you play "Straight Life" in double time?

No, that's just an old tune sped up.

Isn't it "All The Things You Are"?

No it's . . . that's incredible, I just can't think of the name of that song right now—anyhow I try to play the alto like as if I was a singer. Really, though, I like all different kinds of music—I love classical music, I like some [Country and] Western music, I like rhythm and blues, rock, real hard rock. I mean when I was with Buddy Rich's band we played in New York in the Basin Street and it was in the Village and we played opposite Steppenwolf 'round 68, somethin' like that. Boy, the sound that they got. Like, being in the dressing room, it was in this gigantic theatre, steel, it reminded me of being in jail, and there was concrete. They were so loud, man, the whole theatre vibrated, this was the metal and the cement vibrating. I don't know if it's in my mind but no, you could feel it, you could feel the thing. The luggage that they had, they had about twice, even three times as much as Buddy Rich's whole band—they had these gigantic amplifiers and things—but I could see what they were getting at, it was very exciting. . . .

You liked their tunes then, their music?

Yeah, I liked what they were playing—certain things I didn't like but certain things I did—just like any kinda music, y'know.

Like I like very little jazz—I'm more critical of jazz than I am of other music—unless I feel that I'm gonna learn something from it or unless it's really good—yeah, I like almost anything. The only thing I don't like is operettas, light comedy or whatever it is they call it. I keep myself open, y'know. There's a lotta guys that won't listen to anything unless it's really up to their standard. They really don't open their ears, and if you do that you lose a lot. I've played with a lot of different groups. I love Latin music. I played with Rene Tazeth, a piano player, really a great band, Johnny Mandel was in the band—he wrote "Shadow Of Your Smile" and he was playing bass trumpet as well as writing charts for us. And instead of the drums he used timbales. . . .

Is there a certain effect you look for when you're writing a song?

What I do a lot of times, on *Winter Moon* for example, I wanted to write one of the songs to be a new ballad cause I've written quite a few ballads and I've got a few that I haven't recorded. I wanted it to be like a love ballad with my wife—for us, and then to the other people that would be listening. We call it "Our Song" so I wrote it with that idea in mind. I wanted it to be real beautiful, like it was a love-type beauty and also with a little sadness. But the main thing was the beauty.

So I sat down to write it and the first eight bars—see, I never studied composition or arranging or anything like that so with me, I just write from my head. I mean I would just sit down right now and start writing and I can hear what I'm writing because of playing so much I'm able to finger the sound in my mind like I just have a kind of pulse. I was in prison so much I developed that thing of playing in my mind, fingering even though I wouldn't be moving my fingers and I could feel this little thing that comes out, kind of electrical-type force. If I make a mistake I stop—you're able to do that kind of thing in practice. Sometimes when I'm going to sleep I'll start thinking of a particular song that I heard or something—that was the way I practised for some time without a horn and so the writing is the same idea. I don't know exactly what's happening, like the rules and all that, so I just write from off the top of that song I wanted to be a certain thing and I wrote it in that way. The first eight bars came out like lightning but the rest of it took me a long long time to write and I was just sitting around saying, I gotta finish it—and nothing would happen. Finally after Bill Holman wrote four of the arrangements on *Winter Moon* and Jimmy Bond wrote three—I didn't have any choice in the matter, which is a whole other thing about record companies.

At the beginning I wrote songs and I used the chords of songs I liked to write new ones. The first writing I wrote was from the blues tunes—that is jazz, that's the bottom. A lot of cats don't make it as great players because they don't have that foundation in the blues. If you have that you can build on that like Coltrane—that basic feeling like George Cables has even though he was a classical player when he was young. He has that basic feel of the blues, that indescribable thing—like anything he plays, especially a slow blues which we'll have to play tonight, the way he does it, well, that's it and that's what I have and there's no telling where it comes from.

But there's a tension between you because he was classically trained and you were not, but you can play together because of the blues which you both have in common.

Yes, it's that basic thing. The piano player that I was using—Milcho Leviev—he's a great piano player but he's a classical player, that's his thing, and he's from Bulgaria so he didn't have that thing, you know. So playing with him was great for me as far as technically and different . . . mechanically.

It would have made you think a lot of playing with such a technical player—you'd have to keep up with what he was doing.

Yeah that's what he had—I remember once we were in Germany in this beautiful hall with this incredible sound, well, they really have a thing for technical aspects of sound and this place was really beautiful. He sat down at the piano and he just started playing a thing by Bartok and y'know the people that were there, like just a couple people from the bookers and people there for interviews and the people who run the hall—they were flabbergasted, they just couldn't believe it. He can sit down and play "Daphnis and Chloe" by Ravel, like, certain little sections of it that I really like and all of a sudden I found that we had reached a certain impasse and there was just nothing happening any more. He was just playing trills and just . . . I hadda tell him everything I wanted and he would get mad—at first he used to listen to me but after a while he would get angry because he thought I was trying to destroy his thing and I didn't want him to live or to grow—he said, "I want to grow" and I said, "Well I'm afraid you're going to have to grow someplace else!" [laughs]

He had to go.

Yeah, but I really like him and he's a great musician but then I started playing continuously with George Cables—we went to Japan together with the rhythm section on the album *Landscape*.

I read an interesting interview with you by the Rolling Stone writer Grover Lewis when you were working at a bakery and not playing music at all—you claimed that the guy who ran the place was ripping you off. . .

Yeah, well, I was getting ten dollars a week and I kept the books, paid people, the whole thing and I worked from early. you get up at four o'clock in the morning, working, getting stuff ready to ship out, cutting these things of cake and it's hard to cut. And for all of that I got room and board and ten dollars a week—this was in 1972—and this guy wrote the article and my wife nearly had a nervous breakdown, because she has a child, a daughter and her ex-husband had the custody—and the way the guy wrote the article it looked as if she was using heroin herself. The guy had her saying in the article: "Whatever he's doing I'll join him"—it was like she was using too. Then my third wife, she was really crazed, her name was Daphne. Her father was a cop, one of her brothers was an electronics whiz and, like, an alcoholic, and her other brother was an armed robber with violence and a junkie and that's how I happened to meet her—and the article said that she was a night person or a lady of the night or whatever, so her brother rang me up and threatened me because it made her sound, you know, like [laughs] and this guy had been up for forcible rape and armed robbery and he's calling me up and saying it's bad for their name [laughs].

I only agreed actually to do this interview because of Eve Babitz the writer who is my wife's cousin. This guy from *Rolling Stone* was a friend of hers—I didn't want to do the interview because I wasn't going to play music any more. So anyhow this guy comes out and does the interview and says don't worry about a thing and a week or so later he rings me up and he's crying and I thought. On my God, and he's saying I'm sorry and I'm thinking Oh Jesus God what did he do and so this is before the paper had even come out he was, like, apologising and I thought if it's that bad the way he's crying it must *really* be bad. What had happened was that he had seen the proof copy of the article—he must not have typed up his own tape—and realised what it actually said and he had made a promise that what was said would have nothing to do with anything about my wife. But at any rate her brother's dead and I fail to have any feeling for him—I'm kinda glad he is dead 'cause that way I don't have to worry about him any more . . . later on that same paper that that writer worked for wanted to publish our book [*Straight Life*] and Laurie said 'No way, no way.'

What's your philosophy about playing music?

Well I think that you have to realise and find out as soon as possible whether there's any point in your playing, I mean trying to be a soloist, you mean a jazz player?

Yes.

Hmmmm, I've given a lot of lessons over different periods, I've enjoyed giving the lessons but the reason I don't do it any more is because the guys who come for lessons, I tell them the truth. If I don't think they've got it I tell them or if they do have it I tell them that but they seem to think, well, they have this kind of lost look and I keep trying to find out what it is, why they look that way and I finally pinned down one guy and I found out that they think I have some kind of special thing that I'm not telling them 'cause I don't want them to know the secret, I'm jealous or whatever, and I'm worried that they might take my *gig*. Like, there's a certain way to hold the ball if you're a baseball pitcher for a screw ball and I know of something like this for saxophone and if I would tell them, that, you hold it this way or that way . . . and you know they really feel that. So after I found out that from this one guy, grudgingly he told me, so then I started asking the other people and once I asked that question I could tell that that was it because they got all kind of flustered.

But, y'know, there isn't any secret, it's just that you're born with it, you're born with that feeling to be a jazz player I think. I think there's a lot of people who are born to be jazz players and don't play jazz. I think the hardest thing in life is to find out what you really feel is the thing that you can do best. In my own case I was very fortunate because when I was young and I would pass a music store I would get very excited at how pretty the instruments were and I wanted to play them because they were so pretty. My mother's side of the family—she's Italian and her whole family played music—her aunt and uncle played and one of the kids was named Gabor and he played trumpet on the radio and he had this real long, you know the full long trumpet, the classical trumpet and he had his little knickers on and this black curly hair with a little kind of a cravat and so I fell in love with the whole thing of being a musician.

You've said in other interviews that the intensity of your drive to play, the drive to get everything there was out of yourself in your playing was one of the main reasons for your excessive habits in life. Is that still the same now or are you more fulfilled at this present time?

Yeah, I certainly feel much more fulfilled—like, the thing of playing, to really feel that that's what it is, once I started taking lessons on the clarinet I used to just play by ear and I finally found out that that was what jazz was, just playing. There's so many people that they want to be a jazz soloist but they're not made, it just isn't there, it's a certain something. With me it's like a fight to the death, I mean I want to play so bad, I want to play, I want people to really dig what I'm doing. So the thing is as far as playing, is to be honest. I try to play without doing any tricks y'know, playing little nursery rhymes and things like that, to really try to create something different. To really be a true jazz soloist every solo should be different even though I guess that's impossible—but the more you play and the more living that you do, I really believe that what happens to you in your life adds to what you're doing.

I thought at one time that at a certain point you weren't able to create any more, that you didn't grow any more musically as a jazz soloist and I was under the impression that when you were about 30 that was the end of your growing and then from then on you just played a certain way. Now, though, I've found out that that isn't so—a lot of people who are playing now are in their 50s, and a lot of people who would be in their 50s if they were still playing, like Bird, and there are so many people who are still there like Dizzy and they are still growing all the time—so once I realised that, that I could keep growing as far as what I had to say, once I realised that I could continue doing that, that lifted this tremendous weight. I wasn't afraid any more that it was all over, to where I would have to regret the years in prison. But I believe that whatever you go through, that builds, it's like a thing that you're building, it's like learning words if you're a writer. People playing ballads—that's the mark of a real jazz player because there's so few people who can really play ballads. That to me is really the bottom line as being a jazz player is if you can play a ballad and play the blues at whatever speed.

Is that why you play alto saxophone and clarinet which sound like the human voice rather than tenor sax which seems to have more of a voice of its own?

Well, tenor is very easy, when I play tenor I can sound better easier than I can sound better on alto because alto is so hard to get a good tone on—just to play it, the technical aspects of playing alto . . . the clarinet is almost impossible, that's really hard—so the only reason I started playing clarinet again was so many people have asked me about the clarinet, especially in Japan.

All these things have happened to me in the last few years, the thing of being accepted, playing in clubs, going to Europe, going to Japan, I'm going to Japan in November and that will be the fifth time, they keep asking me back, they are just marvellous there and they were asking me how come I don't play the clarinet any more. 'Cause I did a couple of things, I did a thing with Henry Mancini called "Combo" where I played clarinet on the album and I have a lot of solos. And then I did a thing with Barney Kessel, *Some Like It Hot* from that movie and I played 'A' clarinet rather than 'B flat' and the sound is much deeper, it's really a nice instrument. Anyhow they kept asking me about clarinet and when I was a kid I loved Artie Shaw. But the way the sound has gone, you can't hear the sound in a club, it's very loud there and in order to play the clarinet it's got to be quiet and rhythm sections have to play quieter and rhythm sections wouldn't do that.

I had this friend from when I was a kid, well he's just gone to jail for 25 years for conspiracy, it's just ridiculous, and friends are very rare. As a friend I can go to him and say, "Man, I'm in trouble" and the guy, whatever it takes he'll do it for you. That's what

I think of when I think of a friend, so I'm kind of a recluse. I don't have any friends really. Anyhow I'd say "How did I sound that time" and he kept saying "Welllllll, uh"—so everybody put me down. We made this record just recently before we came to Australia, the weekend before, we recorded Thursday, Friday and Saturday live at a place called the Maiden Voyage in Los Angeles. I played clarinet. I played "Begin The Beguine" the first two nights and we were to the third night and nothing had happened right and Laurie said, "Look, just burn the thing," [laughs] "don't try it again" and I knew she was right so I started thinking and I realised that—clarinet, it should be something happy, something that is swinging but real happy and easy and pleasant and I started thinking of something happy. And I thought of "When You're Smiling" so I ran through that the day before we were doing the gig and it went OK—and I was real happy about that because otherwise it would have been a defeat, a real failure, 'cause it would have been a challenge that I couldn't meet, would have been one of the only ones I faced and didn't make, didn't win. So it was really a life and death thing to me. I ran through "When You're Smiling" at home and Laurie was taking a shower and she said, "What was that?" and I said, "that was 'When You're Smiling,'" and she said, "Well, why don't you try that?"

So we went down and I told the people that this was my last chance and that if his doesn't happen I'm never gonna play clarinet again and so I started playing "When You're Smiling" and it came out really good and it sounded like I really knew everything that I, well, I was able to play what I wanted to play on it, which was amazing. The drummer, Carl Burnett, said, "Well, you are gonna have a lot of cats trying to play the clarinet when they hear what you are doing on this record."

So that was like conquering something, to me, like, playing is to be totally honest and try to create something new and not just doing something because people will clap. Like so many musicians play just for the applause. I play for applause too but not to where what I'm doing to get the applause is destroying my thing. That isn't playing, so many musicians do that. They play little nursery rhymes.

You read in the paper that so-and-so died of a heart attack, I read the obituary columns to see the ages of the people that die (laughs) and when I see that, you're more—it's not that it's going to happen but your chances are really increased. So whenever I play I feel that it may be the last time I've ever gonna play and I wanna really go out playing. So whenever I play it's really a challenge and I try to play as well as I can. So far, things have worked out pretty well.

27

ENDGAME

Gary Giddins

When this extraordinary compilation was in the works, Ed Michel, who produced Art Pepper's Galaxy sessions, told Laurie Pepper, "There are still critics in this country who don't take Art seriously as a major jazz artist. . . . The amount and quality of this work will force them to rethink." It's caused me to rethink, and I took him very seriously indeed. Pepper's sudden reappearance in 1975 was something of a second coming in musical circles. For the next seven years, his frequent recordings and tours, and the publication in 1979 of the autobiography he and Laurie wrote, *Straight Life*, transformed him from a gifted altoist who had made a string of semiclassic albums in the Fifties to a touchstone for the very aesthetics of jazz music. He wasn't merely back; he was back with a vengeance.

A tale that made the rounds in those years concerned Arthur Blythe, another California altoist, who was first making his reputation. Pepper is said to have called him at some outlandish hour to tell him he was coming to town to see how good Blythe was, and that he better get ready because Pepper was going to do him in on the bridge to "Body and Soul." In the early thirties in Chicago, Louis Armstrong used to hit the stage and tell everyone, "I'm ready, I'm ready, so help me I'm ready," before he blew the joint down. Well, Art was ready and he made damn sure everyone knew it. This lone gunslinger knew he was running out of time and he had no intention of wasting it.

"While Art was dying, when I was driving him to the hospital," Laurie Pepper recently recalled, "he told me that he figured he was dying and he said it was okay. He said he'd done everything he had to do—'the book, the ballad album, the movie [a documentary, *Art Pepper: Notes from a Jazz Survivor*].' And he thanked me for making it all possible. He said he was satisfied, although he later complained to one of the doctors that he was supposed to play at Carnegie Hall with Phil Woods in a couple of weeks. But I think that was partly bragging. Anyway, I believe those last years were a period of reconciliation for him."

What sobered the critics and fans (many of them musicians) about those years was the aggressiveness of his creativity, a refusal to coast that made every performance a conscientious statement—a "trip," in the prison lingo he favored. If you thought you were going to sit back, sip your whiskey, and drowsily tap your foot, you were in the wrong place. Pepper could draw blood (usually his own), especially on ballads. He was always thinking, thinking, thinking. And he made you think; he reminded you how you came to love this music in the first place.

Armstrong once said, "Jazz is only what you are." Pepper's understanding of that was profound. He had lived a dark, cold life and this was his last stand. He shamelessly set it all out on the table, in writing and in music. He was a drug user, and he put that into his music. He was white in a music in which most of the innovators were black, and he accepted that as a challenge. "It looks to me like life begins at fifty," he wrote, "and I never thought I'd live to see fifty, let alone start a new life at this age." He set up an ambitious agenda for himself (to be the best saxophonist in the world, for starters), and, driven in part by a paranoia that convinced him that everyone wanted him to fail, he found new ways to stretch his endurance. You could hear that in his playing, and it was riveting.

Art always had a distinctive sound, even back in 1943, when he made his recording debut with a halting solo on a Stan Kenton session: cool on the surface, with a skittish undercurrent that often made the prettiness seem restive. In the nearly 40 years he made records, his style became increasingly personal—by turns bitter and timorous, knowing and scared. When he emerged from 16 years of silence in 1976, with the albums *Living Legend* and *The Trip*, both recorded for Contemporary, the label that made him famous in the Fifties, he consciously imitated John Coltrane. His sound became icily strident. It was as though he were trying to show that he'd been keeping himself up to date. That phase didn't last long: the nature of his introspection didn't lend itself to Coltrane's steely embouchure or his effusiveness. At his best, Pepper's solos were shaped by a patient elegance, his phrases sculpted with dynamic logic and an even disposition. He had a miraculous ear for melody notes and a rhythmic sense that was all but imperturbable; he modulated the intensity of his swing to drive home the meaning of his melodies. By 1978, when he recorded *Today* (with its stunning performance of "Patricia") for Galaxy, he was in total command, mating his old facility with a new expressiveness. He could make you laugh at his virtuoso conceits and weep at his unrequited passions. All the albums that followed were savory: *Straight Life*, *Winter Moon* the Maiden Voyage sessions, *Goin' Home*, and the rest. But they were just an appetizer for the set at hand.

The statistics alone are likely to prompt reconsideration. Here are 16 compact discs (18.6 hours of music) recorded in three and a half years, between December 1, 1978 and May 11, 1982. Of the 137 performances, eight have previously been issued only in Japan and 53 have never been issued at all. In other words, 45 percent of the music in this set is new. What does this mean? That he taped a lot of music, much of which wasn't good enough to

release, but is now being scraped together in posthumous tribute? Hardly. Little of the new material can be dismissed as alternate takes, since some of the duplications of the 78 compositions
he recorded were played in varied settings with diverse personnel. Nor was Art ever a repeater pencil, to borrow a pejorative
from Lester Young. What amazes me about *The Complete Galaxy
Recordings* is the consistency of his playing. As you look closely
at the best sessions, you can't help but note the apparent capri-
ciousness about what was or wasn't issued on the original LPs.
For new masterpieces are now added to the Pepper canon.
Except for the magnificent *Winter Moon* set, the sublime duets
with George Cables, and the addition of an occasional fifth man
(guitarist Howard Roberts, percussionist Kenneth Nash), Pepper
is heard exclusively in a quartet setting. Yet the music is always
fresh, compelling, surprising. Pepper had jam session appetites,
but he also had compositional discipline—especially when he
prepared to record. His power of concentration at session after
session, in take after take, is in itself enough to confirm his reputation as a master.

The lives of few artists have been told as comprehensively or
as well as Art Pepper's. I've always regretted that *Straight Life*
was published by a firm associated with music (Schirmer) and
marketed accordingly, because it received insufficient attention
from mainstream media. At the time of publication, Pepper was
compared with Henry Miller, Jack Kerouac, and Malcolm X. Dan
Wakefield, who knows what addiction is and how to write about
it, welcomed *Straight Life* as "an honest and wrenching por-
trayal"; Whitney Balliett credited Pepper with "the ear and
memory and interpretive lyricism of a first-rate novelist." I wrote
that Pepper was better than William Burroughs on the subject of
drugs and better than Malcolm Braly on prison life, an evalua-
tion that is easier to make today, when neither Burroughs's
Junky nor Braly's *On the Yard* are as well remembered. It hardly
matters that Laurie Pepper (Boswell with a tape recorder)
brought the book to life; her ear and editorial instinct turned

Art's stories and obsessions into a hellfire narrative. The collaboration was seamless, and every page is wounding and real. I've gone back to the book, supplementing it with Laurie's recent recollections, to try and set the early years in perspective.

Art was born in 1925, in California, to a merchant seaman and his 15-year-old wife. He was so sickly his family didn't expect him to survive; when his parents divorced, he was placed in the care of his paternal grandmother—"a dumpy woman, strong, unintelligent. She knew no answers to any problems I might have." He grew up afraid of everything and resentful of his family. When he became a cog in the prison system, he adopted those very characteristics he despised in his grandmother to prove his strength. "I wanted to pour my heart out to somebody; probably a lot of the people felt the same way, but you had to be strong and act like nothing bothered you. I had to be tough, I had to ridicule anything that indicated weakness." His arrests followed his surrender to heroin, which he insisted provided the only relief from sexual obsessions that had turned him into a rapist, a voyeur, an obsessive masturbator. In the book, he recounts sexual exploits with relish of a pornographer.

He turned to alcohol and pot to rid himself of anxieties, but nothing worked until a woman band singer cajoled him into a hotel john, taught him to sniff smack and made a beeline for his fly. "I finally found peace," he said. But it was a peace that passeth liberal understanding. He became a raging reactionary, switching his allegiance from musicians to junkies: "I looked at myself in the mirror and I looked at Sheila [a pseudonym for the singer] and I looked at the few remaining lines of heroin and I took the dollar bill and horned the rest of them down. I said, 'This is it. This is the only answer for me. If this is what it takes, then this is what I'm going to do, whatever dues I have to pay. . . . And I *knew* that I would get busted and I *knew* that I would go to prison and that I wouldn't be weak; I wouldn't be an informer like all the phonies, the no-account, the non-real, the zero people that roam around, the scum that slither out from under rocks, the people that destroyed music, that destroyed this country, that destroyed the world, the rotten, fucking, lousy people that for their own little ends—the black power people, stinking motherfuckers that play on the fact that they're black, and all this fucking shit that happened later on—the rotten, no-account filthy women that have no feeling for anything. . . ." He continues in that vein for a while and concludes, with no trace of irony, "All I can say is, at that moment I saw that I'd found peace of mind."

This is alienation with a trudgeon, a narcissist's ravings. Yet it's a side of a man who in those same years revealed in his music a gentility and a generosity of spirit that made him one of the most distinctive and emotive improvisers of his generation. He attempted in his book to justify his indulgences by parading them nakedly, giving and asking for no quarter. As Laurie points out, the transition from musician to junkie (each term implies a moral code, the adoption of a family, the attempt to define one's place in the world) followed hard on two exiles:

He was hanging out, actually working on Central Avenue [the famous strip of jazz clubs in black L.A.] from age 14. He was accepted and admired in a world he loved. Then he was suddenly rejected by that world. That's how, at age 18, he saw it when he experienced racism for the first time in North Carolina. He spent most of the rest of his life in a state of chronic paranoia, only it wasn't only paranoia (as I first believed) because the bad vibes he got from many black musicians—sarcasms, slights, willful incomprehension, onstage shenanigans—were not usually imaginary. . . . And he was incredibly sensitive to that stuff. Always expecting it. . . . Pretty soon he got bitter, suspicious, and nasty. And then prison just exacerbated everything.

That was the first exile. The second was entirely his own doing. Arthur Sr., Art's father (nicknamed by the boy "Moses" because "he was old as Moses and as wise as Moses"), was a real man. Art spent a lot of his life trying to prove to Moses that he was, too. Moses was also the guy who came down from the mountain with the rule book, and one of Moses's most important rules was "thou shalt not be a stool pigeon." In 1953, Art's best friend [a celebrated musician] informed on him and sent him to jail. Another friend [and another musician] stole Art's wife. Art decided that musicians were not "men," they were despicable, amoral sissies. And Art rejected that part of himself that was a musician and an artist, because it was inferior, something to be ashamed of, and spent most of the rest of his life ambivalent—he had the gift and the love of music and he was ambitious, he wanted to be a star, but he had to believe he was also an honorable man, "righteous people," a standup guy, like his father and men like his father—the criminals of East L.A. whom he met when he started using. And since he did happen to be a junkie, he proved his manliness the only way he could—by doing time. And some of the ambition was fulfilled that way; because he was a star in prison.

Remember that Pepper had already achieved a measure of stardom in the straight world. He'd appeared with Benny Carter's band, and for five years (1946–51), following his stint in the Army, he emerged as the most admired soloist in the Stan Kenton Orchestra. Yet he sank deeper and deeper into the netherworld. After his first marriage broke up, his second became a grotesque and vindictive battle between two junkies who tortured each other relentlessly until his wife informed on him. Then Pepper embarked on a maniacal revenge that was short-circuited, like so much else in his life, by the requirements of his addiction. The music seemed to come last, though it's impossible to suspect that when you hear the fugitive recordings from the early Fifties. Two private sessions with Hampton Hawes (a great pianist, whose junk-savaged career is documented in another miraculously literary jazz memoir, *Raise Up Off Me*, by Hawes and novelist Don Asher), recorded in Hollywood in 1952 and released decades later, show the two as unrepentant bebop burners, achingly incisive and wildly energetic. In those days, he seems to have chosen as his models Lester Young, Zoot Sims, Charlie Parker, and Lee Konitz—a matrix of hot and cool stylings, girded by fierce rhythms, rich in exquisite harmonies. Still, except for a couple of beguiling Savoy dates, one in 1952 and the next two years later, Pepper hardly recorded at all.

Then, beginning in 1956, he started making the rounds as a sideman. He appeared on numerous sessions led by Shorty Rogers, Chet Baker, Marty Paich, Hoagy Carmichael, John Graas, Mel Torme, Barney Kessel, June Christy, Henry Mancini, Andre Previn, Helen Humes, and others. During those same years, 1956 to 1960, he hooked up with Les Koenig's Contemporary Records, and produced a series of masterful albums. Those sessions were a respite, a period of grace.

It's astounding to read in *Straight Life* that Art had to be propped up to play on sessions that became epiphanies of the West Coast jazz movement. Pepper's intonation was clear and balmy (on clarinet and tenor as well as alto), but the texts of his solos were shaded with longings. The tensile and deliberated phrasing was a means to a direct and, yeah, manly emotional expressiveness that was virtually antithetical to the cool posturings of those improvising beach boys who tried to recreate California jazz as fun in the midnight sun. Could he really have been nodding out when those cover photos were taken? He appeared so strong and uncomplicatedly handsome. In retrospect, the significance of the titles and contents of those albums is unmistakable: *Smack Up* and *Intensity;* the bold reconsideration of jazz classics, arranged by Marty Paich, for *Plus Eleven;* the driving inspiration he sought from Miles Davis's men on *Art Pepper Meets the Rhythm Section.* He recorded his last Contemporary date in November 1960. Except for a sideman gig eight weeks later, a guest stint with Buddy Rich's orchestra in 1968, and a little-heard featured spot with the Mike Vax Big Band in 1973, Art Pepper disappeared from records and, as far as most people were concerned, from public view for 15 years.

He had made the big time: San Quentin. He was stealing to support his habit, and devoting his most creative energies to planning heists, many of which could have been better executed by Laurel and Hardy. In jail, he thought "how great it would be to kill someone and really be accepted as a way out guy." Prison life made him increasingly racist (which, paradoxically, in no way mitigated his conviction that the great jazz players and, indeed, the moral giants of the music were predominantly black)—he contemplated forming a white vigilante committee. When he was released, he spent time in North Beach in San Francisco; the Sixties were in full gear, and he wore an earring and hit the rock joints with his tenor. Soon enough he returned to heroin to alleviate the hatred over which he had no more control than he did his sexual obsessions. At the nadir of his life, he retreated to Synanon, where he met Laurie, who became his wife, lover, mother, babysitter, manager, editor, and co-author.

Art left Synanon in 1971. Four months later, his father died—a release, Laurie speculates, that may have made it easier for Art to think of himself as a man. He started working as a musician again, playing casuals and working clinics, touring colleges, sitting in. But his ambivalence about music remained, despite a wonderful, challenging experience with Don Ellis's band, for which he added piccolo to his arsenal of instruments; and two movie soundtracks for Clint Eastwood, *The Enforcer* and *The Gauntlet*, the latter a trying situation because he was asked to play baritone, much to the bemusement of the studio guys who knew he'd never played one before. (Jerry Fielding, who composed the score and hired Art, called him that night and raved about how great his playing was.) In 1977, three events, in Laurie's estimation, forced him to reappraise his gift and his life: In March, he played a concert series in Tokyo with Cal Tjader, and the crowds cheered him as though "he might have been the Beatles"; in June, he toured the East Coast for the first time as a leader, playing two dates at the Village Vanguard, the last of which was recorded; in September, he got busted after a car accident that almost killed him. Laurie recalls,

> Art discovered then that he couldn't go "home" again to jail. There was no honor, no welcome there. All his buddies were

dead. He was an old man. He wasn't a bigshot. He went through a long spell of depression, aggravated by sobriety and by Les Koenig's death in November. When he went back to Japan with his own band in February of 1978, he'd just about decided to be a musician. Galaxy signed him in September. That did it. That and the publication of *Straight Life*.

When Art returned to New York in May 1980, he asked me to come by with my copy of his book so that he could inscribe it. One of the things he wrote was, "[Thanks] for being so honest in the last article." That was a review in which I had enumerated many of the least appealing aspects of his character, as detailed in his book. He liked people to be polite, but honest. Our first encounter followed his 1977 debut at the Village Vanguard. I had sat there opening night mesmerized, and then went home to write a reverie in which there were even more egregious puns than the title, *The Whiteness of the Wail*. I really didn't know anything about him, except the Contemporary records and some of his own liner comments, and the way he looked and sounded on stage—gaunt and tenuous, compulsively talkative, searing and punchy in his playing—so I was flying by the seat of my pants in speculating about drugs and race and everything else. My essay was more presumptuous than knowledgeable. You can imagine how surprised (and relieved) I was when Laurie called the day it came out in the *Village Voice* and said, "Art wants to meet you. He wants to know how come you know so much about him." It never occurred to me to say: It's all there in his music.

After Les Koenig's death, Laurie started looking around for a record label. Some companies replied with tentative interest, others ignored her letters. When a call came from Fantasy, Art had suffered a breakdown, possibly a delayed reaction to the car accident: a CAT scan turned up some brain damage. She had to tell the representative from Fantasy, "Art's in the hospital and doesn't even know his own name." She didn't know whether he'd "get better or how much better he'd get or whether he'd ever play again." The representative, Bob Kirstein, persisted, calling week after week to see how he was. Art recuperated and in June they negotiated a contract, Laurie outlining their desires, which included an album with strings. When she finished, Art added, "And a nonrecoupable bonus for signing." Laurie nearly fell off her chair, but Fantasy gave it to them.

Laurie once asked Ralph Kaffel, the President of Fantasy, why he signed Art, especially after producer Ed Michel had warned him that he would be trouble. A practical man, he gave four concise reasons: (1) Asked to name his 20 favorite albums of all time, two would be *Meets the Rhythm Section* and *Plus Eleven,* (2) Art was available, (3) Art was a major jazz name, and (4) Kaffel knew how well the Vanguard albums were doing and figured Art had some commercial momentum going for him. Fantasy's subsidiary, Galaxy, originally an R&B line, was recreated in the mid-'70s as a jazz label. The day after he turned 53, Art signed with Galaxy, and that December he recorded *Art Pepper Today.*

Art was grinding his knuckles to dust when the *Today* session got under way. It was Ed Michel's idea to take advantage of the fact that Stanley Cowell, Cecil McBee, and Roy Haynes were in the Fantasy studios, and he suggested they all have a get-acquainted dinner. It was a disaster. Except for Michel and engineer Baker Bigsby, Laurie recalls, nobody "contributed anything but polite monosyllables." Later that night, Art complained to her, "They hate me. They just figure I'm some ol', white, washed-up junkie from the coast. It's gonna be terrible. I'll have to *show* them who I am!" The next day he and Laurie arrived early to watch the trio lay down tracks for a couple of sampler albums to which Art was also scheduled to contribute. He brought along a few brand new tunes, "Mambo Koyama," "Miss Who," and "Chris's Blues," and a couple of old things he'd recorded back in 1956, "Pepper Pot" and "Patricia." They got under way with "Yardbird Suite," which was slated for one of the Galaxy samplers (*Five Birds & A Monk*), and followed with the new pieces and the ballads, of which "Over the Rainbow" was ransomed for the other sampler (*Ballads by Four*).

Late in the day, during a break, Stanley Cowell started play-ing a tune of such beauty that people stopped talking and looked up. Laurie recalls, "Art, in all innocence, remarked that it was really nice, what was it? When Stanley said it was Art's tune, 'Patricia' (which Art probably hadn't heard in 20 years), and offered that he liked it, Art decided to play it. They all went back into the studio. Art suggested that they do just a bluesy sort of coda, sort of a long tag at the end. He looked dubiously at the guys, not sure whether they knew what he was talking about. They played the tune, and then Cecil carried them into that won-derful ending. They finished, came into the studio, listened to the playback. Wow. Impressed silence. Roy Haynes broke it. To Art: 'Where did you say you were from?' Art: 'Gardena, California.' Roy: 'Is that *South* Gardena?' "

I can confirm one part of that story: the "Wow." That's the way people reacted when the album came out. *Today* was a record everyone talked about, in part because the previous Contempo-rarys, *The Trip* and *Living Legend*, were uneven, transitional. The new level he'd achieved was underscored a few months later when Contemporary issued the first of three volumes recorded at the Vanguard 15 months before the *Today* sessions; the per-formance of "Goodbye" was gripping, but the growth as reflected in the newer (superbly recorded) album was unmistakable. On "Chris's Blues" and "Mambo Koyama," he showed he could still muster the gleaming technique, and the lovely "These Foolish Things" exemplified the clarity of his tone (light, quick, elegant), but "Patricia" was something else. From the opening touches of craggy timbre through the brilliantly modulated closing alto, where he seems to be talking to himself and to the rhythm sec-tion, as though his story were a discrete testimony and their accompaniment the semblance of a good listener who nods and says, "Yeah, go on, I hear you," he was breaking ground. Not for jazz, perhaps, but for Art Pepper. It showed how close to raw feel-ing he could take his music. *Today* was voted best album of the year by the French Jazz Society, and placed high on most of the polls in Europe and Japan.

Now we have the whole session: the six selections that appeared on the album (#1-6), the two selections that were released on the samplers (#7-8), the two cuts that were cut for space (#9-10), and two alternate takes that show how freely Pepper improvised from performance to performance. Note the overdub by percussionist Kenneth Nash on "Mambo Koyama" (named for Kiyoshi Koyama, then the editor of *Swing Journal*, now one of the most admired record executives in the business). When the Peppers traveled to Japan, Koyama let them in on an unlikely coincidence: Mambo had been his nickname as a kid, because of his love for Latin music.

The next session was anticlimactic, to say the least. When Art signed with Fantasy, he stipulated his promise to record for John Snyder's lamented label, Artists House. In part because Art felt Ron Carter was uncooperative, a pall settled over the studio and the result was, in Laurie's words, "an exceedingly uneventful, unsoulful date." The music is not entirely dour, not least because Hank Jones is always a joy and because, even without the edgy inspiration that informed his best work, Art could fashion a sprightly, convincing music. Interestingly enough, the alternate take of "Straight, No Chaser," which Galaxy released in a 1985 set, is more imaginative than the master. "Diane" is yet another lovely original, written for his second wife, and originally introduced on a Tampa album in 1956.

In May the Peppers went to London, Art's first visit there since the war. He cracked a rib in an accident and contracted pneumonia, but still managed to play two successful concerts. When he returned, he did the second session for John Snyder, this time with musicians of his own choosing. He loved Charlie Haden, who had appeared on *Living Legend*, and joked that he was the only person in the world who whined more than Art did. He told Laurie at that time that he thought Billy Higgins might just be the best drummer in the world, and though he was just getting to know George Cables, he admired him. "Blues for Blanche" is built with the kind of short, halting phrases Art often used to construct a solo; here they are built into the structure of the piece itself. "Donna Lee," a Charlie Parker–Miles Davis milestone based on the chords of "Indiana," is an eternal challenge to bop players—a demarcation between the men and the boys. The rhythmically tricky "My Friend John," written for John Snyder, is one of three pieces that Laurie considers "Art's New York Charts" ("Vanguard Max" and "For Freddie" are the others), and in its exploratory fervor evokes much of what Art was working through in his music—the Coltrane influence, backbeat rhythms, disjointed phrases brought together in coherent figures. This session also marked a welcome return of the Pepper clarinet on "Anthropology" and "In a Mellow Tone," as well as the rare experience of three unaccompanied alto solos. The session is also notable for its promise: the Pepper-Cables combination, which would reach empyrean heights before long, is just getting started here (in 1982, Cables would have been more discreet on "Stardust"); and the previously unreleased "Landscape," one of Art's greatest tunes, is heard here in a workshop version that prefigures the incomparable Maiden Voyage performance.

Then the deluge. If you have any doubts about what distinguished journeyman Pepper from great Pepper, go directly to the Tokyo concerts, where from the first note you recognize his soul on fire: the flame is sustained through more than three CDs of music, culled from two concerts. A few weeks earlier, in New York, Art had stopped smoking for the first time, and Laurie suggests that the longer phrases that became emblematic in his playing in the last years was a consequence. She surprised me, however, by alluding to troubles in the ranks. Art never liked the blitz bass (a skinny box with a neck), which couldn't be heard without an amp, and he was occasionally displeased with the lines Tony Dumas played. Tempers flashed from time to time, and Laurie thinks Art's superb playing was inspired as much by the tension as by the importance of the gig. Most of this music has never been heard, and it's a marvelous gift, doubly so because the tracks that had been issued by the Japanese affiliate, Victor, were poorly mixed. After obtaining the original tapes, Laurie, Ed Michel, and engineer Danny Kopelson remixed them and produced a live sound that Laurie describes as "wet, saturated, and not too bright in the upper register."

If you have *The Trip* you'll want to compare the enormous strides he made in the new versions of the title tune and "Red Car." More rewarding still is the opportunity to compare the various performances of the same pieces at the Tokyo concerts. Cables provided a lush, yet crystal and pointed foil: sometimes his solos arrive like a damp cloth, to wipe the sweat off Art's brow. Billy Higgins plays, as was said of Jo Jones, like the wind— a cool breeze or a gale, whatever's called for, and always musical. He's one of the few drummers I know of who is never jarring, no matter how near you are to his set-up. "Sometimes" was written for the tour, to feature Art's clarinet—which, in its lonesome poise and gentle evocation, has always reminded me of Lester Young's. "Over the Rainbow," a strangely satisfying choice for a man who disdained easy sentimentality, exemplified his ability to transmute sentiment into a sagacious, hard-won nostalgia. It became a trademark number, as did "The Shadow of Your Smile."

The Japanese especially requested "Besame Mucho," which he played with more soul than has ever been associated with it, and which became his routine encore. But the real gem was that gnostic original, still unknown to records, "Landscape." Laurie recently noted, "I still remember reading your review of Art's performance of that tune aloud to him. You said it was a blues with two or three 12-bar themes minimizing the subdominant change. I asked Art if that was what 'Landscape' was. He thought and said, with mild surprise, yes, he guessed so. I said, I'd never thought of it as a blues. He laughed and said, 'Me neither.'" Perhaps I had too much faith in the magic number 12. My review was written after hearing Art play it one night at Fat Tuesday's, yet having gotten to know the records, it seems to me that the structure steamrolls its blues roots into a grammar of riffs that is designed by their momentum and direction, to steer the improviser away from the easy formulae associated with blues choruses. The improvised solo must sustain the mood of the composition, or the whole thing falls apart. Each "Landscape" may be counted among Pepper's most concentrated solos: they all repay close examination. Nowhere is Pepper's notion of a solo as a "trip," a cautionary tale, more palpable.

In August, the Peppers went to Chicago, where Art played with Barry Harris, then to New York, where Laurie handed in the manuscript of *Straight Life*, and Art went into the studio with John Snyder to record several solo tracks: only two of them, "But Beautiful" and "When You're Smiling" (on which he reminds me of a jauntier Lee Konitz), were deemed good enough to release here. A month later, Art was back in the studio at Fantasy, this time with two gloried veterans, bassist Red Mitchell, who has played with everyone, and Tommy Flanagan, with whom everyone would like to play. Again, Laurie surprises me by insisting that neither she nor Art thought the results were "any great shakes," though now, she admits, "I really love it . . . It's kind of moist, sexy and warm." When the album, *Straight Life*, was released in early 1980, it was widely greeted as a fitting successor to *Today*, especially for the ballads "Nature Boy" and "September Song," and for the original "Make a List (Make a Wish)." And therein lies a tale.

"One reason I think 'Make a List' is so exciting," Laurie says, "is that the chart is so formal and disciplined and yet so primordial and almost scary, and then the blowing part, which is punctuated by these disciplined little formal fragments, get so completely crazy. At least that's what's supposed to happen." At the session, Tommy had trouble with the formality of the head; he and Art spent three hours working on the contrapuntal parts. "I never saw such a demonstration of good manners," Laurie recalls. When they finally got it down, Tommy played it through, sighed, and asked Art, "Okay, so after we play that, then what do we do?" Art said, "Then we blow." As Laurie describes it, "Tommy stared at him for an eloquent moment. Then he said— with the most exquisite little shading of sarcasm I ever heard (it was high art)—'Oh, *then* we blow.'" *Straight Life* is one of my favorite albums, not least because all of the piano solos are pithy gems that perfectly complement the leader. Flanagan's solo on "Nature Boy" is a classic, and when Pepper returns, shadowed dramatically by the avuncular Red Mitchell, he goes beyond playing: he's singing, slowly and tenuously, almost humming to himself. The alternate take is a welcome bonus.

A year passed before Art recorded again, but the next date was one he'd waited a lifetime to make, and I guess if I were sentenced to a desert island with only one Art Pepper album, *Winter Moon* would be high on the short list. I don't know why it isn't better known—perhaps because strings petrify jazz fans in a way that, say, Gil Evans's brass arrangement for Miles Davis don't. Yet in many ways *Winter Moon* seems to me as perfectly realized. The choice of material, Bill Holman's voicings of the violins and his use of cellos to darken the edge, and the quietly arresting rhythms of the quartet (especially Carl Burnett's restrained yet firm touch), all combine to inspire the soloist. And, my God, is the soloist inspired. His expertly captured sound is chilling; his high notes break the inevitability of crashing waves, and his concentration is such that everything he plays highlights the arrangement as, indeed, they highlight him. It's a mesmerizing album, especially the Holman selections. The four Jimmy Bond arrangements are more conventionally lavish or, in the instance of the surprisingly funky "That's Love," hot. Holman allowed Art to peer into the darkness.

The choice of material was a collaboration that drew on many resources and recollections. "Winter Moon," a virtually unknown Hoagy Carmichael ballad, was recorded by the composer with Art in tow in 1957; Laurie told him he had to do that one. She took him to see *The Eyes of Laura Mars,* and he responded to the theme song, "The Prisoner"; they heard "Here's That Rainy Day" on the Muzak in a department store, and they remembered how he used to play it with Clare Fischer in 1977, and bring everyone to tears; he wanted to do "Ol' Man River" because he loved the Sinatra version. Note that the entire ensemble consists of only ten strings and the quartet, and that it was recorded live, a departure from standard practice. Surely that's one reason the intensity of his playing is so vivid. Laurie remembers "Art standing in front of the mike, at the first session, ready to rehearse, and the strings played an introduction, and Art was supposed to come in but he didn't. And Bill Holman turned to Art who just grinned at him and apologized. Art said that he was listening to the strings, and they sounded so beautiful he just forgot to play."

On September 5, the day after *Winter Moon* was completed, the studio and the rhythm section were still on call, so they went back to work and recorded *One September Afternoon,* a solid blowing date, with an unexpected shuffle tune in "Mr. Big Falls His J.G. Hand," a reminiscence of Central Avenue days that received quite a bit of radio play. There followed a month's tour of Japan, then two months in the Northwest with a tour that took the band into Canada. Art had been having trouble finding the right bass player, and was happy to have finally landed David Williams, who had worked with Elvin Jones. But the trip was plagued by personnel problems and by the time they arrived at Fat Tuesday's in New York, practically everyone in the band was subbing for someone else, and they all found one another's playing abrasive. It was a bad time, but not totally and not for long. Art had filmed his documentary in March, and by the time he made his second European tour of the season, in July, he had his band of choice again—George Cables, David Williams, and Carl Burnett. After all that time together, they were primed for the microphones that captured their return to Los Angeles and the Maiden Voyage, in August.

In some ways, the four and a half hours of music recorded on August 13, 14, and 15 in the L.A. club are a definitive document of what it was like to see Pepper in the final phase of his career. Over the years, three LPs were released—*Roadgame, Art Lives,* and *APQ*—and a fourth was prepared but abandoned when it was decided to embark on the present collection. Two new pieces were written for the engagement, "Roadgame" and "Road Waltz"; more importantly, Art succeeded in playing a possibly definitive account of "Landscape," as well as the first usable rendering of one of his best pieces, the provocative and very witty "For Freddie" (on *Art Lives,* the tune listed as "For Freddie" is actually "Thank You Blues"). Art and Freddie Hubbard greatly respected each other, despite the fact that Art lured away Carl Burnett, whose playing on these sessions once again justified Art's enormous pride in him. In 1980, both men had participated in an all-star lineup at the Royal Festival Hall. Art's band included John Lewis and Roy Haynes, and although he had trouble communicating to them what he wanted, the audience went wild when he finished. Afterwards, as Laurie recalls, Freddie said, "Man, you got the biggest hand of all of us." Roy Haynes said, "Yeah, why was that?" "Because," Freddie answered, putting his arm around Art's shoulder, "he's the greatest alto saxophone player in the world, that's why."

Listening to Art's between-numbers talk, you can't miss the admiration he had for the players in the band, and how much he expected from them and from himself, and how impelled he was to talk. I used to think of him as a Samuel Beckett character, marking every second of his life on stage with an assertion of selfhood, either in music or words, it hardly mattered which: the point was to connect with people—and not just any people but an audience, captive witnesses to the art of Art, to the pain of Art, to the phenomenon of Art. His motto might have been. "I talk, therefore I triumph." Sometimes, he was funny: always, he was honest.

Ed Michel gave him the tapes from the gig and asked him to make notes on the selections, some of which were reproduced on the covers of the original albums. Of the unreleased "Arthur's

Blues," he wrote, "My whole life went into this." The four choruses of his opening solo are characteristic of what he brought to
jazz at a time when too many of his peers were selling out for
commercial formulas that today are merely embarrassments to
all the players they seduced: a time when bands were the thing,
and young soloists were often content to make names for themselves with flashes of virtuosity. What Pepper reaffirmed was the
sacred trust of great jazz: the individualist in the throes of creativity. "Arthur's Blues" is so old-hat it's exhilarating. In four
choruses, played with a slow undulating rhythm that swells every
beat into its own measure, he begins with a sketch of the blues,
in which the rests are as dramatic as the notes (George Cables
covers them with incomparable finesse, never playing too much).
Art builds to a grace-note lick that gets the second chorus off the
ground, and then, with perfect logic, builds higher still on his
foundation, enlarging the scope or range of his ideas: growling;
arching into squeals; mumbling thirty-second-note figures as
though they were off-banded asides; building to the climactic
volubility that closes the third chorus; and settling with unshak-
able resolution into the fourth.

Let the Peppers have the last word on a no less remarkable
ballad, also recorded at the Maiden Voyage. Laurie: "His whole
life also went into 'Everything Happens to Me,' which should
have been Art's theme song. He played the tune fairly frequently
during his early years. But he never played it—or in my opinion
anything else—the way he plays it here. In my opinion, which
may be worth very little because it's so subjective, nobody ever
played anything quite as wonderful as this 'Everything Happens
to Me.' I'll tell you Art's opinion. One afternoon he sat down and
listened to it seriously. When it was over he looked up at me and
shook his head. He was absolutely dazzled. He said, 'I don't know
... am I crazy?' I knew exactly what he meant. He meant that he
didn't think anybody had ever before played anything quite as
wonderful as this 'Everything Happens to Me.' But obviously, he
must be crazy, because the world was not beating a path to his

door or crowning him with lilies or electing him emperor—or even putting his picture on the cover of *Down Beat.*"

After the Maiden Voyage, they went to Australia—"made a lot of money and had a hell of a good time." Then Canada, then the best tour yet of Japan. In March of 1982, the documentary film was released to good reviews. In April, he was back at Fat Tuesday's and he looked awful. . . . His playing remained nervy, edgy, urgent. Laurie remembers it as "a heavenly, unforgettably good week." Yet they both knew time was running out. They went home to record the *Goin' Home* album, duets with George Cables. The first session was ineptly recorded with digital equipment, a new phenomenon then, and they had to do it over again in May. For *The Complete Galaxy Recordings*, all the April sessions have been remastered and the selections presented as they were played, though not necessarily in order. The tunes cover new as well as familiar ground: George wrote "Tête-à-Tête" at the session, and suggested "Isn't She Lovely," which Art referred to as "that weird Stevie Wonder tune." A devoted Ray Charles fan, Art brought in a tape of Charles singing "Don't Let the Sun Catch You Cryin'." The "free" ending on "'Round Midnight" came about because Laurie complained that everyone always tacked on the same ending. On "Last Thing Blues," which ended the first day of recording, Art plays alto and clarinet. "I've been to a lot of record dates," Laurie says,"but none to equal those for sweetness and light." You hear it in every selection. Always a formidable technician, Cables displays the touch, creativity, and finesse associated with Art Tatum. Pepper had found an ideal bandmate, and his last sessions are poignant and gorgeous.

Laurie: "Ed Michel once remarked, Art's *favorite* high was the adrenaline high. You said in one review that he was at his best with something to prove. Art knew that very well, so if the odds weren't formidable, he made them that way. Blood was often shed. Art's blood. He became dreadfully accident-prone before important sessions. And, of course, he insisted everyone was against him, wanted to see him fail. He'd show them. I used to try to soothe him until I realized that he was working himself up on purpose, and it was useful and necessary" There was a final tour in May, which took him to Chicago, Milwaukee (where, for a brief moment, he finally worked up the nerve to sing on stage), and Washington, D.C., where he had a chance to hang out with Zoot Sims for the first time in many years. He played his last in D.C., at a Kool Festival. Ten days later, at home, he complained of a headache. Later that day, June 9, he went into a coma, and on June 15 he died. The funeral was packed with admirers, a fitting tribute, and the centerpiece was a wreath contributed by George Cables, David Williams, and Carl Burnett, which read: "To the Greatest Saxophone Player in the World."

After my first encounter with Art, in 1977, I wrote, "Jazz legends never die; they become self-fulfilling prophecies." Art fulfilled his legend in seven astonishing years, and this collection is something of a notarized testimony to his accomplishment. He would have loved it. He'd have said, "Why shouldn't I love it? It's exactly what I deserve."

28

STRAIGHT LIFE

Ted Gioia

Serve the Master

Any account of Art Pepper's tumultuous career risks being a pale shadow of the story Pepper tells in his autobiography, *Straight Life*. Even the most candid outsider's description of the altoist's life and times would have a hard time matching Pepper's unflinching honesty, while even the most diligent investigative reporter would never dig up the kind of nasty details on Pepper's life that the altoist calmly presents himself. Pepper's worst enemies could hardly outdo his self-incriminations, but then again few panegyrists could match his self-praise.

While most jazz autobiographies are a predictable recital of honorary degrees received and polls won, Pepper eschews the surface gloss and digs deep into a gritty account of his passage from Stan Kenton to San Quentin and his ensuing attempts, none of them entirely successfully, to put his life together again—all told with a clinical detachment almost as fascinating as the story itself. He neither relishes the seamier details, in the manner of so many kiss-and-tell books, nor whitewashes the tale of his life.

"Straight Life" is an edited chapter that originally appeared in *West Coast Jazz: Modern Jazz in California, 1945-1960* by Ted Gioia. Copyright © 1995 by Ted Gioia. Reprinted by permission of Oxford University Press, Inc.

Nor finally does he assume the smug attitude of the born again, justifying his transgressions through the self-righteousness of his final conversion to the straight life. Like all real redemptions, Pepper knew, his had to be earned again every day. At the end of the book he comes across as no self-confident victor over his problems, but a man every bit as anxiety-ridden and haunted as the convict incarcerated in San Quentin. Art Pepper almost certainly never read St. Augustine or Rousseau, but this latter-day confession is rooted in those predecessors, just as his blistering alto sound grew out of Charlie Parker, Benny Carter, and Willie Smith.

Pepper the musician is portrayed vividly in the pages of this book, but so are Pepper the addict, the thief, the pervert, the narcissist, the voyeur, the convict. As if this self-revelation were not enough, Pepper quotes his "friends" at length as they add to the charges.

Has any entertainer's autobiography ever gone to such lengths to tell the whole story, to present a rounded and unflinching portrait of the artist as a young scumbag? Certainly other jazz autobiographers have included passages written by friends of the subject, but most outside contributions have all the authenticity of speeches made at a testimonial dinner—for the ultimate example see Dizzy Gillespie's comprehensive *To Be or Not to Bop*, where the platitudes never stop. Pepper's friends and acquaintances come across, by comparison, as participants at a celebrity "roast," albeit one in which the implicit good humor typical of such events is noticeably absent.

Pepper the addict may incur our criticism; Pepper the writer may draw our amazement; but it is Pepper the musician who earned his place in the history of jazz. Yet an individual does not exist piecemeal; links between life and art have been the critics obsession at least since the time of Vasari. And rightly so. Who can deny that, in Pepper's case, this extraordinary candor, which overwhelms the reader of *Straight Life*, also played its part in the man's music? Emotional honesty of an extreme degree gave Art

Pepper's music its raw edge. If Pepper told all in his 1979 auto-biography, he was also letting it all hang out night after night on the bandstand. Especially at the end of his life. It was almost as if writing the book had a cathartic effect on his playing; there too his attitude was increasingly "Here I am, warts and all." The missed notes, the painfully bent tones, the honks, the distorted sounds—all mixed with the sweetest lyrical passages.

His late ballad "Everything Happens to Me"—which was being prepared for release on the *Roadgame* album at the time of his death on June 15, 1982—brings all these things together, and though you would swear that so many disparate elements could never cohere in the context of a thirty-two-bar solo, somehow Pepper pulls it off. Pepper never agreed with Lester Young's statement that you need to know the lyrics to play a ballad. "I don't know the words to any song. Maybe 'America the Beautiful,'" he said in 1981—then added: "No, I don't even know that." [1] But the poignant world-weariness and self-pitying lament of these lyrics seemed echoed in every note of this gripping performance. If Pepper was an egomaniac (And could anyone who spent more than five minutes in conversation with him deny it? When I interviewed him, he dwelled at length on the injustice *Down Beat* had done him by never putting him on the cover.), it was only another side of the intense self-assertion that brought his music so tellingly to life. The whole man, with all his contradictions and flaws and pains, entered into his music.

The music of Art Pepper from the 1950s had more of the sweetness and less of the *Angst* that one finds in his later playing, and this, too, was reflective of the man. Thirty years before *Roadgame*, Pepper recorded "Everything Happens to Me" as part of one of his first dates as a leader for the Discovery label. The easy, relaxed mastery of the song was as fitting then as his later anguished rendition was in his charged circumstances. In 1952, everything bad had yet to happen to Art Pepper. For two years running, he had finished second in the *Down Beat* poll, placing behind only the legendary Charlie Parker. If not universally accepted as the greatest alto saxophonist in the world—that being his often stated goal—Pepper was recognized as one of the masters of his instrument. At only 27, Pepper must have felt his best was yet to come.

By then Pepper had already come a long way. His troubles began MacDuff-like, according to his autobiography, while still in the womb. His teenage mother tried various methods of inducing miscarriage. Although she failed, her child was born—on September 1, 1925, in Gardena, California—sickly and frail. Pepper attributed his early poor health, including rickets and jaundice, to her attempts at self-induced abortion. At age five he left home to live with his grandmother on a ranch farm near Perris, California; and soon they moved to Los Angeles before finally settling in the nearby beach community of San Pedro. At nine Pepper began studying clarinet—he wanted to learn trumpet, but a local music teacher advised him that his teeth were not strong enough for the instrument—and at twelve he started playing the alto saxophone. By the age of fifteen, he had lost his interest in school bands, and he began looking for opportunities to sit in with working jazz groups.

Soon Pepper was gigging on Central Avenue, where he learned about an opening in Gus Arnheim's band in San Diego. It took little prodding for him to leave school—his attendance at Fremont High was sporadic at best—and take the job. After three months in San Diego, he returned to Central Avenue, where, from Dexter Gordon, he heard of an opening in Lee Young's band at the Club Alabam. Pepper auditioned for the spot at the black musicians' union—the unions would remain segregated in Los Angeles for years to come—and won the job.

Lee Young's band provided heady company for a seventeen-year-old white alto saxophonist from San Pedro. Lee's brother Lester was Pepper's earliest idol. (Pepper described Lester as "one of the greatest saxophone players that ever lived in the world. The most fantastic—equalled only fairly recently by John Coltrane. Better than Charlie Parker. In my humble opinion, better than Charlie Parker, just marvelous, such beauty.")[2] While gigging on Central Avenue, Pepper also played with some of his most promising LA contemporaries, such as Dexter Gordon and Charles Mingus. After work he would go to the nearby after-hours clubs to hear the legendary players of the older generation: Louis Armstrong, Lester Young, Art Tatum, Ben Webster, Coleman Hawkins, Johnny Hodges, and others. Little wonder Pepper would claim, years later, "I attribute whatever ability I have to play jazz to those times on The Avenue. I didn't know what chord it was, but I was in an atmosphere of great jazz feeling, and I think it stayed with me."[3] Pepper's musical education at the Alabam took place both onstage and in the back room. The precocious altoist was getting by on his strong ear at this time; not only did he lack any knowledge of harmony, but he was also a poor reader. Between shows, fellow saxophonist Jack McVea gave Pepper impromptu music lessons on reading stock arrangements. "I'd go into the dressing room with Art and I'd go over his parts with him, "McVea relates. "He learned real fast, you know."[4]

Central Avenue was home turf for the leading black jazz musicians in Southern California, and though integrated bands were something of a rarity, they posed no problem in the black district (in striking contrast to some other Los Angeles neighborhoods). Harry James, Artie Shaw, Buddy Rich, and Vido Musso, among others, were known to sit in on Central Avenue when they were in town. Lee Young had already featured Jimmy Rowles in his band before Pepper joined on. Barney Kessel, Russ Freeman, and other white musicians of the period invariably describe their experiences on the Avenue as positive ones in which racial tension rarely came to the fore.

The Central Avenue days perhaps also contributed to the essentially black aesthetic that remained at the heart of Pepper's music for the rest of his life. The experiences of the black underclass have long served, in the words of critic Gary Giddins, as "the best possible source for self-examination" for the most probing white jazz musicians. The oppression of a minority—whether political, religious, or ethnic—has long borne an uncanny relation to the production of art of lasting value. (I recall a literary critic once pointing out to me that the history of poetic masterpieces in English literature characteristically showed that poets produced their finest works when their own political party was out of power. The argument, however tendentious when set out in such an extreme form, contains more than a grain of truth.) The undaunted vitality of black music during much of this century is no accidental circumstance. It is the bitter fruit harvested by a race that has been forced, by its very existence, into constant self-awareness and uneasy self-assertion. This was an element of the jazz experience white musicians could appreciate, at best, only secondhand. The tension and intensity characteristic of the jazz experience had, for the black creators of the music, all too many corollaries in their nonmusical lives.

The best white jazz artists have often felt, whether consciously or subconsciously, that they belonged to an underclass. And even if the black/white dichotomy was not the cause of this inner sense of isolation, the situation of their black colleagues must have served as an apt symbol for the alienation they experienced in their own lives. Pepper's autobiography is full of telling anecdotes in this regard, and one imagines that the psychology of a Chet Baker, a Bill Evans, a Stan Getz, or even a Bix Beiderbecke, were it probed as deeply as Pepper has done in his book, would reflect similar feelings of isolation from the norms and expectations of society. Perhaps such musicians were initially attracted to jazz because it was (and is) the art of an oppressed, underclass sensibility. Jazz is the art form of the outsider, whether racially, musically, or psychologically. In 1979, Pepper recalled the roots of his early identification with jazz musicians: "At the beginning, when I was very young, playing on Central Avenue, I asked someone about [alto saxophonist] Willie Smith and that he looked so white, and they told me that he was a seventh-grain negro, and

I remember wishing that I was. I wanted to be black because I felt such an affinity to the music."[5] Years later when Pepper recorded as a sideman under the pseudonym "Art Salt," he was delighted to learn that some listeners thought Salt was a black alto player. Freddy Rivera, amplifying on this undercurrent in Pepper's self-image, suggests that the altoist was very much at home during his later prison terms, because he was then in "an environment where he could *identify*, believing unconsciously that he was a black sheep, ostracized from the 'respectable' world. Feeling that way all of his life, he could readily identify with all these other outcasts."[6] Jack Sheldon recalls that Pepper retained the isolated convict mentality even when on the outside: "He would stay in his room all the time. His life was like he was still in prison."[7] Drugs, legal problems, alcohol, eccentricity, isolation—perhaps these are not haphazard elements in the biographies of Pepper, Baker, Getz, Evans, Beiderbecke, but are as representative of their true selves as their affinity with jazz. They craved the position of the outsider, the loner, the oppressed.

For the young Art Pepper, his music, even more than his lifestyle, was well suited to the Central Avenue setting of his first efforts at public performance. Only a few years later, West Coast Jazz would gain notoriety for its supposed emphasis on complex compositional structures, unique instrumentation, and a laid-back improvisational style, but Central Avenue in the 1940s gave little hint of this emerging sound. The music in the air at Lovejoy's, the Downbeat, or the Last Word was typically hard-swinging, loosely arranged, often informal, with an emphasis on improvisational brilliance rather than compositional ingenuity. Throughout his career Pepper's music would bear the stamp of these same mercurial qualities: With few exceptions (the most noteworthy being his collaborations with Marty Paich), the best work of his career came from informal small-group sessions, often done with little preparation.

It is telling that Pepper, in his autobiography and various interviews, tried to understate the amount of preparation he actually did—for example, he explains that he had not touched his horn for months when he recorded *Art Pepper Meets the Rhythm Section*, yet his discography shows that he participated in several sessions in the weeks preceding the date. Similarly, he always claimed to practice the horn very little, implying that his technical fluency simply emerged through native talent. "I don't practice much, but I think about music all the time," Pepper told me during our interview. Obviously there is a fair degree of truth mixed with the hyperbole in Pepper's assertions, but it is equally clear that his ideal of what a jazz musician should be involved a rejection of conventional notions of diligence, practice, and decorum. His ethos was of inspiration, not preparation.

In the same vein, Pepper prided himself on his compositions, but he never followed the model of Mulligan, Giuffre, Rogers, and other West Coast players in pursuing writing as a serious form of self-expression. His compositions were invariably vehicles for his own soloing, and they succeeded or failed on that basis. Indeed many of his pieces follow the bebopper's practice of adding a new melody to a standard chord progression—Pepper's composition "Straight Life," for example, is based on the chords to "After You've Gone"—the result being new compositions that remained familiar and comfortable settings for straight-ahead blowing. Above all, Pepper followed the Central Avenue model in his unrelenting emphasis on swing. More than any other white jazz musician's of his day, Pepper's sense of swing was at the very heart of his music. Stoking the rhythmic fire was second nature to him, akin to breathing or walking. In each of these respects Pepper stayed true to the culture of this early setting for his musical exploits.

Through Lee Young's intervention, Pepper got an audition for the open saxophone chair in the Benny Carter band. Pepper made the band, and though he played second alto behind Carter, occasionally the latter would let the youngster take the lead and play his solo spots. It is easy to hear echoes of Carter in the later Pepper, especially in his appealing manner of combining sweet-toned lyricism with a strong sense of swing. The older altoist was a past master at this rare hybrid: There were plenty of "hot" players around at the time, but few could match Carter at driving the band without losing this underlying sweetness. Pepper flourished in this conducive setting for his musical development.

At this point Pepper was still playing by ear, unaware of chord structure and harmonic progressions, but his strong musical talent let him go further within these limitations than most could go even with the deepest grasp of theory. His colleagues with the Carter band were as impressive as his musical companions at the Alabam. In addition to Carter, the group brought him into contact with such present and future jazz luminaries as Freddie Webster, J. J. Johnson, and Gerald Wilson. The band played in and around Los Angeles, and Pepper also accompanied the group to Salt Lake City. But when Carter was preparing to embark on a tour of the South, he was forced to drop Pepper from the band. It was far too risky to bring an integrated group to that part of the country.

Carter talked to his manager, Carlos Gastel, who also represented the Stan Kenton band. Soon Pepper was part of the Kenton orchestra, just in time for its new recording association with Capitol Records. His experience playing with Carter held him in good stead in the new ensemble; at the same time, the more complex arrangements of the Kenton orchestra forced him to learn to read chord changes instead of relying on his ear alone. Pepper was with the group for only about three months before receiving his draft notice, but before leaving he made his recording debut with a solo on two takes of "Harlem Folk Dance," recorded on November 19, 1943. He was barely eighteen years old. He was inducted at Fort MacArthur on February 11, 1944, and soon sent to Fort Sill, Oklahoma, for basic training. Right before he was scheduled to be shipped out to combat, he was transferred into a military band. Most of his remaining time in the service was spent playing in bands and serving as an MP in England.

At the close of 1946 Pepper left the army and returned to California, where he soon discovered, much to his dismay, that a musical revolution had taken place during his absence. While overseas he had not even heard the word *bebop*, let alone encountered the music being played by Parker, Gillespie, and the new generation of modernists. "When I came out, I didn't know anything about what was happening over here," Pepper later explained.[8]

> I got home, a friend of mine came by and said, "I want you to hear these records." He had two records, and one he had was with Sonny Stitt and Dizzy—"Oop Bob Sh'Bam" and "That's Earl, Brother." That record was the first one I heard, and I said, "Oh, my God," and I just got sick. I just couldn't believe it. And then the next record I heard was, I think it was "Salt Peanuts," and that other real fast one—it was "Shaw Nuff." That thing was so fast. . . . When I heard Bird I just got deathly sick. I couldn't stand any more, and he was going to play something else, and I said, "No, no, I can't stand it. I can't listen to any more."

The initial sense of musical vertigo soon gave way to the altoist's kindled desire to master the new music. Already an accomplished professional, having gained notoriety with Benny Carter, Stan Kenton and others, Pepper was forced to return to the woodshed to keep pace with the rapidly changing musical environment of the postwar years. Eventually he would forge a partnership between swing and bop, hot and cool, that would stand out as one of the most authentic alto sounds of the 1950s. Indeed, much of the beauty of his later style stems from the lyrical prebop underpinnings that meld with the modern and postmodern jazz inflections in his playing: "I really dug Bird, but I didn't want Bird to destroy me. I didn't want that to happen to me that I heard so many other guys do. . . . I really worked at that very hard. I more or less gave myself a pep talk that I've got to go out and play, and I couldn't ignore the new thing because I had to be modern but I had to keep me, I couldn't lose myself."[9]

Two decades later Pepper would weather another crisis of confidence in the face of the new music of John Coltrane—so much so that he even temporarily switched to tenor saxophone—but here, too, he eventually succeeded (and reached a higher level in his own playing) by incorporating the more modern approach into his own distinctive alto voice. Much of Pepper's genius lay in this serpentine ability to swallow whole the styles of his most illustrious contemporaries while remaining true to himself.

Resettled in Los Angeles, Pepper worked on assimilating the new bop sounds, meanwhile doing casual gigs. This same time period found the altoist becoming increasingly dependent on alcohol, marijuana, and pills. For a brief time Pepper took a day job in a meat-packing plant, until an unexpected phone call from Stan Kenton led to Pepper's rejoining the band. Soon he was again living the nomadic life of a road musician. During the second Kenton stint, Pepper's music continued to develop, and his solo work with the band began to show the mature presence of a strongly personalized saxophonist.

Pepper's music from the period reflects what seems a different man from the anguished addict portrayed in *Straight Life*. In due course, his playing would communicate more than a small dose of these painful emotions, but his solos with the Kenton band are another thing entirely. On his feature number, the Shorty Rogers composition, "Art Pepper," the altoist begins with a long, slow interlude that is simply and unaffectedly pretty. Like Getz, who did something similar in his "Early Autumn" feature with the Herman band, Pepper somehow was able to pull this off without sounding saccharine or sentimental. It came across not as a shallow or contrived prettiness, the calling card of so much popular music, but more like the innocent beauty of a child. Even when the tempo doubles on this piece, Pepper's complex melodic lines do not destroy the earlier impression. There is something carefree about this whole performance, almost in defiance of the pretentious instrumentation.

Rogers obviously found this particular aspect of Pepper's playing especially moving, because his several later attempts at writing and composing for the altoist typically tried to recapture this same kind of simple sweetness. Rogers's arrangement of "Over the Rainbow" is noteworthy here, but perhaps the most striking example is "Bunny"—the piece named for Art and Patti's French poodle—from the January 12, 1953, session for Rogers and his Giants. (Rogers's predilection for naming compositions after pets borders on the extreme: "Popo," "Didi," and "Sam and the Lady," for example, all are dedications to various cats owned by producer Gene Norman.) Like its predecessor "Art Pepper," "Bunny" begins with a meditative calmness that is broken by a lilting up-tempo section.

At the close of 1951, Pepper left the Kenton band. Although he was one of the highest-paid members of the orchestra and developing a national reputation for his alto work, Pepper was tired of the hassles of life on the road—aggravated by the difficulties of scoring heroin in constantly changing locations—and anxious for more musical freedom than the modest degree allowed him in a big band setting. His departure was part of a larger exodus from the Kenton band at this time, which also saw Shorty Rogers and Shelly Manne leaving the fold. Pepper's decision to go on his own put him, at least temporarily, in an uncertain financial state. With the expenses of married life and his increasing drug dependency, Pepper found himself with a number of outstanding bills and no regular source of income. The almost immediate opportunity to record with Shorty Rogers and his newly formed Giants was a godsend. Pepper's feature on "Over the Rainbow" became one of the most popular recordings of his career (he kept the number in his repertoire until the end of his life, recording a much more harrowing version of it in the late 1970s) and was an important success at a time when he was about to form his own group.

Largely on the strength of the notoriety earned with Rogers and Kenton, Pepper formed a group under his own leadership early in 1952. He brought the band into the Surf Club, a tiny jazz

nightspot located at the corner of 6th and Manhattan in Hollywood. Despite the name, the Surf was no hangout for jazz-lov-
ing beachcombers, but rather a ramshackle saloon, located miles
from the nearest surfing spot, which could hardly seat more than
fifty or sixty fans. In contrast to the low-key surroundings, the
caliber of the entertainment was world-class: Pepper's sidemen
included pianist Hampton Hawes, Shelly Manne, or Larry
Bunker on drums, and bassist Joe Mondragon. Richard Bock,
then an unemployed student taking classes at Los Angeles City
College on the GI Bill, was one of the enthusiastic listeners who
first heard Pepper in person during this engagement. Bock had
recently completed a two-year apprenticeship as Albert Marx's
assistant at Discovery Records. Although Marx had ceased operations, his former understudy tried to interest the new owner of
the Discovery masters, New York distributor Jack Bergman, in
letting him produce the Pepper quartet for the label. With
Bergman's go-ahead, the musicians assembled on March 4,
1952, at MacGregor Studios in Hollywood to cut Pepper's first
date as a leader. The four tracks recorded that day, in particular
the fast-paced "Surf Ride," showcased Pepper's exuberant and
effortless alto stylings, with Hawes providing a perfect piano
counterpart. It is easy to view Hawes, like Pepper, as a tragic figure, an anguished victim of addiction, but the music here seems
more a statement of pure exultation. Perhaps this is the other
side of the junkie's live-for-the-day mentality: This is uplifting
music of the here-and-now.

Three days after this session, a glowing article on Pepper, written by Bock, appeared in *Down Beat*. (Such disregard of obvious
conflicts of interest were—and are—not uncommon among a few
of the "old school" critics.) "This year may well prove to be the
most important one yet in the career of Art Pepper. . . . He has
earned an enviable reputation and large following as one of the
most consistent of the modern jazzmen."[10] Bock's questionable
impartiality aside, Pepper clearly had come into his own by the
time of the Discovery date. He had always been a distinctive

soloist, but now for the first time he began to focus his attention on composing original material. Two of his finest compositions—his ballad "Patricia" and the barn-burner "Straight Life"—were penned during this period. The former piece was named for his daughter, whom he finally grew to know and love during this relatively happy time in his life. Pepper's career was on the upswing. With his earnings from the Surf Club and other venues, he was able to buy a tract house on the GI Bill. In a manner typical of his topsy-turvy ethics, Pepper refused to use his music earnings to support his drug habit, instead relying on the money he made from dealing to subsidize his own use.

Finally, on the urging of his father, Pepper entered a sanitarium in Garden Grove, where during a several-week stay, he was slowly broken of his addiction through a process of gradually decreasing injections of morphine. His father had taken out a mortgage on his home to pay for the treatment, and Pepper had entered the program in good faith, but after only a short period on the outside he was using again. Finally, in 1953, he was forced to quit cold turkey under less comfortable circumstances. He was arrested on heroin possession charges and incarcerated in the Los Angeles County Jail. Later he claimed that during this anguishing period of breaking the habit, he went seventeen days and nights without sleeping, plagued by chills and pains, constantly vomiting and unable to eat. The only "treatment" available at the jail was an occasional aspirin. At his trial, Pepper pled *nolo contendere* and was sentenced to two years in the federal hospital at Fort Worth.

The Route

In 1954, Pepper was paroled from Fort Worth and returned to Los Angeles. Some casual gigs with tenor saxophonist Jack Montrose led to a recording session for the two horn players on the Discovery label. On August 25, they entered the studio, where they were ably supported by a rhythm section comprised of Claude Williamson, Larry Bunker, and Monty Budwig. Montrose proved to be an ideal collaborator with Pepper—years later Pepper would mention that only with Montrose and Warne Marsh was he able to share the front line and still play freely. The group's performance of "Deep Purple" bears witness to this claim with its spontaneous opening counterpoint, which segues nicely into Pepper's lead-off solo. A more tightly arranged opening graces the equally compelling "Nutmeg." (Spices seemed to be on the altoist's mind during this session. In addition to "Nutmeg," the other originals include "Cinnamon," "Art's Oregano," and "Thyme Time." Drug culture cognoscenti of the time might have appreciated the titles—ingestion of large amounts of spices was one of the few legal highs available to an addict cut off from contraband.) More noteworthy than the kitchen cabinet song titles was Pepper's playing on the date. Here we begin to hear a more probing, impassioned soloist than the one who graced the Kenton or Rogers bands, or even the Surf Club quartet. Despite, or perhaps because of, the tribulations of his private life, Pepper's music comes across here as stronger and deeper than ever.

The Montrose date would be Pepper's only studio recording before another period of imprisonment. By the end of 1954, Pepper was using forty caps of heroin a day, and his weight was down to 128 pounds. On December 7, 1954, he was arrested while trying to score heroin, but the only charge that could stick was possession of codeine tablets—for which he was sentenced to six months in the county jail. The arrest was perhaps a hidden blessing. Later he would say, "I could have been using maybe a hundred caps a day in another month if I had access to that much, because the demand just builds and builds."[11] Given his past record, Pepper was forced to serve nineteen months, most of it at the federal penitentiary on Terminal Island, near his boyhood home in San Pedro.

In the late spring of 1956, Pepper was released from Terminal Island. Despite his newfound freedom, his situation at this time was far from enviable. His marriage had failed; he had lost his house and car; and he had not worked a steady jazz gig since November 1954. Moreover, his reputation was tainted by the now widely publicized details of his addiction. To make matters even worse, he was soon using again. Pepper was befriended by a big-time drug dealer, Mario Cuevas, who became enamored of the altoist's talent and provided him with a regular (and steadily increasing) supply of heroin. Pepper later wrote and recorded a song for Cuevas: the poignant 5/4 blues "Las Cuevas de Mario" from the altoist's 1960 *Smack Up* album. In his autobiography Pepper calls Cuevas, in another example of the altoist's odd value system, "one of the greatest people I've ever met in my life."

By the beginning of 1957, Pepper's increasing dependency on heroin was taking its toll on his career. He missed gigs. He stopped looking for work. He did not return phone calls or would not take them even when he was in. With the exception of an occasional record date, he stayed at home behind locked doors and windows and, in his words, would "fix all day and night." Whatever money he had went to Cuevas in return for drugs: "Whenever I came to I'd just cook again. Sometimes the spike would be lying on the floor or still stuck in my arm so when I woke up I'd have to clean it out, get it unplugged. I'd start cutting the light fixtures. I'd be cutting the cords and the plugs to get wires to stick into the spike to clean it. I would have ripped up anything in the house to unplug that needle."[12]

One Saturday morning near the close of January, Pepper was awakened by his girlfriend Diane (soon to become his second wife) and told that he had a record date scheduled for that day. Les Koenig and Diane had arranged the session behind his back, fearing that he would back out unless it was set up as a *fait accompli*. Miles Davis was performing in Hollywood that week, and Koenig had arranged to bring Davis's world-class rhythm section into the studio for a session with Pepper. Davis's band featured drummer Philly Joe Jones, bassist Paul Chambers, and pianist Red Garland—perhaps the finest working rhythm session in jazz during that period. Koenig, one of the altoist's staunchest supporters, felt this was the perfect opportunity to feature Pepper in a setting that would challenge him to the utmost.

In Pepper's circumstances, the challenge must have seemed almost too great. He had played the alto only infrequently during the six months since his release from prison. Trying to prepare his horn for this unexpected session, Pepper discovered that he had not taken it apart since the last time he played. Now, when he tried to remove the mouthpiece, the cork on the neck of his saxophone came off with it. With no time to repair the damage, he put the mouthpiece back on—the cork still in it—and taped it into place. Before leaving the house, Pepper fixed one more time, so he would be steady for the recording. Arriving at the studio, he met the other players. The title of the eventual album, *Art Pepper Meets the Rhythm Section*, was no exercise in poetic license; he truly met them for the first time at the session. Needless to say, he had never played with them before, and there was obviously no time for a rehearsal. Even the basic task of choosing songs had not yet been done.

Despite these unpropitious circumstances, Pepper recorded one of the finest albums of his career. His playing here begins to show the mature qualities that would characterize his work to the end. In the past, it seemed, two different musical personae had made up Art Pepper: a lyrical, sweet side, epitomized in the several feature pieces Shorty Rogers had written for him, and the saxophone virtuoso, whose biting improvisations on the earlier recordings of "Straight Life" and "Cherokee" were full of spark and flash. By the time of his early thirties—he was thirty-one when he recorded *Meets the Rhythm Section*—these two selves had begun to coalesce. From now on, even Pepper's ballads probed deeper and took on the biting intensity formerly reserved for up-tempo work; at the same time, his fast work no longer relied so heavily on technical displays. Now each phrase came across as deeply felt, a personal statement that refused to be reduced to a manifestation of virtuosity. In time, Pepper would develop almost an antivirtuosity, one in which his missed notes, jagged phrases, distorted tones, honks, and cries would stand side by side with the passages of effortless fluency. Hints of this transformation can be heard on *Meets the Rhythm Section.* In the 1970s, this aspect of Pepper's playing would reach full flower in a series of brilliant recordings for the Galaxy and Contemporary labels.

What comes across on this 1956 recording is the focused vitality of a player for whom every note counts. Describing music in words is always a challenging task, but pinpointing the change in Art Pepper's music during this period is especially elusive. Above all one gets a sense here of musical conviction, difficult to define but easy enough to feel, which goes beyond Pepper's previous efforts. Even when he lets his fingers fly, as on the group's re-recording of "Straight Life," one hears a deeper level of commitment than on the earlier version of the tune. That this should happen at a point in Pepper's life when his involvement in music seemed most detached is difficult to comprehend. Perhaps the musical side of him, which for so long had been undernourished, asserted itself in reaction to the dissipation of his personal life. One can only speculate, and perhaps such speculations should be left to the psychologists. In any event, Pepper's performances during these darkest days recall the truism of the spirit being willing while the flesh is weak. This playing exemplifies willing and willfulness *par excellence.*

Not that all of Pepper's performance from this period are at a uniformly high level. Almost immediately after his release from Terminal Island, he was slotted by Richard Bock to record with Chet Baker for Pacific Jazz Records. The combination of Art Pepper and Chet Baker, the two bad boys of jazz, must have seemed to many West Coast jazz fans like a musical match made in heaven. Beyond the compatibility of their boyish good looks and fast-paced lifestyles (the pairing was marketed as the "Playboys of Jazz"), their playing indicated a powerful affinity. As much as any two musicians of the 1950s, Baker and Pepper represented the most telling mixture of the sweet and the hot: Their playing was pretty without being saccharine or shallow, and their souls could burn without ever losing their melodic integrity. Their music could be appreciated on the surface, where it glistened with all the mellow beauty that *was* "West Coast jazz" according to the pundits, but those who wanted to probe deeper could hear a raw honesty that was anything but superficial. Truly one had high hopes for such a pairing.

The Baker–Pepper collaboration, to be sure, produced some noteworthy performances, but one leaves them vaguely disappointed. The first session, from July 26, 1956, finds the duo joined by Richie Kamuca in the front line and supported by a rhythm section consisting of Leroy Vinnegar, Pete Jolly, and Stan Levey. On "Minor Yours" and "Little Girl" both Baker and Pepper contribute individually strong solos, but there is no sense of chemistry between the two—as one finds, for example, in Baker's collaborations with Desmond or Mulligan or, to perhaps a slightly lesser degree, in Pepper's work with Jack Sheldon. Johnny Mandel's sophisticated arrangements, which would have been well suited for the Lighthouse All-Stars or Shorty Rogers's Giants, are too constricting for Baker and Pepper. On "Tynan Time," written for *Down Beat's* West Coast correspondent John Tynan, Pepper sounds like a parody of himself. His playing always had a swashbuckling quality in which the jagged rhythms of his phrases were set off by pregnant pauses, but here the phrases are uncommonly stark and the rests uncomfortably protracted. Put simply, Pepper sounds angry: "This is my session and I'll sulk if I want to." "The Route" is much better and noticeably unarranged, with Pepper's blues solo starting sweet as honey and slowly building to a heated conclusion. Baker follows, and he makes it clear that he wants to follow a different road map on this route. He begins gently, as though he were playing a lullaby to a toddler, and only barely raises the energy level during the solo. He sounds as though he is back in the Mulligan Quartet and trying to be as low-key as possible.

This playing at cross-purposes is representative of the whole session. Baker and Pepper (and for that matter Kamuca) do not seem to be listening to each other. It is perhaps no coincidence that the altoist's best work from this session took place when

Baker and Kamuca sat out, leaving Pepper to stretch out on the "Cherokee"-based "Ol' "Croix." This gradual attrition, whether planned or spontaneous, continued with Jolly departing and Pepper attempting two numbers with just bass and drums. The whole event, especially given Bock's piecemeal way of releasing the music, has the look of a desperate attempt to find some combination of these talented musicians that might click.

Follow-up work from a Halloween date follows a similar formula. Again Baker and Pepper are joined by a third horn player, this time tenor saxophonist Phil Urso. Again a guest arranger is brought in, this time Jimmy Heath, who relies heavily on his own compositions. The addition of pianist Carl Perkins is quite welcome, especially in light of the exceptional later collaborations between Perkins and Pepper, and the supporting presence of Curtis Counce and Lawrence Marable promised a first-rate recording date. While a step above the first session, this second Baker-Pepper pairing still gets bogged down by the overly elaborate arrangements and the unnecessary third horn. One craves hearing just Pepper and Baker, backed by the rhythm section, work their way through some standards.

Perhaps part of the problem was simply that, for all their shared peculiarities of lifestyle, Pepper and Baker never really warmed up to each other as individuals. Baker, in an unprecedented display of prudery, has gone on record as being aghast at Pepper's lifestyle. Pepper, in contrast, stops short of this pot-calling-the-kettle-black mentality. He remained oddly silent on the subject of Baker. It comes as some surprise that Pepper had absolutely nothing to say about Baker during the course of some five hundred pages of *Straight Life*. In many articles published on Pepper, the journalist or interviewer reached for the obvious comparison with Baker, but Art never did so. This uncharacteristic reticence combined with the duo's surprisingly few collaborations suggests that some hidden feud or bad blood separated the two. Perhaps the answer is simpler still: Each may have seen too much of himself in the other.

Despite the mixed results of the Baker collaboration, these works have been reissued in many formats and are widely known. The same cannot be said unfortunately, for the masterful work Pepper recorded a short time later for Omegatape. These January 1958 performances are far less known than the celebrated work with Miles's rhythm section, but they are no less compelling. If one is looking for a neglected Pepper masterpiece from the 1950s, this is where to go. The reason for the neglect no doubt stems from the strange fact that these performances were originally issued solely on reel-to-reel tape format, and thus were unavailable to the vast majority of jazz record buyers. These electrifying performances, long overlooked, should now take their rightful place as key jazz recordings from the late 1950s.

The original session was instigated by Manny Koppelman, a sometime record producer with no track record in jazz. In early 1958, he brought Pepper's working quartet into a small Hollywood studio to record a project for what he hoped would be a growing home market for reel-to-reel tapes. Even then Pepper and his bandmates must have realized that this was a fairly arcane project, not likely to be widely heard, and this perhaps contributed to the relaxed informality of the session. Over a dozen successful takes were made, possibly in a single session, of a uniformly high quality.

The supporting cast of Carl Perkins, Chuck Flores, and Ben Tucker may be less well known than the Garland/Chambers/Philly Joe unit, but on the strength of these works they must be considered one of the strongest rhythm sections on the West Coast during the decade. Perkins's tremendous talents were, of course, no secret in Los Angeles. Although his reputation never made much headway on the East Coast (despite the deep admiration Miles Davis had for his ability), he retains a cult following among California jazz aficionados some quarter-century after his death. January 1958—some six weeks before Perkins's death—was a fruitful period for the pianist, with the Pepper date as well as sessions with Curtis Counce and Harold Land producing outstanding work. Pepper told *Down Beat* in October of that year that Perkins's work on the Omegatape recordings was the finest of the pianist's career. Pepper's praise, at least on this occasion, represented neither empty hype nor sentimental eulogizing.

As for the other members of the band, Flores and Tucker were not viewed as major innovators in West Coast jazz during the 1950s, but you might think otherwise on the strength of these recordings. Bassist Tucker, a Tennessee native born in Nashville on December 13, 1930, graced the bands of Pepper, Bill Perkins, Warne Marsh, and Chico Hamilton before moving to New York in 1959. Chuck Flores, a Californian born in Orange on January 5, 1935, had recorded with Shorty Rogers, Woody Herman, and Al Cohn, among others, by the time of the Omegatape date. Both were strong journeyman players on the LA scene, and both were at peak form for the Pepper/Perkins date. The band is tight and swings like crazy.

Some might attribute the cohesion of this group to their long experience as a working band. Yet though these four did in fact work together, their engagements were anything but steady. Flores recalls the band working on no more than a half-dozen occasions between 1956 and 1958. Pepper's prison record may, in fact, have resulted in a blacklisting in many Southern California nightspots. In any event, work for the altoist was sporadic at best. Moreover, when the band did work, Perkins was never a permanent member, often being replaced by Russ Freeman or Pete Jolly. Yet this was as close as Pepper ever got to a working unit during the decade, and the chemistry between the band members is quite apparent. All three musicians had also recorded with Pepper in the past, Flores and Tucker in particular having shared several sessions with him.

The previous May, *Down Beat's* John Tynan had reviewed the group during their two-week stay at the Tiffany Club. "Pepper never has sounded better," Tynan wrote. "The sidemen provide superior support and solo well. Eastern exposure is strongly recommended—fast."[13] "Despite Tynan's admonition, Pepper received virtually no East Coast exposure with this group—or any other of his bands from the 1950s. However, the recorded evidence suggests that this band might have taken Manhattan by storm with its easy mastery of a variety of musical moods. On "Without a Song" Pepper's opening break sets a powerful bluesy mood, and from then on it sounds as though he and Perkins are trying to outdo each other in down-home funkiness—a duel that culminates in a memorable series of exchanges between the two soloists. "Fascinating Rhythm" serves as an ideal up-tempo feature for Pepper—Gershwin wrote the melody, but its quirky syncopation sounds like something Pepper would compose himself—and he stretches out comfortably on its changes. The rap against Perkins was that he couldn't play ballads, but on "Body and Soul" he takes a majestic two-handed solo that proves otherwise, while Pepper merely states the melody, but with a kind of conviction that looks forward to his anguish-laden later work. The all too short Latin vamp leading into "Begin the Beguine" was also anticipatory: His later extended use of such vamps would bring out the very best in Pepper, so much so that they would come to dwarf the song they introduced or completed. Here the vamp lingers briefly before settling into a comfortable medium-groove rendition of this convoluted (a 108-measure-long form!) Cole Porter composition.

Pepper's large-group collaborations with Marty Paich struck a different vein entirely. Both Pepper and Paich had been impressed with Gerry Mulligan's ten-piece group, and they decided to emulate that instrumentation, but the similarity with the Mulligan band ended there. Their conception was to create a hotter, more bop-oriented sound than typically found in the nonets and tentettes that were a staple of West Coast jazz during the 1950s. Paich recalls that the original model for the *Art Pepper plus Eleven* album was not, as most have assumed, the Miles Davis Nonet or the similar ensembles headed by Rogers and Mulligan but the small combo music of Charlie Parker.

Lester Koenig, who owned Contemporary records, put us together and said, "Why don't we do an album of Charlie Parker songs?" That's exactly the way it came about. So I got together with Art and we had about 25 songs, then it got down to 20, then down to 15, and it got down to the normal 10 or 11 songs that were on the album. . . . The Charlie Parker stuff up until that time was just done with two front line, alto and trumpet. . . . Our idea was to do the same thing with a band.[14]

Certainly the influence of the Miles Davis Nonet is not totally absent in these recordings, but to focus on that element alone is to miss most of the story. The enduring appeal of these performances resides in their willingness to break out of the Miles/Evans/Mulligan mold, to combine the birth of the cool with the coming of age of the hot. In this regard, Pepper was the ideal soloist. He had deep roots in the cool, melodic approach followed by Miles and Mulligan, but he also instinctively knew how to push up the energy level of a performance, how to kick a band into overdrive. His unique blending of gentle lyricism and raw passion brought the Paich arrangements to life.

Tears Inside

The Paich big band sessions for Warner Brothers, coming only a few weeks after the recording of *Art Pepper plus Eleven,* serve in many ways as a counterpart to that work. Once again Pepper is featured prominently, and Paich, relying heavily on Ellington compositions, shows that he has also learned Duke's technique of fitting the arrangement to the players involved. On "It Don't Mean a Thing (If It Ain't Got That Swing)" and "Violets for Your Furs," the charts are perfectly built around Pepper's sound. The collaborations between these two artists remain among the most satisfying meetings of musical minds West Coast jazz produced. Paich recognized this compatibility and went out of his way to include Pepper as often as possible in the various projects he pursued—for Tormé, Jesse Belvin, the Hi-Los, and others—at a time when Pepper's drug-related notoriety made him *persona non grata* in most studio sessions. Between 1958 and 1960, Paich was directly or indirectly responsible for almost half of the recordings in the Pepper discography. Although many of these sessions find the altoist making only an occasional contribution as a soloist, still Paich's advocacy was vital in documenting much of Pepper's recorded legacy from this period. Paich recalls:

> Art would not conform like the other musicians in town. . . . He was such a devoted saxophone player, he didn't want to try to double on flute or do any of the stuff that the usual musicians had to do in order to make a living. So a lot of guys didn't hire him for that reason. I hired him because he was such a great alto saxophone player that I had to have that sound on my records. . . . When I first heard Art Pepper I just couldn't believe what a beautiful sound he had. . . . He and Chet Baker were, I think, the two most important people in West Coast jazz.

Paich's sensitivity to Pepper's distinctive talent is evident throughout *Art Pepper plus Eleven*. Other arrangers had been able to capture specific sides of Pepper's musical personality;— Shorty Rogers, for example, had created several successful settings to feature the lyrical quality in Pepper's ballad work—but Paich was able to develop settings that wrapped perfectly around the full range of Pepper's sound, not only utilizing his alto voice in different contexts, but also effectively exploiting his seldom-heard playing on clarinet and tenor sax. The former finds perhaps its ultimate bebop expression on "Anthropology," while the tenor solo on "Move" ranks among the finest of Pepper's career. He comes out of the opening ensemble with a simple repetition of a single note, but the quality of swing he is able to put into that one note is remarkable. Pepper was a master of precisely this kind of device; the repetition was almost like a melodic stutter, an opening incantation, a moment of hesitation that throws the listener temporarily off balance. From this musical mantra, Pepper moves into a free-flowing, rapid-fire phrase that cuts through the initial tension. At their best, as on this solo, Pepper's improvisations seemed to suggest that he was discovering his craft anew each time he played. Listening was like watching a child just learning to ride a bicycle, fearful that at any moment he would topple, when suddenly he balances himself, picks up speed, and races off with the wind. Earlier in his career, Pepper's solos seemed to demonstrate his alto virtuosity at every opportunity, but by the middle of the 1950s, he had learned to keep such displays in reserve for the most telling moment. By the time of *Meets the Rhythm Section* or *Art Pepper plus Eleven*, he had become a master at merely suggesting a phrase; a few hundred notes convey the impression that one is hearing just the extracts of a more elaborate musical demonstration, which has been compressed and concentrated for our benefit.

Pepper's nonmusical life continued to show all the terrible symptoms, if anything aggravated, of the addict's lifestyle. To support his drug habit, Pepper's day-to-day activities began to include burglaries, shoplifting, forgeries, armed robbery (in a reference to the last in *Straight Life*, the only regret Pepper espouses is that he wished his partners had let him hold the gun). This was the lowest point Pepper would reach in his whole career, and it was a period that also, in many ways, would seem to be his last hurrah. After 1960, fifteen years would go by before Pepper would again record as a group leader. For all intents and purposes his career appeared to be over, but this last year of recording found Pepper at absolute top form. It was almost as if he sensed that he needed to make these musical statements while still in a position to do so.

The year 1960 is chock full of recording projects in which Pepper's music literally explodes out of the starting gate, including three leader dates of the highest caliber. On Leap Day, Pepper reunited with the Miles Davis rhythm section, this time comprised of Wynton Kelly, Paul Chambers, and Jimmie Cobb, with trumpeter Conte Candoli joining the front line. As with the earlier *Meets the Rhythm Section* date, this project was squeezed into one day, with half of the project devoted to basic blues and rhythm changes. On "Rhythm-a-Ning," Pepper plays with the fate-tempting abandon that would come to characterize his later style. "Diane," named for Pepper's second wife, is aptly described by Martin Williams, in the liner notes to the album, as "an *emotionally* sustained piece of improvised impressionism" and forms a kind of Sadie Hawkins Day tribute to a relationship on the rocks. ("The tune was way too beautiful for her," was Pepper's later comment.)[15] The other ballad, "Why Are We Afraid?"—an André Previn piece Pepper had played on the soundtrack of the film *The Subterraneans*—is only a notch lower in quality. *Intensity* and *Smack Up*, two other albums from this time, are equally powerful. The former finds Pepper teaming up with pianist Dolo Coker in a hard-hitting series of performances, while the latter shows Pepper digging into daring material, including Ornette Coleman's "Tears Inside."

These projects, despite their marked excellence, could do little to boost Pepper's career. By the time of their release Pepper was back behind bars, this time at San Quentin.

Time on My Hands

The name notwithstanding, no patron saint—Quentin or otherwise—looks over this stark federal penitentiary, incongruously situated in prosperous Marin County, California. The city and its eponymous institution are named for an Indian leader Quintin, slain on the site sometime in the last century, who was mysteriously canonized when the township was founded. Other oddities persist in the most desolate of West Coast prisons; perhaps the most striking is the perennial crop of outstanding jazz musicians brought within its walls. In 1942, a San Quentin-based dance band gained enough renown to broadcast regularly on the Mutual radio network. The group was, needless to say, unable to follow up this success by going on the road—although the band members would no doubt have been willing. The group's theme song was—what else could it be?—"Time on My Hands."

Each of the California prisons of the 1950s had a character of its own: Chino provided a minimum security environment for relatively nonviolent offenders; Soledad was known for its vocational programs; Vacaville was a medical institution/prison; Folsom was for older offenders who were seen as beyond rehabilitation. San Quentin was reserved for the most violent younger prisoners, repeat offenders with serious records. Dupree Bolton, another jazz musician turned professional inmate, declared to me without hesitation that "San Quentin was the worst"—and Bolton's twenty-plus years of experience in the Big House give his judgment some weight. Prison is never a picnic, but this Marin County institution was perhaps the worst the West Coast had to offer.

After his October 1960 arrest for heroin possession and subsequent conviction, Pepper was incarcerated at San Quentin. He was sentenced to two to twenty years—an ambiguous although comparatively light punishment given his previous convictions. Pepper was a three-time loser, with a record that could have resulted in a sentence that would last the rest of his life. But Pepper viewed this as harsh treatment. It was, he believed, a response not to his criminal record, but to his unwillingness to give evidence against his connections. With his topsy-turvy sense of values, Pepper prided himself more on this fidelity to his dealers than on almost any other moral decision related in his life story. Not being a "rat," a "snitch," was his recurring boast, but one that must have provided little consolation in the degrading surroundings in which he now found himself. To survive, Pepper amplified on the technique he had developed while at Terminal Island. He pretended to be crazy, adopting a repertoire of eccentric behavior in an attempt to keep other inmates at bay: stumbling, mumbling, slobbering, throwing things—a whole series of oddball actions designed to give him breathing space. During his working hours, he labored in the paymaster's office in the South Block, near the walkway to the gas chamber. In his spare time he played music and looked for ways to get high.

In 1964, Pepper came up for parole. Shelly Manne wrote to the authorities, indicating that he had a job waiting for Pepper at the

Manne Hole, Shelly's Los Angeles club. This made the difference, and soon Pepper was gigging at the Manne Hole, followed by an engagement at the Jazz Workshop in San Francisco. Pepper's style had undergone a major transformation since his last period on the outside, largely under the influence of John Coltrane and, to a slightly lesser extent, Ornette Coleman. Pepper's new sound was something of a surprise, if not a disappointment, to those familiar with his earlier work. For a while he seemed to have lost much of the individuality that had characterized his seminal work from the 1950s. But with time the altoist was able to blend these new influences into his own sound effectively.

During the comeback years of the 1970s, Pepper was a driven soloist with a slashing, pointillistic style that cut to the quick. Pepper's up-tempo numbers were cathartic in their fiery discharges, but his ballads were even more remarkable. On late ballads, such as "Everything Happens to Me," "Goodbye," and especially "Patricia," with its gripping coda, Pepper pulled together his whole range of musical and personal experiences into a riveting sound that mixed equal doses of the raw and the cooked. The lessons of jazz history suggest that it is music made best by young men, but Pepper seemed ready to turn the tables on this truism. Has any saxophonist played with such newfound energy so late in life? These late recordings stand as crowning achievements in Pepper's career. Unlike virtually every other musician examined in this book, Pepper created his greatest work at the end of his life, long after the glory days of West Coast jazz had passed.

When I interviewed Art Pepper, only a few weeks before his death, he showed the vitality of a player at the start of his career. He spoke of his plans and goals for the future—an album with Toshiko Akiyoshi's band, a recording of "down-home" bluesy music, another solo saxophone project, more performances in New York, and—his big goal—seeing his picture on the cover of *Down Beat*. None of these ambitions came to pass. Within a month, Art Pepper was dead, struck down by a cerebral hemorrhage. Toward the end he knew his days were numbered. He recorded prolifically in an attempt to set down as much music as he could while he could.

At that last stage of his career, Pepper's monomania would settle for nothing less than being acknowledged as the greatest also saxophonist in jazz. Such arrogance may have been off-putting, but his playing was backing him up. His was heady music; seeing Art Pepper even on an off-night, at this time, was a memorable experience. There may be no one best player in today's pluralistic jazz environment, but if such an accolade existed, Pepper had to be in the running. Even back east, where he had rarely played, word of his music was going strong, and after his death a consensus slowly began to develop granting him the status of a jazz master. The praise he so wanted to hear, and so long eluded him, is now a matter of record.

NOTES

1. David Pepperell, "I Want to Play So Bad," *Wire*, June 1986, p. 26.
2. Art and Laurie Pepper, *Straight Life*, (New York: Schirmer, 1979), 44.
3. Quoted in Todd Selbert's notes to *Art Pepper Discoveries* (Savoy 2217), 1977.
4. Bob Rusch, "Jack McVea: Interview," *Cadence*, April 1986, p. 18.
5. Brian Case, "Straight Life," *Melody Maker*, June 9, 1979.
6. Quoted in Art and Laurie Pepper, *Straight Life*, 174.
7. Interview with author, June 13, 1987.
8. Ira Gitler, *Swing to Bop: An Oral History of the Transition in Jazz in the 1940s* (New York: Oxford University Press, 1985), 153.
9. Ibid., 224.
10. Dick Bock, "Scanning," *Down Beat*, March 7, 1952, p. 2.
11. John Tynan, "Art Pepper . . . Tells the Tragic Role Narcotics Played in Blighting His Career and Life," *Down Beat*, September 19, 1956, p. 16.
12. Art and Laurie Pepper, *Straight Life*, 191.
13. John Tynan, "Art Pepper Quartet," *Down Beat*, May 16, 1957, p. 34.
14. Interview with author, April 30, 1988. All further unattributed Marty Paich quotes are from this interview.
15. Art and Laurie Pepper, *Straight Life*, 216.

29

ART PEPPER
The Second Career

John Litweiler

ART PEPPER
With Duke Jordan in Copenhagen 1981 * Galaxy 2GCD-
8201-2(2-CD set)
ART PEPPER-ZOOT SIMS
Art 'N' Zoot * Pablo 2310-957-2
ART PEPPER
Tokyo Debut * Galaxy 4201-2

Was Art Pepper a greater artist during his second career (the mid-'70s to his death in 1982) than during his first career as a mature artist (the 1950s to 1960)? Gary Giddins and Laurie Pepper certainly seem to think so, in the expanded 1994 Da Capo edition of the book *Straight Life*, and moreover, Laurie maintains that Art recorded with more major jazz names during his second career—quite an assertion, considering all those 1950s dates with singers and the likes of Chet Baker, Jimmy Giuffre, Warne Marsh, Hampton Hawes, Red Norvo, the Red Garland Trio, and on and on, including the Kenton band and crowds of ex-Kentonites.

"The Second Career" by John Litweiler is a slightly revised and expanded piece that originally appeared in the January/February 1998 issue of *Coda* magazine, and is reprinted by permission of the author.

There's no question that Pepper was a different artist in his second career. The wonderful Galaxy recordings have been, up to recently, the best available evidence of that. And now during the 1990s Laurie Pepper has begun leasing, to the Fantasy combine, broadcast recordings of Pepper's second career, material that originally appeared on Japanese and European releases according to Todd Selbert's Pepper discography. The prospect of future issues is a real matter of intrigue, for Art Pepper was billed as a sideman on a number of sessions ostensibly led by Sonny Stitt, Lee Konitz, Jack Sheldon, Milcho Leviev, and others. The purported sidemen on those tend to be Pepper's regular quartet, as in Sheldon's Angel Wings LP (Atlas LA27-1001), which includes 3 originals, 2 by Pepper and one Sheldon–Pepper collaboration. As a matter of fact, Sheldon plays fine lyric trumpet throughout the date, but Pepper, in beautiful form, takes the lion's share of solo space, and the cover photo tells the story: A glum Sheldon, on the right, points to Pepper, center, gloating over all his loot.

What happened to Pepper between his first and second careers? Prison and the Synanon cult, of course, and a much-reported period of obsession with Coltrane that you'd hardly have anticipated from the earlier, distinctively original Pepper, a bop era artist with swing era origins. Terry Martin's 1964 *Jazz Monthly* essays indicated the opposing pulls of black and white jazz on Pepper's early development, the models of Benny Carter and Lee Konitz (Pepper liked to cite the Lester Young tradition as his principal inspiration), the growth of Pepper's mastery of improvised form and linear flow. Joined by Martin, I heard Pepper for the first time in 1974 at a college jazz band conference. Pepper was teaching clinics for Buffet saxophones in those days; prior to his set, chaperoned by an obviously worried Ken Yohe of Buffet, Pepper showed all the symptoms of stark, paralyzing terror. Yet, joined by trombonist Bill Watrous and accompanied by an uncoordinated student rhythm section, he played excellently and at length.

The differences between the first and second Art Pepper, including the influence of Coltrane, became evident later, when he began touring in clubs and concerts. Pepper liked to draw attention to the differences, by performing, along with his new songs, new versions of his early triumphs. As Martin wrote, one of Pepper's early breakthroughs was his lovely 1951 solo feature on Shorty Rogers' "Over the Rainbow." Of course Sun Ra's satiric solo versions point up for all time the song's inherent emotional dishonesty, with the yearning octave leap that begins and the comforting major thirds and soothing cadences that follow. But Pepper, who played it again and again in his second career, seemed to wish the "Rainbow" fantasy would come true.

In his '70s and '80s versions, Pepper liked to open "Over the Rainbow" with an unaccompanied alto intro, beginning with a cascading phrase, that had no direct reference to the theme. The version in *Art 'N' Zoot* has his intro in something of a pure form, with variations on that opening phrase notable for fourths and flatted intervals that evade the theme or at best dwell on its yearning qualities. He then interpolates minor notes into his theme variations and this opening solo includes a high, harsh, anguished tone to indicate that Harold Arlen's world is in fact far from his. That high note predicts the harshness (sheets of sound) that begins his second solo and the strained, climactic octave leap. He finds no comfort in the concluding cadence, either, for he creates sheets of sound yet again in the rubato coda. His *Copenhagen* version develops rather similarly, though after the cascading opening phrase his intro is quite diffuse; this version has the advantage of Duke Jordan's solo, for in contrast to the tormented yearning in Pepper's broken phrases, the pianist creates long lines of flowing bop melody.

On the other hand, there's "Winter Moon," a near-masterpiece in the 1956 Hoagy Carmichael recording: Pepper's opening solo is the plaintive, long-tone, minor-key theme with spare decorations, and the sorrow that emerges from his simple 24 bars is unforgettable. The long Galaxy solo (1980), over a string arrangement intended to dramatize the song's starkness, is itself admirable but sounds melodramatic by contrast. One of his very best blues solos is "Las Cuevas De Mario" in the 1960 *Smack Up*, a marvelous trip through strange melodies and dislocated accents in 5/4 meter; Pepper's 1977 Village Vanguard version by contrast struggles to be coherent. There are the fast, biting, brittle, staccato Pepper solo in the 1960 "Rhythm-A-Ning," ending in an ecstatic chorus of pure accents—surely this is rhythmic virtuosity to rival Charlie Parker—and his *Copenhagen* "Rhythm-A-Ning" solo, slower but with a similar tension of varied phrase shapes and silences, with sheets of sound erupting in the third chorus and recurring thereafter; Pepper may be preferable in the earlier version, but Duke Jordan's 1981 piano solo, in delightful long lines, all the brightness of Bud Powell without the mania, is quite superior to Wynton Kelly in the earlier.

One more comparison: "Besame Mucho," in which Pepper, in a great 1956 Tampa recording, concentrated a lifetime's tragedy into two wrenching choruses. In his second career he played the minor-key piece often, including a comparatively subdued ballad version in that 1979 Tokyo Galaxy disc. There's a 1978 version not to be missed in *Art Pepper Live In Japan Vol. 1* (Storyville 4128), with squalls of Coltranelike fury in the intro and coda vamps. The *Copenhagen* version has less dramatic dynamic contrasts but does include strained tones and sheets of sound. These later versions are in considerably more broken phrases than the Tampa "Besame Mucho," and these solos' very length determines that they're more diffuse solos. Admirable though these solos are, they're coarser works that deliberately attempt to evoke the tragedy that grew naturally from the lyric tensions in the early version.

What are the differences between early and late Art Pepper? Like his first master, Benny Carter, his alto sound, always beautiful, acquired a firmer quality over time, and it probably never sounded so brilliant as when Rudy Van Gelder recorded him in that 1979 Elvin Jones Quartet session, originally on a Japanese

45 r.p.m. LP (Evidence CD 22053). His vibrato, always so slow that it was more like a little quaver, widened. The later Pepper played longer solos, of course; now that he was a full-time bandleader, he structured performances on a large scale, and he especially liked routines such as the vamps that often opened and closed his pieces. Necessarily, the forms of his solos, ever a crucial concern with Pepper, also changed. While he was recurringly capable of creating beautiful melodic phrases, the more crucial element of his soloing was tension sustained and developed through fine sensitivity to phrase lengths, accenting, and rests. Slightly off-pitch tones, emphatically bent tones, low register passages became more frequent. High, strained tones, or overtones; multiphonics tones; momentary flurries of 16th notes to end phrases, all appeared, adding further stresses to his lines. All these expressive elements added to the tension of his solos, but then his sheets of sound that became climactic developments of vamps recalled an aspect of Coltrane's cyclic forms, too. Interestingly, Pepper's sheets of sound were not rising chromatic scales, like Coltrane often used, but arpeggios—even at his most extreme his harmonic vocabulary was founded on pre-bop practices.

Altogether, the body of his solos offered the early Art Pepper kinds of tension and phrasing, with more elaborate details and settings. The newest formal element was the one-chord intros and codas, which by their absence of mobile harmony demanded a different approach to shaping solos. That these changes did not, to him, devalue his earlier kind of lyricism was shown by his many clarinet solos and many of his last duets with pianist George Cables. As a generalization, joy, tragedy, pure beauty, and the emotions between them arose from Pepper's lines themselves in the 1950s. The later Pepper often consciously sought to evoke these emotions in his late career, especially in his extended routines. But throughout his career, early as well as late, he was an uncommonly self-aware artist, and his fine care for solo creation led to intimate revelations in both periods.

Tokyo Debut comes from his first tour of Japan (4/5/77), upon which he was accompanied by members of Cal Tjader's rhythm section. Unlike Charlie Parker and most other jazz players of his generation, Pepper had a real affinity for Latin phrasing, fitting accents and phrase lengths to mambo and samba patterns. So the Latin specialties, "Manteca" and two standards from *Black Orpheus*, in which he joins Tjader's full, quite extroverted band, are thoroughly sparkling. As usual, he played "Straight Life" very fast, at a "KoKo"-like tempo, like a diatonic Parker. Considering that Pepper always denied any direct Parker influence, let's say that his great freedom of accenting surely had affinities with Parker's discoveries. There's a medium-up blues, "The Spirit Is Here," that brilliantly shows Pepper's sense of structure. It begins with a little riff theme that he varies for a few successive choruses; variations of that riff then pop up in every second chorus that he improvises, resulting in an unusually unified solo.

Art 'N' Zoot(9/27/81) has a changing cast of characters including Victor Feldman, Ray Brown, Charlie Haden, Billy Higgins, and Barney Kessel; there's Pepper's solo feature, "Over the Rainbow," and three solo features for Sims plus "Wee" ("I Got Rhythm") and the blues for the saxes together. It's revealing that Sims, with his uplifting swing, meant more to Pepper than Getz, with all his virtuosity, and it's interesting that on this concert Zoot plays a cheerful, riffing "Girl From Ipanema" at a faster tempo than Getz did, with no hint of Getz's melancholy. Alto and tenor open and close the slow blues as duo improvisations, but the remarkable empathy of Pepper, Warne Marsh, and Ted Brown in two 1956 albums is impossible here. Instead, Pepper and Sims provide a more conventional battle-of-the-saxes show; they make interesting contrasts, with the altoist (the bluesier of the pair anyway) interjecting funky phrases and the tenorist swinging with a rude swagger and a sometime broad, dramatic sound that recalls Coleman Hawkins and Ben Webster.

None of these three concert albums is with Pepper's standard rhythm section. Despite all his work with forceful bop pianists, for his own sessions he preferred less aggressive, less distinctive accompanists who supported with simple but hip harmonies and who soloed in pretty melodies, on something less that Pepper's own high creative level; think of the likes of Ronnie Ball, Pete Jolly, Marty Paich, Dolo Coker in earlier years, and later the many tours and recordings with the ingenious Cables. All of which makes the two-disc *Copenhagen* (7/3/81) especially attractive, for Duke Jordan is truly the costar throughout the program, complementing Pepper's complex self-examinations with their emotional opposite: long lines of melodies that flow inevitably, yet with surprise and delight. Moreover, Jordan's intensity is of Pepper's own quality, so the concert is uncommonly well-sustained—was the altoist, at any other time in his career, matched with another pianist this inspired? Too bad there wasn't more rehearsal time, because I for one would have loved to hear Pepper take on the challenge of excellent, and once-familiar, Jordan themes like "Flight to Jordan" and "Jor-du."

The album has a flying start in the terrific "Blues Montmartre"—Pepper was at his best in up-tempo blues—with the theme generating his developments in early choruses, then riff choruses alternating with melodic choruses, new material alternating with developments of earlier ideas, and exultant sheets of sound by the 18th chorus, an ingeniously structured solo followed by particularly witty Jordan playing. The vocalized elements in "What Is This thing Called Love?" rise to the climax of another especially well-formed alto solo. He generates tension in the vamp intro to the fast "Caravan" by alternating bars of brittle sound with bar-long rests, playing broken phrases that become unsnarled with the accompanying rhythm, all confined in a half-octave in the lower middle register. Not until the theme bridge does he break free, but only briefly, for the punchy, low, minor piano chords call him back to brittle, eventually convoluted phrasing throughout his solo on the chords. There is a driving piano solo, and the vamp alto coda is the finishing development of an extended, harrowing performance.

The ultra-fast tempo of "Cherokee" segues into the ultra-slow "Radio Blues"; the tempo extremes finally defeat the musicians. After all the complexities of the preceding selections, the relative respite of "Good Bait" is welcome. It's a lyrical clarinet solo, intense but without strained passages, with early low-register choruses over only bass and drums, then by the fourth chorus higher tones that suggest something of the sound of Lester Young's metal clarinet. The final piece, at the same tempo, is "All the Things You Are," with a perfectly appropriate conclusion: Pepper and Jordan alternating eights and fours, playing off and fulfilling each other's lines and finally pointing up the good musical feelings between the pair. As you'd expect, throughout the 11 songs bassist David Williams and drummer Carl Burnett provide very alive accompaniment.

Pepper obviously believed in Lester Young's dictum that a solo should tell a story. Even without the book *Straight Life*, you can hear themes of his life in his playing—the affinity for darkness in his minor-key pieces; his quest for ecstasy especially in his ultra-fast-tempo pieces; the broken phrasing that suggests a disrupted consciousness; above all else, the great tension that sustains all of his solos. The quest for beauty is in all of his music and the vocalized techniques of his second career are an almost visceral reflection of the pain involved in his quest. You may hear his phrasing now and then in improvisers like Frank Morgan and Bud Shank, but unlike some songs of, say, Jordan, none of his themes became standards, and by and large Pepper had no more direct influence on his fellow saxophonists than Jelly Roll Morton had on other pianists of his era. The music, the beauty, the intensity were Pepper's story and his alone.

30

ART PEPPER, 1925-1982

Gary Giddins

It was no surprise to hear that Art Pepper died of a stroke June 15. The surprises were his annual appearances in New York since 1977, when he made his belated debut here. He was living on borrowed time, and he knew it. You could hear it in every note he played. The last time I saw him, at Fat Tuesday's a few months ago, his face was bluish white, and his lower legs—he pulled up his trousers to demonstrate—were as bloated as beer barrels. He told me he couldn't shake hands because he'd cut himself that afternoon and, not feeling any pain, didn't know it until he saw the streaming blood. He was obsessed with the miracle that he was still ambulatory and breathing; difficult to be around. How, I wondered, did his amazingly patient wife Laurie, whom he'd met at Synanon when he got out of jail in the late '60s, who'd put together his powerful autobiography, *Straight Life*, and kept him on the road and working—how did she put up with it?

Well, there was, as she once said in a moment of candid desperation, the music. Pepper had achieved the most ragingly expressionistic music of his career, and he made so much depend on the integrity and substance of each chorus that watching him play was an eerie sort of adventure. When the proof was in, when the payoffs rained—for example, in ballad performances as his alto stuttered a few clipped strained phrases and then suddenly found the wind and inspiration for a long, looping, richly evocative melody—you couldn't help but be impressed. Other musicians could play as well from beginning to end, with little fuss. But it was part of Pepper's art that he didn't let you take anything for granted. His solos were a series of small victories. You paid for them, couldn't turn your head from them; they had suspense. Listen to the ballads, especially "Good-bye" and "Cherokee," on the three records he made at the Village Vanguard in 1977 (Contemporary); in their own tenuous, occasionally unpleasant ways, they are as nerve-shattering as the unholy cries of late Coltrane. John Coltrane was living on borrowed time, too. Perhaps it's only in the recognition that we all are that the unpleasantness of their music becomes meaningful, acceptable, and even beautiful.

Coltrane's influence transfigured Pepper when he resumed his career after 20 years of hospitals and jails. In the early years, Lester Young, Zoot Sims, Lee Konitz, and Charlie Parker had been his models. He had a lithe, dry-ice sound, and though his playing was always intense, he knew the values of bebopping proficiency. By the early '50s, he was the sharpest white player in California—a qualitative and racial distinction that remained profoundly important to him. Crazily competitive, in his later years he wanted nothing less than to be the first white player to loom as "the inspiration for the whole jazz world"; in the 1950s, however, he was content to prove his originality in a series of brilliantly realized Contemporary albums—+11, *Art Pepper Meets the Rhythm Section*, *Intensity*—that were occasionally recorded in a junkie haze so complete that he listened to the results in amazement: am I *that* good? The Coltrane influence was tortuous at first—*The Trip*, *Living Legend*—but it resolved itself into a harsher version of the old Pepper, as witness the Galaxy albums, *Straight Life*, *Today*, and the nervously wistful *Winter*

Moon. Finally, there were two Peppers—the supple and professional recording artist, and the neurotically emotive concert performer. If he was never going to be at the center of jazz, he was
nonetheless a center of sorts. You couldn't file him in a category.
He wasn't L.A. cool, white bop, hype, '50, or '80s, but an impassioned musician with an alto sax and a rhythm section that never
completely satisfied him. Despite the facile clichés of the music
he mastered, he made you know that, facility and clichés
notwithstanding, no one else could ever play like that.

Capitol

REG. U. S. PAT. OFF.

Album ECD-248
(6045)
Y

Instrumental

ART PEPPER
Created and Scored by Shorty Rogers

STAN KENTON
and His Orchestra
8-28008

MANUFACTURED BY CAPITOL RECORDS, INC • HOLLYWOOD, CALIFORNIA • U.S.A.

RECOMMENDED RECORDINGS

All recordings by Art Pepper are worthwhile, but the following are particularly recommended. For a complete discography, see *Straight Life: The Story of Art Pepper* (Da Capo Press, New York, 1994).

STAN KENTON AND HIS ORCHESTRA

Jolly Rogers	*Retrospective* Capitol CDP 7 97350
Blues in Riff	Creative World of Stan Kenton 1036
Art Pepper	*Retrospective* Capitol CDP 7 97350
Round Robin	Creative World of Stan Kenton 1036
Dynaflow	*Retrospective* Capitol CDP 7 97350
Street of Dreams	Creative World of Stan Kenton 1042

These recordings from 1950–51 are among the first to display Pepper's own style. His solos on these pieces are like wildflowers in fields of Kenton brass.

SHORTY ROGERS   *The Birth of the Cool Vol. 2*
AND HIS GIANTS   Capitol CDP 7 98935
The 1951 *Modern Sounds* date that launched West Coast Jazz, including "Over the Rainbow," one of the most beautiful examples of jazz ballad playing on record.

ART PEPPER QUARTET   *The Discovery Sessions*
AND QUINTET   Savoy Jazz 92846

Pepper's first recordings as a leader. Four tracks with the original quartet with Hampton Hawes, the quartet with Russ Freeman, both from 1952, and the quintet with Jack Montrose from 1954.

SHORTY ROGERS AND   *Short Stops* RCA
HIS GIANTS   Bluebird 5917

A frisky Rogers nonet, with Pepper wailing, from January 1953, containing "Bunny," a ballad Rogers wrote for Pepper, coupled with the *Cool and Crazy* big band date from March 1953 with stirring Pepper on alto and tenor.

SHORTY ROGERS AND   *Blues Express* (French) RCA
HIS GIANTS   FX1 7234

The *Cool and Crazy* date (see above) plus 4 titles recorded in 1956 to bring the ten-inch lp up to the twelve-inch *The Big Shorty Rogers Express*. Two of the added 4 titles, "Pay the Piper" and "Blues Express," feature lapidary solos by Pepper. "Art . . . remains to this day one of our greatest jazz artists." (Shorty Rogers, *Down Beat*, 7/10/58)

THE RETURN OF ART PEPPER   Blue Note CDP 7 46863

The "return to society" recording, with a quintet rounded out by Jack Sheldon, Russ Freeman, Leroy Vinnegar and Shelly Manne in August 1956, plus 4 tracks with Red Norvo and Joe Morello from 1/57 as an aperitif. "It's fine having Pepper back. He has grown musically since his last recordings, and now is certainly one of the leading jazzmen on his horn. He plays with immediate emotional warmth, with a fuller tone than some of his contemporaries, and with an invention that is now becoming more his own than that of any of his influences. Pepper was seriously missed; I hope he's back for a long, productive time." (Nat Hentoff, *Down Beat*, 1/9/57)

MARTY PAICH QUARTET FEATURING ART PEPPER   V.S.O.P. 10

The Tampa session with Marty Paich. ". . . another invigorating indication that Pepper has returned to the scene with even more to say than before. He is one of the relatively few young altoists to have worked through Bird and other influences into a voice of his own. Art plays with a combination of guts and lyricism, good time, and intelligent, stimulating conception." (Nat Nentoff, *Down Beat*, 2/20/57)

ART PEPPER QUARTET   Original Jazz Classics OJC-816

The Tampa session with Freeman recorded in November 1956. "I am increasingly impressed with Art's growing command of the horn, the ease with which he executes, and his full but not overweight tone. As mentioned before, his time is also a gas to follow. He often understates, thereby projecting a feeling of latent emotional power as well as the warmth that is already evident. His conception is lucid and consistent in quality, although I think he will develop a considerable distance yet in the breadth and originality of his ideas." (Nat Hentoff, *Down Beat*, 3/6/57)

THE WAY IT WAS   Contemporary OJC-389

The quintet session with the astonishing tenor saxophonist Warne Marsh from November 1956, plus quartet tracks with two Miles Davis rhythm sections (from 1957 and 1960) and one from 1960 with Dolo Coker that somehow got left off the albums for which they were destined.

MODERN ART   Blue Note CDP 7 46848

Sessions with Freeman from December 1956 and January 1957, plus 3 alternate takes from the Omegatape session (see below). "He best gets his legs under him on 'Blues In' and 'Out,' which actually is nearly 10 straight minutes of Art crying out his story, accompanied only by Tucker, split into two sections. He is at once moving and sobbing and laughing and protesting, as if playing all alone in a dark, empty hall. Despite the flaws and slips that are almost inevitable in an entirely improvised speech of this length, it is a memorable performance. Pepper has seemingly found his voice. He could well be the most important altoist about today—he has something to say and the means with which to express it." (John Tynan, *Down Beat*, 6/27/57)

THE ART OF PEPPER   Blue Note CDP 7 46853
The Omegatape session with the buoyant Carl Perkins from April 1957.

ART PEPPER MEETS THE   Contemporary OJC-338
RHYTHM SECTION
The "Surprise!" session with Red Garland, Paul Chambers and Philly Joe Jones (Miles Davis's rhythm section at the time) from January 1957. "The solos of all concerned are of consistent interest, with Pepper at times reaching heights he's seldom attained even under most congenial conditions in a club. This memorable meeting deserves a favored place in anybody's collection." (John Tynan, *Down Beat*, 6/12/58)

ART PEPPER + ELEVEN   Contemporary OJC-341
Be-bop and other tunes with punchy arrangements by Paich in 1959 for an eleven-piece band with Pepper riding over it on alto, tenor and clarinet. "Pepper, in the context of this group, turns out one of his best performances on record. As an alto saxophonist, he immediately assumes his place again in the front rank with the added virtue of successfully escaping the tyranny of Charlie Parker's spirit and keeping that full-blown swing." (Ralph J. Gleason, *Down Beat*, 2/18/1960) "A superb album in every way. Not only does it showcase one of the really important soloists of our time but it focuses attention on one of jazz's brightest arrangers. For some years I have looked on Art Pepper as the greatest alto player in jazz since Charlie Parker and this present

lp, which I cannot recommend too highly, merely reinforces that opinion." (Alun Morgan, *Jazz Monthly,* 11/60)

GETTIN' TOGETHER   Contemporary OJC-169
A quartet session with Wynton Kelly, Chambers and Jimmie Cobb (another Miles Davis rhythm section) with, on 3 titles, some stellar trumpet playing by Conte Candoli. Recorded in February 1960 with Pepper on alto or tenor. "Art Pepper has never made a better record than this one. Like many West Coast regulars, he has recorded extensively, but never before with such a consistent and mature musical purposefulness. It seems to me that Pepper has a romantic musical vision similar to that of Lester Young. Like Prez, he has a sense of almost poetic sadness in his ballad interpretations, a kind of declamatory reading of deeply personal feelings. His playing on 'Why Are We Afraid?' and 'Diane' seems to indicate a search for something more than the musical idea—an almost destructively intense examination of interior motives. This is not to misstate his singular musical effectiveness. Thelonious Monk's tune, 'Rhythm-A-Ning,' includes one of Pepper's best solos to date. His improvisatory method is to fragment, breaking the lines into short bits, often in different registers. Pepper also heightens his rhythmic excitement by the use of heavily accented, angular bursts of sound. In this particular solo he extracts material directly from the theme, developing it with stingy economy and adding just the right touch of tongue-in-cheek joviality. An interesting aspect of Pepper's solos here and on 'Whims of Chambers' is that they are constructed of extremely short pieces of material, sometimes only 3 or 4 notes; as in pointillistic painting, this approach works beautifully, bringing out shades of depth and contrast that are not immediately apparent from the sparseness of the material employed." (Don Heckman, *Metronome,* 7/61)

"SMACK UP"   Contemporary OCJ-176
   Although the album title was borrowed from the name of a Harold Land composition, it was prophetic, since Pepper was

busted upon the completion of the second of two days of sessions for it. A quintet date with Sheldon and Pete Jolly, containing the hypnotic 5/4 blues "Las Cuevas de Mario," recorded October 24 & 25, 1960.

INTENSITY   Contemporary OCJ-387

Despite being made rather hastily, while Pepper was out on bail before what was sure to be a stiff sentence for his third narcotics conviction, and a program of standards with a less-than-fancy rhythm section, Pepper displays a searing lyricism that makes this one of the most satisfying of all Pepper recordings. "Perhaps the most striking Pepper characteristics here are his tone, phrasing, and rhythmic concept. All three can best be illustrated by the way he plays melody. Like Charlie Parker, Lester Young, and Billie Holiday, among others, Pepper is able to express himself while playing what at first sounds like straight melody. But he, like the others, shades and shapes the melody, emphasizing and de-emphasizing certain notes, perhaps unconsciously displaying certain hidden facets of the tune and of himself simultaneously, turning the "melody" into a strong personal statement. This stamp of strong personality—and the aforementioned characteristics cast the stamp—carries into Pepper's heated, sometimes tortured-sounding improvisations. There is little note-wasting, which gives his best work a surging urgency that, surprisingly, produces a poignancy that is moving in the extreme. His best comes forth on 'I Can't Believe That You're in Love with Me,' 'Come Rain or Come Shine' (a touching performance in which Pepper conjures up a mood of despair much as Billie Holiday did in her late recordings), 'I Wished on the Moon,' and 'Long Ago and Far Away' (his solo consists mostly of short phrases that come at the listener like bullets.)" (Don DeMicheal, *Down Beat*, 5/23/1963)

ART PEPPER TODAY   Galaxy OJC-474

Recorded in 1978, Pepper is rejuvenated by a tight rhythm section comprised of Stanley Cowell, Cecil McBee and Roy

Haynes. A varied program including a blues, "Miss Who?–his take on "Sweet Georgia Brown," the pulsating "Lover Come Back to Me," the strutting "Mambo Koyama," and some ballads including his own plaintive "Patricia."

PETE JOLLY AND HIS WEST   *Strike Up the Band*
COAST FRIENDS   (Japanese) Atlas LA27-1003
    Although he was under contract to Fantasy (Galaxy), Pepper was permitted to make a series of albums as "sideman" for Yupiteru Industries and the Japanese market. With an inspired and inspiring rhythm section comprised of Jolly, Bob Magnusson and Roy McCurdy, this is easily the best of them. Recorded in February 1980.

CHRONOLOGY

Sep 1, 1925	Born in Gardena, California to alcoholic parents of German (father) and Italian descent.
1934	Begins clarinet lessons at 9.
Sep 1, 1937	Receives an alto saxophone from his father for his 12th birthday.
1940-42	Plays in jam sessions on Central Avenue in Black Los Angeles.
late 1942	Leaves high school during his senior year to join Gus Arnheim's orchestra in San Diego along with Joe Mondragon. Quits band after two months, saying "it was too commercial."
early 1943	Joins Lee Young's band with Dexter Gordon and Charles Mingus at the Club Alabam. Shortly thereafter, adds an after-hours gig around the corner at the Ritz Club.
mid-1943	Joins the Benny Carter orchestra with Gerald Wilson, Freddie Webster and J.J. Johnson.
Aug 11, 1943	Joins the Stan Kenton orchestra at age 17.
Jan 13, 1944	Leaves Kenton following receipt of Army draft notice.
Feb 11, 1944	Inducted into U.S. Army.

May 21, 1946	Returns to U.S. from England, receives Army discharge, and hears be-bop and Bird for the first time and is awestruck. Spends the following one-plus years working in a meatpacking plant and absorbing and mastering this new language.
mid-1947	Freelances and tours briefly with the Lou Olds Group.
Oct 22, 1947	Rejoins Kenton orchestra.
Dec 17, 1948	Leaves Kenton when Kenton disbands.
Jan 10, 1950	Rejoins reorganized Kenton 40-piece orchestra for the "Innovations in Modern Music for 1950" tour of 80 concerts. (Kenton downsized to dance band from June 30, 1950 to October 1951.)
1950	Studies informally with Bill Russo and Shorty Rogers while with Kenton to learn modern harmony and chord progressions.
circa Dec 1950	Uses heroin for the first time. (Pepper always said he first used heroin in 1947 or, maybe, 1948. In the original manuscript of *Straight Life*, he says it was in 1947. He was incredulous when it was pointed out to him that, based on the circumstances and those involved—several alumni of Woody Herman's Second Herd—the date almost certainly had to have been late-1950. But the chapter heading remained "Heroin 1946-1950" because he wasn't entirely convinced.)
Oct 8, 1951	Participates in the *Modern Sounds* recording that launched West Coast Jazz as a member of Shorty Rogers' Giants.
Dec 8, 1951	Leaves Kenton for the last time following the "Innovations in Modern Music for 1951" tour when Stan dismantles his 40-piece behemoth.
Dec 1951	Joins Shorty Rogers at The Lighthouse on Hermosa Beach.

Feb 1951	Launches his own quartet, with Hampton Hawes, Joe Mondragon and Larry Bunker, at the Surf Club in Hollywood.
March 4, 1952	Cuts first recordings with the above group—4 titles.
Spring 1952	Enters private sanitarium, with the urging and financial support of his father, in an effort to kick heroin habit. Kicks after two weeks but resumes habit immediately after leaving sanitarium.
Sep 2, 1952	Arrested on suspicion of narcotics possession, but there was no disposition of the case.
Apr 30, 1953	Arrested for possession of heroin. Booked May 1, charged June 23 and, on July 6, sentenced to two years at the U.S. Public Service Hospital at Fort Worth.
May 17, 1954	Receives conditional release after serving 10 months.
Nov 1954	Appears as guest soloist with Barney Kessel's trio at Jazz City.
Dec 7, 1954	Arrested on suspicion of possession of narcotics, and charged December 8 with possession of heroin. Spends almost 3 months in Los Angeles County Jail awaiting trial.
Feb 25, 1955	Sentenced to 6 months when the only charge he could be convicted of was possession of codeine pills. Serves 5 months of this sentence.
July 26, 1955	Charged with violation of the terms of his release from Fort Worth and sentenced August 3 to one year at the Federal Correctional Facility on Terminal Island.
June 1956	Released from Terminal Island after serving 314 days.
Jul-Oct 1956	Leads own groups and records prolifically.
Dec 1956	Signs with Contemporary Records for one album and makes one session with Warne Marsh, with whom he was gigging.

1957	Continues prodigious output in clubs and recording studios. Appears on "The Steve Allen Show" and "Stars of Jazz" on KABC-TV in January and reappears on "Stars of Jazz" in March.
Nov 1, 1957	Arrested on suspicion of narcotics possession and released after 3 days.
Dec 1957	Wins *Down Beat* Critics Roll, Talent Deserving Wider Recognition, and finishes second to Paul Desmond in the Readers Poll.
1958	Records just once, with a John Graas nonet. In the 4th Quarter, though, signs a long-term contract with Contemporary; this would help offset the drain on his cash flow caused by his lingering addiction because, by this time, he had been reduced to selling accordions door-to-door by day and playing in rock-and-roll and Latin bands by night.
Winter 1958-9	Plays in the house band of the Rossmore Hotel in Palm Springs.
1959	Begins work with Marty Paich on the first album under his new contract with Contemporary. Plays in the Latin band of René Bloch and records frequently.
early 1960	Joins a Bud Shank group with Gary Peacock and Kenny Hume at The Drift Inn in Malibu for two months.
late-Feb 1960	Joins the Lighthouse All-Stars with Conte Candoli, Bob Cooper, Vince Guaraldi, Howard Roberts and Nick Martinis, playing 5 nights a week and Sunday afternoons.
late-Jun 1960	Leaves the LHAS (with Candoli) and turns up at the Blue Beet in Newport Beach in early August. Records with June Christy, Rogers, Paich, Henry Mancini, Mel Tormé and Helen Humes.
July 25, 1960	Arrested for needle marks, pleads guilty to

	heroin addiction, is sentenced to 90 days, and serves one month in the Los Angeles County Jail.
Oct 25, 1960	Arrested for heroin possession the day he completes the second of two days of sessions for *Smack Up.*
Feb 9, 1961	Tried for heroin possession. Sent to Los Angeles County Jail, then Chino, to await sentencing.
Mar 8, 1961	Sentenced to 2-20 years in San Quentin.
March 1964	Transferred to Tehachapi, after serving 3 years in San Quentin, and paroled March 22 as a result of a letter from Shelly Manne guaranteeing employment at Shelly's Manne Hole.
April 1964	Forms group with Frank Strazzeri, Hersh Hamel and Bill Goodwin. Playing tenor with strong Coltrane influence. Plays Manne Hole and the Gold Nugget and Jazz Workshop in San Francisco.
Spring-Summer 1964	Tapes "Jazz Casual" with Ralph J. Gleason for public television. Plays return engagements at the Manne Hole. Returns to alto briefly for a slight Paich-led date with the pop singer Frankie Randall.
Sep 2, 1964	Gives himself up after failing to report for Nalline tests, a condition of his parole, and is sentenced to 6 months in Chino.
Feb 19, 1965	Released from Chino.
Apr 10, 1965	Arrested for being under the influence of narcotics; sentenced to 120 days suspended, with 2 years summary probation.
May 21, 1965	Remanded to San Quentin for parole violation.
Jun 18, 1966	Released from San Quentin after serving 13 months.
late-Aug & Sep 1966	Returns to the Manne Hole.
March 1967	Returns again to the Manne Hole with Tommy

Flanagan, Hamel or George Morrow and Will Bradley Jr. or Ed Thigpen.

Spring-Summer 1967

Gigs in LA; leads own group at Cold Nugget in June and September with Dick Whittington, Hamel and Jerry Granelli. Records with this group for Contemporary without eventual release. Work drying up due to onslaught of rock.

1968

Joins Buddy Rich orchestra late-June in Las Vegas using borrowed alto. Records with Rich in July. Suffers ruptured spleen while with Rich at Basin Street West in San Francisco and spends three months recuperating from operation at St. Luke's Hospital. Cirrhosis diagnosed. Benefit to help defray hospital bills held at Jazz Workshop on September 29. Repairs to LA to convalesce in October when ventral hernia diagnosed. Rejoins Rich band in New York for two weeks at The Riverboat late-October through November 6. Plays Fillmore East November 8 and 9. Returns to LA and heroin. Plays two weeks with Rich at Hong Kong Bar beginning November 10. Leads own group at Donte's on November 24 with Joe Romano from the Rich Band and house rhythm section—Strazzeri, Chuck Berghofer and Nick Ceroli.

1969-1977

Checks into Synanon 1969-1971. Leaves Synanon circa Christmas 1971 after 33 months. Works as bookkeeper for eight months at Good Stuff Bread in Venice. Applies for and is granted Aid to the Totally Disabled by the State of California, which guarantees him a lifelong income of $177 per month provided he does not earn any taxable income. Begins taping his autobiography May 11, 1972. Admitted to methadone program by Veterans Administration. Invited by

University of Denver in August 1972 to hold clarinet clinic. Resumes career, holding clinics for Buffet and playing weddings and bar mitzvahs. Records with Mike Vax Big Band in San Francisco July 1973. In 1975, records for Contemporary with Hawes, Charlie Haden and Manne. Begins using cocaine (in conjunction with methadone), a habit he would continue up until his death. Works with Don Ellis Orchestra for one year from mid-1976 to mid-1977, and records with Art Farmer and as soloist on soundtrack of Clint Eastwood picture *The Enforcer*. Leads one recording date with George Cables, David Williams and Elvin Jones, and is sideman on another with Coker. Now a clinician for Selmer. Records with own group in 1977, and plays three concerts in Japan as guest artist with Cal Tjader. Tours U.S., plays the Village Vanguard in June and, for the first time, the Newport Jazz Festival in July. Records soundtrack for another Eastwood picture, *The Gauntlet*, as featured soloist in September. Wins *Down Beat* Critics Poll as Talent Deserving Wider Recognition in 1977.

1978   Tours Japan for three weeks with Milcho Leviev, Bob Magnusson and Carl Burnett in February-March. Following tour of Oregon, is admitted to hospital in June. Spends two months in hospital; diagnosis: brain damage. Records with Freeman, Magnusson and Frank Butler in September. Signs with Fantasy to record for its Galaxy label later the same month. Completes autobiography November 14. Records first album for Galaxy in December with Stanley Cowell, Cecil McBee and Roy Haynes.

1979	Records as leader and sideman (with Bill Watrous, Elvin Jones) and as featured soloist on soundtrack of *Heart Beat* in first half of the year. Tours Japan in July with Cables, Tony Dumas and Billy Higgins. Records with own group with Flanagan in September. *Straight Life*, his autobiography, is published in November.
1980	Records as sideman with Sheldon and Jolly in February. Tours Europe in the month of June, and records at Ronnie Scott's in London. Records as sideman with Sonny Stitt in July, and album with strings in September. Wins *Down Beat* International Critics Poll.
1981	Records as sideman with Manne in May. Tours Europe in July and Australia in August. Records with his quartet in August and September.
1982	Films *Art Pepper: Notes from a Jazz Survivor*, a 48-minute documentary by Don McGlynn. Records as sideman with Lee Konitz in January, Richie Cole in February and Joe Farrell in March. Records duo with Cables in April. Makes short tour (Chicago, Milwaukee, Washington, D.C.) in May with Roger Kellaway, Williams and Burnett. Dies from cerebral hemorrhage in Los Angeles June 15, at the age of 56. Is voted into *Down Beat* Hall of Fame by its readers later the same year.

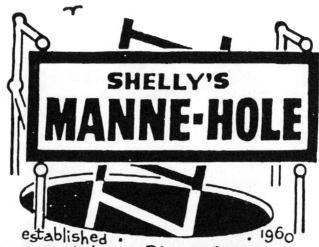

established • 1960
Jazz Nightly • Dinner from
1608 N. CAHUENGA BLVD.•HOLLYWOOD
464-6900 or 464-4774

PERMISSIONS AND
SOURCE MATERIALS

THE ART PEPPER COMPANION

"No Limit/Among Friends/Art Pepper Today" by Terry Martin originally appeared in the September 6, 1979 issue of *Down Beat*. Reprinted by permission of the author.

"Addict" by Whitney Balliett originally appeared in the January 7, 1980 issue of *The New Yorker*. Reprinted by permission of the author and Conde Nast; copyright © 1980. All rights reserved.

"Art Pepper Threatens the Groove" by Gary Giddins originally appeared in the May 12, 1980 issue of *The Village Voice*. Copyright © 1980. Reprinted by permission of Georges Borchardt, Inc., on behalf of the author.

"The 'Straight Life' of Art Pepper" by Michael Zwerin originally appeared in the July 8, 1980 issue of *The International Herald Tribune*. Reprinted by permission of The New York Times Syndicate.

"Art Pepper Talking" by Les Tompkins originally appeared in the August 1980, September 1980, November 1981, and September 1982 issues of *Crescendo* magazine. Reprinted by permission of *Crescendo and Jazz Music* magazine.

"Art Pepper: The Living Legend Moves On" by Steve Voce originally appeared in the August 1982 issue of *Jazz Journal*. Reprinted by permission of *Jazz Journal*.

"A Tribute to Art Pepper" by Arthur F. Kinney originally appeared in the September 1982 issue of *Crescendo* magazine. Reprinted by permission of *Crescendo and Jazz Music* magazine.

"Art Pepper: The Legend" by Hal Hill originally appeared in the June 1985 issue of *Coda* magazine. Reprinted by permission of the interviewer.

"I Want to Play So Bad" by David Nicholson Pepperell originally appeared in the June 1986 issue of *The Wire* magazine. Reprinted by permission of *The Wire*.

"Endgame" by Gary Giddins originally appeared as the liner notes for the Galaxy Boxed Set. Copyright © 1989 by Gary

OTHER COOPER SQUARE PRESS TITLES OF INTEREST

WAITING FOR DIZZY
Fourteen Jazz Portraits
Gene Lees
Foreword by Terry Teachout
272 pp.
0-8154-1037–9
$17.95

OSCAR PETERSON
The Will to Swing
Updated Edition
Gene Lees
328 pp., 15 b/w photos
0-8154-1021-2
$18.95

SWING UNDER THE NAZIS
Jazz as a Metaphor for Freedom
Mike Zwerin
with a new preface
232 pp., 45 b/w photos
0-8154-1075-1
$17.95

UNFORGETTABLE
The Life and Mystique of Nat King Cole
Leslie Gourse
352 pp., 32 b/w illustrations

0-8154-1082-4
$17.95

REMINISCING WITH
NOBLE SISSLE
AND EUBIE BLAKE
Robert   Kimball   and   William Bolcom
256 pp., 244 b/w photos
0-8154-1045-X
$24.95

HARMONICAS, HARPS,
AND HEAVY BREATHERS
The Evolution of the People's Instrument
Updated Edition
Kim Field
392 pp., 44 b/w photos
0-8154-1020-4
$18.95

Available at bookstores; or call
1–800-462–6420

COOPER SQUARE PRESS
150 Fifth Avenue
Suite 911
New York, NY 10011